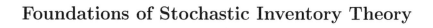

Foundations of Stochastic Inventory Theory

Foundations of
Stochastic Inventory Theory

EVAN L. PORTEUS

Stanford Business Books
An Imprint of Stanford University Press
Stanford, California

Stanford University Press
Stanford, California

© 2002 by the Board of Trustees of the Leland Stanford Junior University

Printed in the United States of America on acid-free, archival-quality paper

Library of Congress Cataloging-in-Publication Data

ISBN 0-8047-4399-1(cloth : alk.paper)

Original Printing 2002

About the Author

Evan L. Porteus is the Sanwa Bank Professor of Management Science at the Stanford Graduate School of Business. A graduate of Claremont Men's College and Case Institute of Technology, he has also worked in the Office of the Assistant Secretary of Defense (Systems Analysis) and at RAND Corporation, and was a Fulbright-Hays Senior Research Fellow in 1976–1977 in Australia. Professor Porteus has published more than 50 articles and book chapters in the areas of supply chain management, technology management, product and process design and management, computational and foundational theory for repetitive operations, financial operations, optimization, and education. His current research focuses on supply chain management and technology management. He is an associate editor of *Management Science* and *Operations Research,* and is a senior editor for *Manufacturing and Service Operations.*

At the Stanford Graduate School of Business, Professor Porteus teaches in both the MBA and PhD programs and is an active PhD dissertation advisor, as well as the current director of the doctoral program. He has served as co-director of the Stanford/Singapore Executive Program and as Area Coordinator of the Operations, Information, and Technology group in the Stanford Business School. He was a founding co-director of the Product Development and Manufacturing Strategy Executive Program, a joint venture of the School of Business and the School of Engineering, and is a founding board member of StartUp, a nonprofit organization in East Palo Alto that seeks to empower local residents to become entrepreneurs. He is married to Ann Wilson and has three children: Matthew, Kimberly, and Bradford.

To Ann, Matt, Kim, and Brad

Contents

Preface

This book is an outgrowth of a doctoral course that I have taught at the Stanford Graduate School of Business for many years. My intent is to equip readers to build and analyze stochastic inventory models, models of inventory management in which uncertainty plays a key role. I present foundational results, concepts, methods, and tools that readers may find useful in this regard. My primary emphasis is on the foundations of dynamic optimization models. However, rather than presenting the general theory of dynamic optimization, I have selected topics with applications to inventory theory in mind. I emphasize understanding and using the foundational results I present, rather than extending them, and I illustrate their application to a number of particular inventory models in detail. I also emphasize insights that can be gained from analysis of these models, rather than of numerical solutions and algorithms. For example, I devote considerable energy to a general framework for characterizing the structure of optimal policies in dynamic problems. I apply this framework to numerous contextual examples. (Nevertheless, I do include two chapters on computational issues in infinite horizon models, because these concepts may be useful to readers seeking to illustrate their work on infinite horizon models with numerical examples.) Although I seek to prepare the reader to build and analyze inventory models, I do not attempt to present a coherent picture of stochastic inventory theory; many important stochastic inventory models get no mention in this book. The idea is to present useful tools and methodology, including illustrations of their application.

Although the book focuses on foundations of stochastic inventory models, readers may find the material useful for building and analyzing dynamic optimization models of other operational phenomena, such as queueing, telecommunications, capacity management, new product development, economic competition, and so on.

I begin with a chapter on two basic classical inventory models, the EOQ model and the newsvendor model. I build on these models throughout the book.

The progression of chapters moves through dynamic models, starting with recursion, which is important enough to merit a chapter of its own. The next several chapters emphasize the foundations needed to characterize the *form* of the optimal policies, rather than simply compute them. I include one chapter each on myopic policies and monotone optimal policies. I also present three chapters on applications to inventory models, including the classical (s, S) model, the generalized (s, S) model, and the empirical Bayesian model.

I then devote three chapters to infinite horizon problems and their numerical solution. Stationary such problems are usually easier to solve numerically than are finite horizon ones (with long horizons). These concepts can be useful to researchers in two basic ways: Those who develop approximate approaches to complex dynamic problems may wish to numerically compute optimal solutions to examples to illustrate how well their approximations perform. Others may wish to identify insights for particular kinds of problems by exploring the solution of numerical examples. This approach offers an alternative to Monte Carlo simulation when it is computationally expensive to get the confidence intervals down to desired levels. The approach can also be useful when it is important to identify the optimal contingent decisions for a large variety of situations. I end the book with a chapter on continuous time models.

The appendix on convexity includes results and concepts that are used repeatedly throughout the book. Thus, instructors may wish to devote an early class to it. The results in the remaining appendices are referred to substantially less. They are included because they prepare the reader to formulate and analyze inventory models using different approaches from those utilized in the main chapters of the book. The appendix on duality suggests ways to deal with multiple products that compete for scarce resources. The one on discounted average value shows how to convert discounted regenerative models, such as the EOQ model, into (approximately) equivalent undiscounted models. It illustrates the effect of the variance of the regeneration time using an EOQ model with random yields. The appendix on preference theory and stochastic dominance reviews concepts that are used in Chapter 8. It also prepares the reader to build and analyze inventory models in which the decision maker is not risk neutral.

I am grateful to more people than I can name. I particularly want to acknowledge the influence that three great teachers have had on my intellectual development: Francis (Miki) Bowers taught me calculus in high school despite my lack of interest. I memorized pi to nearly 37 places in his class. John Ferling imbued me with a fascination for practical uses of mathematics in college. Bill Pierskalla took me to the frontier of inventory theory in graduate school.

Being engaged in an intellectually stimulating place has been much more important to my growth than I expected. My colleagues and students at the Graduate School of Business have pushed me in ways I did not recognize at the time. I have had the pleasure of working with many coauthors who have shaped my thinking on numerous topics. I am particularly grateful to Albert Ha, Joe Hall, Dave Kreps, Marty Lariviere, Lode Li, and Hongtao Zhang for their collaborations that appear explicitly in this book. The many students who have seen earlier versions of this manuscript in my course helped me to convert a sequence of bullet points into a book. They also identified innumerable corrections and essential clarifications. I want to thank Yuval Nov, who, as a student in my class, meticulously read the manuscript and made many important suggestions for improving it. I also want to thank Marcelino Clarke and Linda Bethel for their help in preparing the figures, Lee Friedman for his visually onomatopoetic cover design, and Anna Eberhard Friedlander for her editorial tutelage, including educating me on the importance of Chicago. Finally, I want to thank my family for their patience and support during this long process.

Conventions

Results (lemmas, theorems, and so on) are sometimes stated without proof. In such cases, proofs can be found in the cited references. References cited as sources for results are intended to be accessible rather than original. A citation in an exercise provides either a pertinent context for the problem or a proof. The page of a citation is sometimes given. For example, Zangwill (1969:28) refers to page 28 of the work by Zangwill that was published in 1969 and is cited at the end of the chapter. "We" refers to you, the reader, and me, the author.

Equations, lemmas, sections, exercises, and so forth are numbered separately within each chapter. The appendices are lettered rather than numbered. For example, Theorem A.2 refers to the second theorem in Appendix A. Many conventions are standard: $x^+ = \max(x, 0)$, $x \vee y = \max(x, y)$, and $x \wedge y = \min(x, y)$ for $x, y \in \mathbf{R}$, the real line. Two common acronyms are used: "iff" means if and only if, and "i.i.d." means independent and identically distributed. I use the notation ":=" for definitions. For example, $f(x) := \sup_{y \in Y} g(x, y)$ means that $f(x)$ is defined to be the result of maximizing (finding the supremum of) $g(x, y)$ over $y \in Y$. I use direct language when possible, to keep the exposition simple, yet exact. In particular, I use *strictly* when I want a strict inequality. When "strictly" is missing, I mean the weak inequality. For example, a real number x is *positive* if $x \geq 0$ and *strictly positive* if $x > 0$. Similarly, the real number y is *above* x if $y \geq x$. A real valued function f defined on $\mathbf{R}$ is *increasing* if $x \leq y$ implies $f(x) \leq f(y)$ and *strictly increasing* if $x < y$ implies $f(x) < f(y)$. Similar conventions are followed for negative numbers and decreasing functions. I say that $-\infty$ is a minimizer of the function f if f is increasing on $\mathbf{R}$. Similarly, $+\infty$ is a minimizer of a decreasing function.

A set X is *discrete* and *countable* if its elements can be put into a one-to-one correspondence with a sequence of positive integers. A discrete set is *finite* if it has a finite number of elements. (The empty set is finite.) A discrete set that is not finite is *denumerable*.

If x is an n-vector, then x_i refers to the ith component of that vector, and I write $x = (x_1, x_2, \ldots, x_n)$, even though x is considered to be a column vector. Suppose y is also an n-vector. The transpose of x is denoted by x^T, and the inner product of x and y is $x^\mathrm{T}y = \sum_{i=1}^{n} x_i y_i$. Here, $x = y$ means $x_i = y_i$ for every component i, $x \neq y$ means there exists a component j such that $x_j \neq y_j$, $x \geq y$ means $x_i \geq y_i$ for every component i, $x > y$ means $x \geq y$ and $x \neq y$, (that is, there exists some j such that $x_j > y_j$,) and $x \gg y$ means $x_i > y_i$ for all i. The same conventions apply to matrices.

The notation $f : X \to \mathbf{R}$ signifies that f maps X into $\mathbf{R}$: f is a real valued function defined on a set X. Suppose that X is a subset of $\mathbf{R}^n$. We always assume in this context that n is a strictly positive integer, and we write the function f evaluated at a point $x \in X$ as both $f(x)$ and $f(x_1, x_2, \ldots, x_n)$.

Suppose further that f is partially differentiable with respect to each of its arguments. The *gradient* of f evaluated at the point x is the n-vector of partial derivatives of f and is denoted by $\nabla f(x)$. Thus,

$$\nabla_i f(x) = \frac{\partial f(x)}{\partial x_i}$$

is the partial derivative of f with respect to its ith variable, evaluated at the point x. We indicate when we deviate from this notation, such as in Chapter 8 when we denote partial derivatives using subscripts and superscripts.

If, in addition, $n = 1$ (f is a differentiable function of a single real variable), then both $f'(x)$ and $\nabla f(x)$ denote the derivative of f evaluated at the point x.

Suppose that f is a real vector valued function defined on a subset X of $\mathbf{R}^n$. That is, $f : X \to \mathbf{R}^m$, where m is a strictly positive integer. For example, if

$$f(x) = \begin{pmatrix} x_1 + x_2^2 + x_3 \\ x_1^2 + x_2 + x_3 \end{pmatrix},$$

then $n = 3$ and $m = 2$. Subscripts refer to the components of the vector. For example,

$$f_1(x) = f_1(x_1, x_2, x_3) = x_1 + x_2^2 + x_3.$$

(We do not have occasion to take partial derivatives of vector valued functions, so the meaning of subscripts will be clear from the context.) In general, we have

$$f(x) = \begin{pmatrix} f_1(x) \\ f_2(x) \\ \vdots \\ f_m(x) \end{pmatrix} = \begin{pmatrix} f_1(x_1, x_2, \ldots, x_n) \\ f_2(x_1, x_2, \ldots, x_n) \\ \vdots \\ f_m(x_1, x_2, \ldots, x_n) \end{pmatrix}.$$

Unless indicated otherwise, I assume that all expectations of random variables exist and are unique.

Evan L. Porteus

Stanford, California

May 2002

1
Two Basic Models

This chapter introduces two basic inventory models: the EOQ (Economic Order Quantity) model and the newsvendor model. The first is the simplest model of *cycle stocks*, which arise when there are repeated cycles in which stocks are built up and then drawn down, both in a predictable, deterministic fashion. The second is the simplest model of *safety stocks*, which are held owing to unpredictable variability.

1.1 The EOQ Model

A single product is used (or demanded) at a continuous fixed and known rate over time, continuing indefinitely into the future. Shortages or delayed deliveries are not allowed. Replenishments are received as soon as they are requested. The ordering cost consists of a setup (fixed, redtape) cost that is incurred each time an order of any size is placed plus a proportional cost incurred for each item ordered. A holding cost is incurred on each item held in inventory per unit time. See Figure 1.1 for a typical plot of the inventory level as a function of time.

The product may be an item that is used internally by your organization and the issue is how many items to order each time an order is placed (equivalently, how often to replenish the stock of the item). The product may also be a man-ufactured product that is used at a uniform rate at downstream stations, in which case the issue is how long the production runs should be. In a manufacturing setting, the order quantity is called either the batch size, the lot size, or the production run, and the setup cost is the fixed cost to set up the equipment to produce the next run. It can include direct costs, the opportunity cost of the time it takes to carry out the setup, and the implicit cost of initiating a production run because of learning and inefficiencies at the beginning of a run. Technically, we assume that all completed units become available at the same time, such as when all units are processed simultaneously and completed at the same time. However, we shall see that the case of sequential manufacturing, under a fixed manufacturing rate, reduces to a form of this model.

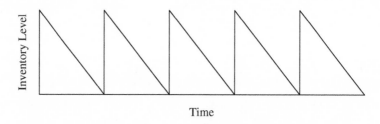

Figure 1.1   Inventory Level as a Function of Time

There are economies of scale in ordering in that the average order cost (per unit ordered) decreases as the size of the order increases. This effect favors large orders, to average the fixed order cost over a large number of units ordered, leading to long cycles, with infrequently placed orders. However, the holding costs favor lower inventory levels, achieved by short cycles, with frequently placed orders.

Notation

$K =$ fixed (setup) cost.

$c =$ direct unit ordering cost.

$\lambda =$ mean demand rate per week.

$h =$ unit holding cost incurred per unit held per week.

$Q =$ order quantity (decision variable).

$C(Q) =$ cost per week (objective function).

Formulation of Objective Function

A *cycle* is the amount of time T that elapses between orders. We first determine the cost per cycle. Dividing by the time length of the cycle yields the cost per week, which we seek to minimize. Exercise 1.1 verifies that we should assume that the cycle length T is the same for every cycle and that replenishment takes place when the stock level drops to zero.

Suppose the first cycle starts at $t = 0$ with the inventory level at zero and ends at $t = T$. An amount Q is ordered and is received immediately, incurring an ordering cost (per cycle) of $K + cQ$. Let $x(t)$ denote the inventory level at time t. Then, for $0 \leq t < T$, $x(t) = Q - \lambda t$. (See Figure 1.1.) Thus, to calculate T: we set $Q - \lambda T = 0$, so $T = Q/\lambda$. The inventory cost per cycle is therefore

$$\int_{t=0}^{T} hx(t)dt = h \int_{t=0}^{T} (Q - \lambda t)dt = h(QT - \lambda T^2/2) = \frac{hQ^2}{2\lambda} = \frac{hQT}{2}.$$

Thus, the total cost per week is

$$\frac{K + cQ + hQT/2}{T} = \frac{K\lambda}{Q} + \frac{hQ}{2} + c\lambda.$$

The first term gives the average setup costs per week. The second gives the average holding cost per week, which is simply the product of the unit holding cost per week, h, and the average inventory level over time, $Q/2$. The last term, $c\lambda$, is the required direct cost per week. Because it is independent of the replenishment policy, we follow the usual practice of ignoring it and write our objective function, consisting of the remaining relevant costs, as follows:

$$C(Q) = \frac{K\lambda}{Q} + \frac{hQ}{2}.$$

The Economic Order Quantity (EOQ)

To find the optimal order quantity, we differentiate the objective function $C(Q)$ with respect to decision variable Q and set the result equal to zero. The resulting first-order conditions are

$$C'(Q) = \frac{-K\lambda}{Q^2} + \frac{h}{2} = 0.$$

Checking the second-order conditions, we find that the second derivative is $2K\lambda/Q^3$, which is strictly positive for $Q > 0$, so the objective function is (strictly) convex on $(0, \infty)$. Hence, the first-order conditions are sufficient for a minimum. The resulting solution is

$$Q^* = \sqrt{\frac{2K\lambda}{h}},$$

which is the famous square root EOQ formula, introduced by Harris (1913) and popularized by Wilson (1934).

Interestingly, this problem represents a special case, illustrated in Figure 1.2 below, in which, to minimize the sum of two functions, we set the two functions equal to each other. An empirical consequence for a practical setting in which this model applies is this: If holding costs for cycle stocks are more [less] than setup costs per week, then order quantities are too large [small].

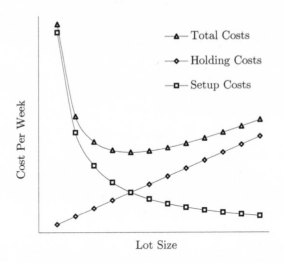

Figure 1.2   *Relevant Costs as Functions of the Lot Size*

Optimal Cost per Week

Plugging the EOQ back into the objective function leads to

$$\sqrt{\frac{\lambda h K}{2}}$$

as the optimal level of setup costs per week. The optimal level of holding costs per week is exactly the same. The resulting, induced optimal setup and holding cost per week is

$$C^* = C(Q^*) = \sqrt{2\lambda hK},$$

which is an increasing concave function of each of the parameters. (Its first derivative is positive and its second derivative is negative.)

Comparative Statics

If volume (demand rate) is doubled, you don't double the order quantity. You multiply by $\sqrt{2} \cong 1.414$, so the order quantity gets increased only by about 40%. Similarly, the total cost per week goes up by about 40%, an economy of scale. Each additional unit per week of volume requires a smaller additional cost. Another way to view this phenomenon is to compute the *elasticity* of the optimal cost as a function of the demand rate

$$\frac{\lambda \frac{\partial C^*}{\partial \lambda}}{C^*} = \frac{1}{2},$$

which can be interpreted as (roughly) the percentage increase in optimal costs for each 1% increase in the demand rate. Thus, for every 2% increase in the demand rate (or setup cost or holding cost, for that matter), the optimal cost will increase by about 1%.

A central feature of many Just-In-Time (JIT) campaigns in manufacturing practice is setup reduction. Suppose such a campaign is implemented in an environment in which the assumptions of the EOQ model hold. If you cut the setup cost in half, you don't cut the order quantity in half. You multiply by $\sqrt{1/2} \cong 0.707$, so the order quantity gets cut by about 30%. Similarly, the induced optimal cost per week goes down by about 30%. Each additional reduction of \$1 in the setup cost yields a larger cost savings. Thus, there are increasing returns to setup reduction, which can lead to underinvestment in setup reduction if only local marginal returns are taken into account. However, if the analysis is done in elasticity terms (percentage changes) instead of absolute terms, then each 2% decrease in the setup cost will yield about a 1% decrease in the order quantity and the total cost. See Porteus (1985) for examples where the optimal amount of setup reduction can be found analytically.

Robustness of Cost to Order Quantity

Suppose, for a variety of possible reasons, such as misestimated parameters, the implemented order quantity is a times the (optimal) EOQ. The resulting cost is

$$\left(\frac{\frac{1}{a} + a}{2}\right) C^*.$$

For example, if the order quantity is either 50% higher than the EOQ $(a = 3/2)$ or the EOQ is 50% higher than the order quantity $(a = 2/3)$, then the resulting cost is $(13/12)C^*$, which means that actual cost is about 8% higher than optimal. The EOQ is famous for being robust in this sense: large errors in the implemented order quantities lead to small cost penalties.

Extension to Sequential Manufacturing

It usually takes time to produce something. If all completed units become available at the same time, after a fixed time for processing/production, then the production run can be scheduled in advance, so that all completed units become available exactly when needed (when the inventory level drops to zero). However, under sequential manufacturing, there will be a buildup of completed units until the end of the production run, at which time the inventory level will start to decrease again. Figure 1.3 illustrates that each cycle consists of the time to complete the production run plus the time for the inventory level to drop to zero. This subsection shows that the essential structure of the EOQ model is maintained in this case.

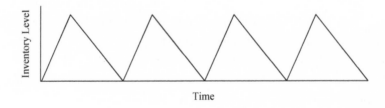

Figure 1.3   *Inventory Level under Sequential Manufacturing*

Let r denote the (finite) rate at which units are produced. (Note that we must have $\lambda < r$ for this analysis to work: If $\lambda = r$, then there will be only one production run, which will continue for the lifetime of the product. If $\lambda > r$, then all demands cannot be met, as we assume they must be.) In this case, the maximum inventory level is less than the run size Q, namely, $Q(r - \lambda)/r$, so the average holding cost per week is $hQ(r - \lambda)/(2r)$. The resulting optimal lot size is

$$Q^* = \sqrt{\frac{2K\lambda}{h(1 - \lambda/r)}},$$

which is sometimes called the *Economic Production Quantity (EPQ)*. By replacing the original holding cost parameter h by $\tilde{h} := h(1 - \lambda/r)$, the (smaller) *effective holding cost* parameter, we can retain the original EOQ notation, terminology, and results.

1.2   The Newsvendor Model

An unknown quantity D of a single product will be demanded (requested for use) during a single period. While the probability distribution of demand is known, the actual number demanded will not be known until after a decision y, how many to order (or make), is made. In short, order y first, observe the *stochastic demand* D second. The amount sold/delivered will be $\min(D, y)$: You can't sell more than you have or than are demanded. Under some demand distributions, such as the normal distribution, it is impossible to always meet all demand, so the prospect of unmet demands must be accepted. The ordering cost consists of a proportional cost incurred for each item ordered. Units are sold for more than they cost. Units purchased but not sold become obsolete by the end of the period and have no salvage value.

The name of the model derives from a newsvendor who must purchase newspapers at the beginning of the day before attempting to sell them at a designated street corner. However, the model applies to products that must be produced to stock (commitment to the quantity, whether procured or produced, is required before observing demand) under the following two conditions: (1) Only one stocking decision is allowed (with no opportunity for replenishment), and (2) The financial consequences can be expressed as a function of the difference between the initially chosen stock level and the realized demand. Actually, we shall see later that there are conditions when it also applies to products that can be replenished infinitely many times.

The tradeoff is between too many and too few. If we make too many, then we have some left over, and we paid for more than we need. If we make too few, then we could have sold more if we had bought more. Inventories held, as they are in this setting, because of unpredictable demand are called *safety stocks*. If there is no variability in the demand, then we would stock the mean demand. Any more than that is safety stock. (Safety stock can be negative.)

Notation

$p =$ unit sales price $(p > 0)$.

$c =$ unit cost $(0 < c < p)$.

$D =$ unit demand in the period $(D \geq 0)$ (continuous random variable).

$\Phi =$ cumulative distribution function of demand.

$\bar{\Phi} = 1 - \Phi$.

$\phi =$ probability density of demand.

$\mu =$ mean demand.

$\sigma =$ standard deviation of demand.

$y =$ stock level after ordering (available) (decision variable).

$v(y) =$ expected contribution (objective function).

Formulation of Objective Function

The contribution in a period equals the dollar sales from the units sold less the cost of the units purchased: $p\min(D, y) - cy$. We assume henceforth, unless indicated otherwise, that $\Phi(0) = 0$: demand will be strictly positive with probability one. Using Lemma D.1 (Lemma 1 of Appendix D) and $\bar{\Phi}(y) = 1 - \Phi(y)$, the expected contribution is

$$v(y) = E[p\min(D, y) - cy] = p \int_{\xi=0}^{y} \bar{\Phi}(\xi)\, d\xi - cy. \qquad (1.1)$$

Expanding the expression for the expected units sold leads to the alternative representation

$$v(y) = -cy + p \int_{\xi=0}^{y} \xi\phi(\xi)\, d\xi + py\bar{\Phi}(y). \qquad (1.2)$$

Recalling that $x^+ := \max(x, 0)$ we can also write (Exercise 1.5)

$$v(y) = p\mu - cy - pE(D - y)^+$$
$$= p\mu - cy - p \int_{\xi=y}^{\infty} (\xi - y)\phi(\xi)\, d\xi,$$

which are dollar sales on expected demand less cost of the stock purchased less opportunity losses (revenues not received for lack of product),

$$v(y) = (p - c)y - pE(y - D)^+$$
$$= (p - c)y - p \int_{\xi=0}^{y} (y - \xi)\phi(\xi)\, d\xi,$$

which is the profit margin on the units stocked less unrealized revenues on unsold units, and

$$v(y) = (p - c)\mu - L(y), \tag{1.3}$$

where

$$L(y) := (p - c)E(D - y)^+ + cE(y - D)^+,$$

which is called the expected one period *holding and shortage cost function* and also the expected *loss function*. The contribution therefore consists of the profit margin on the mean demand less the expected holding and shortage costs. Thus, since $(p - c)\mu$ is fixed, we can equivalently minimize the expected holding and shortage costs. It is also convenient to express $L(y)$ as follows:

$$L(y) = E\mathcal{L}(y - D),$$

where

$$\mathcal{L}(x) := cx^+ + (p - c)(-x)^+.$$

The Critical Fractile Solution

To find the optimal order quantity, we differentiate the objective function with respect to the decision variable y and set the result equal to zero. By Exercise 1.7, the resulting first-order conditions are

$$v'(y) = p - c - p\Phi(y) = 0.$$

Checking the second-order conditions, we find that the second derivative exists
and equals $-p\phi(y)$, which is negative, so the objective function is concave.
Hence, the first-order conditions are sufficient for a maximum. Let S denote
an optimal stock level after ordering. The first-order conditions lead to

$$\Phi(S) = \frac{p-c}{p}, \tag{1.4}$$

which is the famous *critical fractile* solution, first appearing in Arrow, Harris,
and Marschak (1951), that is illustrated in Figure 1.4. Arrow (1958) attributes
the newsvendor model itself to Edgeworth (1888). To avoid certain technical
details, assume henceforth, unless indicated otherwise, that an optimal solution
to the newsvendor problem exists and is unique.

It is useful to define $\zeta := c/p$, which is the *optimal stockout probability (OSP)*

$$\bar{\Phi}(S) = \zeta.$$

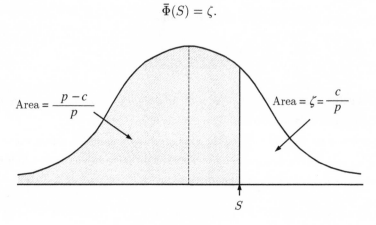

$$\text{Area} = \frac{p-c}{p} \qquad\qquad\qquad \text{Area} = \zeta = \frac{c}{p}$$

$$S$$

Figure 1.4   *Critical Fractile Solution in the Continuous Case*

Interpretation

If $p = 2c$, which corresponds to a 100% markup over cost (but is called a 50%
markup by retailers who like to think of the markup as a percentage of the sales
price), then it is optimal to stock the median demand. In this case, it is optimal
to stock out (run out) half the times the product is stocked and to have leftover
stock half the times. The lower the wholesale cost or the higher the retail price,
the less likely you are to run out. Thus, if your retailer of perishable goods
rarely runs out, you are probably paying a big markup.

Note, however, that while the stockout probability may be fairly high, the optimal probability that a randomly selected demand is unsatisfied is typically much smaller. For example, the ratio of expected unsatisfied demand to expected total demand, namely, $E(D-S)^{+}/E(D)$, can be substantially smaller than the stockout probability. In particular, it will be illustrated shortly that the optimal *fill rate*, defined here as the ratio of expected satisfied demand to expected total demand when stocking optimally, namely, $E\min(D,S)/E(D)$, can be substantially larger than the critical fractile.

Discrete Demand

This subsection explores the consequences of dropping the assumption that demand is a continuous random variable. In particular, suppose that demand D is discrete in the sense that there exists a sequence of real numbers, $\{x_1, x_2, \ldots\}$, representing all potential demand quantities, and $0 \le x_1 \le x_2 \le \cdots$. Furthermore, suppose all these quanities are admissible stock levels. These assumptions hold if the stock level must be an integer and demands arise only for integer quantities. These assumptions also hold if the admissible stocking units are continuous and demands are discrete but not necessarily integers. For example, the product might be gravel that can be produced to reach (essentially) any fractional level requested but is sold in full containers of various specific sizes, which are not necessarily integer multiples of the smallest size.

By Exercise 1.11, under these assumptions, the optimal stock level S is the smallest admissible y such that

$$\Phi(y) \ge \frac{p-c}{p}.$$

Figure 1.5 presents an example in which $(p-c)/p = 0.75$. In this example, the optimal stock level S is a fractional quantity between 2 and 3 that satisfies $\Phi(S) > 0.75$ and such that the next smaller potential demand quantity x satisfies $\Phi(x) < 0.75$.

Informally, the optimal stock level is found as follows: Start at the height of the critical fractile on the vertical axis, move horizontally to the connected representation of the distribution function and then down vertically to the horizontal axis to read off the optimal stock level. The same approach applies when demand is a mixture of continuous and discrete random variables. However, if

all potential demand quantities are not necessarily admissible stock levels, then
further considerations are required. (See Exercise 1.12.)

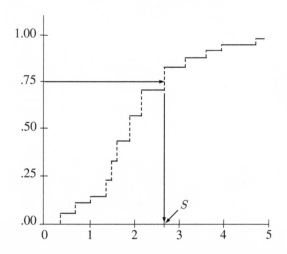

Figure 1.5   Solution under Discrete Demand

Normally Distributed Demand

Let Φ_N and ϕ_N denote the unit normal distribution and density functions,
respectively. Define I_N as

$$I_N(z) := \int_{x=z}^{\infty} (x - z)\phi_N(x)\,dx,$$

which is called the *unit normal loss function*, which should be distinguished
from our expected loss function L. I_N is commonly tabled and, as is verified
by Exercise 1.14, can be readily computed in terms of Φ_N and ϕ_N, as follows:

$$I_N(z) = \phi_N(z) - z\big(1 - \Phi_N(z)\big). \tag{1.5}$$

$I_N(z)$ can be interpreted, in a setting in which negative demands are possible
(corresponding to more previously sold units being returned for credit than
newly sold), as the expected number of unmet demands $(E(D - z)^+)$ if z
units are stocked and demand is normally distributed with mean equal to zero
and standard deviation equal to one.

If D is normally distributed with mean μ and standard deviation σ, then use of the transformation $z = (y - \mu)/\sigma$, which represents the stock level y in standard deviations above the mean, leads to

$$E(D - y)^+ = E(D - \mu - z\sigma)^+ = \sigma E \left(\frac{D - \mu}{\sigma} - z \right)^+ = \sigma I_N(z), \qquad (1.6)$$

and the following form for the holding and shortage cost function:

$$L(y) = L(\mu + z\sigma) = [cz + p I_N(z)]\sigma.$$

Let $z^* = z^*(\zeta)$ satisfy $\Phi_N(z^*) = (p - c)/p = 1 - \zeta$, which is independent of the mean μ and the standard deviation σ of demand. It is straightforward to see that the optimal stock level is $S = \mu + z^*\sigma$, so z^* is the optimal stock level, expressed in number of standard deviations above the mean, as a function $z^*(\zeta)$ of the optimal stockout probability ζ. The safety stock $z^*\sigma$ is proportional to the standard deviation of demand. Note that if $p < 2c$, then $z^* < 0$, and the safety stock is negative. Let

$$L_N(\zeta) := z^*(\zeta) + I_N(z^*(\zeta))/\zeta.$$

Then (Exercise 1.17) the induced optimal holding and shortage costs can be written as

$$L(S) = c\sigma L_N(\zeta) = p\sigma \phi_N(z^*(\zeta)), \qquad (1.7)$$

which is proportional to the standard deviation and independent of the mean and can be easily computed. In addition, the optimal fill rate is given by

$$1 - \frac{\sigma}{\mu} I_N(z^*(\zeta)).$$

For example, suppose $c = 1$, $p = 4$, $\mu = 100$, and $\sigma = 30$. Then $\zeta = 0.25$, so, using Table 1.1 (p. 26), $z^*(\zeta) = 0.674$, $I_N(z^*(\zeta)) = 0.1492$, and $L_N(\zeta) = 1.271$, so the optimal stock level is $S = 100 + 0.674(30) \cong 120$, $L(S) = 1(30)(1.271) \cong 38.1$, and, using (1.3), $v(S) = (4 - 1)100 - 38.1 = 261.9$. In this case, the expected contribution is reduced by more than 12% (to 261.9 from 300) because of the existence of uncertainty in the demand. Furthermore, although the critical fractile is 0.75, the optimal fill rate equals $1 - 0.3(0.1492) \cong 0.955$, which is much higher.

If we could invest in a system (such as a reservation system) that reduced the variability of demand (but kept the mean constant), we would face the optimization problem of finding the optimal standard deviation of demand.

Economies of Scale in Market Size

Suppose there are n independent customers, each of whom will demand a random amount of the product (with mean μ_0 and standard deviation σ_0.) The (total) mean demand is therefore $n\mu_0$, and the variance in total demand is $n\sigma_0^2$. The standard deviation in demand is therefore $\sigma_0\sqrt{n}$, which is another instance of a square root law, leading to economies of scale. For convenience, let's assume that the distribution of total demand is normal. (Such an assumption is justified by the central limit theorem of statistics when n is large.)

Exercises 1.21–23 verify and interpret the essential results of this model in the remainder of this subsection. Suppose that the number of customers is doubled. The mean and variance of demand both double, but the standard deviation increases only by about 40%. If $p \geq 2c$, then the safety stock is positive and increases only by about 40%, while the order quantity increases by somewhere between 40 and 100%. In general (whether $p \geq 2c$ or not), the resulting optimal contribution is

$$(p-c)n\mu_0 - \sigma_0\sqrt{n}k,$$

where $k := cz^* + pI_N(z^*)$, and z^* satisfies $\Phi_N(z^*) = (p-c)/p$. Here, k is independent of n and is always strictly positive, assuming $p > c$, and $n > 0$.

Expected Value of Sample Information

Suppose we cannot affect the demand variability, but we may be able to sample one or more correlated random variables that will let us forecast demand outcomes more accurately. We (1) observe the sample outcome (which may be of several random variables), (2) use Bayes's rule to compute the *ex post,* revised probability distribution of demand, (3) compute the optimal decision (stock level) for the new distribution and the resulting optimal expected return, and (4) compute the expected return (conditional on the sample information) from the optimal decision we had without any sample information. The difference is the ex post value of that sample information. We repeat this process for every possible sample outcome and compute the expected value. (Weigh each of the respective ex post values by the probability of it arising.) The result is the *ex ante* value of sample information. It is more commonly called the *Expected Value of Sample Information (EVSI)*.

Expected Value of Perfect Information

The best we can do with *any* sample information is to predict the actual demand exactly in each case. Assume the sample gives a perfect indication of the actual demand, which is equivalent to observing demand first, then deciding how much to stock. (In the newsvendor model, provided the sales price exceeds the unit cost, we would always stock the actual demand.) In this case, the *EVSI* is called the *Expected Value of Perfect Information (EVPI)*. Because *EVSI* $\leq$ *EVPI* for all sample statistics, the *EVPI* can be used to rule out the gathering of any sample when the cost of getting a sample exceeds the *EVPI*: the cost of obtaining a sample would exceed the best possible expected return that could result from it. In the newsvendor model, the *EVPI* equals the optimal expected holding and shortage costs, $L(S)$, which explains why $L_{\mathbf{N}}$ is called the *EVPI* factor in Table 1.1 (p. 26).

More General Formulation

In general, suppose a quantity y must be specified, a random variable X is then observed, and the resulting cost is of the form

$$c_{\mathbf{O}}(y - X)^+ + c_{\mathbf{U}}(X - y)^+.$$

That is, if $X \leq y$, then the *unit overage cost* $c_{\mathbf{O}}$ is incurred for each unit of the difference, and, if $X \geq y$, then the *unit underage cost* $c_{\mathbf{U}}$ is incurred for each unit of that difference.

Assuming that X is statistically independent of y, and that ϕ and Φ denote the density and distribution of X, respectively, the resulting expected costs are

$$v(y) = \int_{\xi=-\infty}^{y} c_{\mathbf{O}}(y - \xi)\phi(\xi)\,d\xi + \int_{\xi=y}^{\infty} c_{\mathbf{U}}(\xi - y)\phi(\xi)\,d\xi.$$

Setting the derivative equal to zero yields

$$v'(y) = c_O \Phi(y) - c_U[1 - \Phi(y)] = (c_O + c_U)\Phi(y) - c_U = 0,$$

which becomes

$$\Phi(S) = \frac{c_U}{c_O + c_U}.$$

The *optimal probability of underage (OPU)* equals $\zeta = c_O/(c_O + c_U)$. When this model applies (the overage and underage costs are proportional to the amount of the overage and underage, respectively), the following guidance is often useful in identifying the correct values of c_O and c_U. The unit overage cost c_O is the amount that could have been saved (gained) if the level y had been reduced by one unit in the event of an overage (having specified too large a level). Similarly, the unit underage cost c_U is the amount that could have been saved (gained) if the level had been increased by one unit in the event of an underage (having specified too low a level).

If X is normally distributed, then the optimal value of the objective function is

$$v(S) = c_O \sigma L_N(\zeta).$$

Exercises 1.24–26 explore this model further.

Exercises

1.1   Suppose, in the EOQ model, that K and h are both strictly positive, that the inventory level at time $t = 0$ is zero: $x(0) = 0$, and that strictly negative inventory levels are not allowed. Let Q_i denote the amount replenished at the beginning of (replenishment) cycle i, and T_i the length of that cycle, for $i = 1, 2, \ldots$. That is, letting $t_0 := 0$ and, for $i \geq 1$, $t_i := t_{i-1} + T_i$, replenishment i consists of the delivery of Q_i units at time t_{i-1}. Let $f_n(Q_1, Q_2, \ldots, Q_n, T_1, T_2, \ldots, T_n)$ denote the (average) cost per week, calculated over the time horizon $[0, t_n]$, corresponding to n complete (replenishment) cycles.

(a) Write an expression for the inventory level $x(t)$ for $t \in [0, t_n]$.

(b) Write a constraint on T_i for each $i = 1, 2, \ldots, n$ that guarantees that $x(t) \geq 0$ for all $t \in [0, t_n)$.

(c) Consider the following optimization problem. The number of cycles is fixed at $n > 0$. The decision variables are $Q_1, Q_2, \ldots, Q_n, T_1, T_2, \ldots, T_n$. The objective function, to be minimized, is $f_n(Q_1, Q_2, \ldots, Q_n, T_1, T_2, \ldots, T_n)$. Finally, the constraints are those of part (b) plus $Q_i \geq 0$ for each i.

Show that every optimal solution to this problem has the property that replenishments are delivered only when the inventory level drops to zero

$$\lim_{t \uparrow t_i} x(t) = 0 \quad \text{for every } i \ (\in \{1, 2, \ldots, n\}).$$

Hint: Show that the cost per week of a cycle can be reduced by extending its length until the inventory level drops to zero.

(d) Show that every optimal solution to the problem in part (c) has the property that all cycles are of the same length: There exists $T > 0$ such that

$$T_i = T \quad \text{for every } i.$$

Hint: Use part (c) and a substitution argument to improve the objective function value if any of the cycle lengths differ.

(e) Show that the optimal value of the objective function to the problem in part (c) is the same for all n.

(f) Argue informally why, in formulating the EOQ problem, which has an infinite time horizon, we may assume without loss of generality that replenishments are delivered only when the inventory level drops to zero and that all cycle lengths are the same.

1.2 Find the optimal order quantity in the EOQ setting in Section 1.1 when the objective is to minimize the cost per cycle (time between regenerations) rather than the cost per week. Give the intuition for why the solution differs from the EOQ in the way that it does.

1.3 *(Quantity Discounts)* Suppose, in the EOQ setting, that quantity discounts are offered: The ordering cost to obtain Q items is $K_i + c_i Q$ if

$Q_i \leq Q < Q_{i+1}$, for $i = 1, 2, \ldots, n$, where $0 = Q_1 < Q_2 < \cdots < Q_n < Q_{n+1} = \infty$, $c_1 > c_2 > \cdots > c_n$, and, to ensure that quantity discounts arise, $K_i + c_i Q_{i+1} \geq K_{i+1} + c_{i+1} Q_{i+1}$ for $i = 1, 2, \ldots, n-1$. How would you efficiently compute the optimal order quantity in this case?

1.4 *(Delays and Shortages)* Suppose, in the EOQ setting, that all demands must be met but that delays in meeting them are permitted, at a cost of p per week late per unit.

(a) Find the new optimal order quantity and the induced optimal cost per week. Hint: Let negative inventory represent backlogged demand, which will be met after some delay.

(b) Express the new optimal quantity as a multiple of the original EOQ (where no delays are allowed).

(c) Compared to the original EOQ model, is the average inventory level increased or decreased?

(d) Apply the results of this model to the following assertion: "If you never run out of inventory and never delay any customers, then you are carrying too much inventory."

1.5 (a) Verify that $v(y)$ of Section 1.2 can be written as

$$v(y) = p\mu - cy - pE(D - y)^+$$
$$= p\mu - cy - p \int_{\xi=y}^{\infty} (\xi - y)\phi(\xi)\, d\xi.$$

Hint: $\min(a, b) = \min(a - a, b - a) + a$ and $\min(x, 0) = -\max(-x, 0)$.

(b) Verify that $v(y)$ can also be written as

$$v(y) = (p - c)y - pE(y - D)^+$$
$$= (p - c)y - p \int_{\xi=0}^{y} (y - \xi)\phi(\xi)\, d\xi.$$

1.6 *(Leibnitz's Rule)* Let $g(x) := \int_{t=a(x)}^{b(x)} f(t, x)dt$, and let X denote an interval subset of the real line. Suppose that $b(x) > a(x)$ for all $x \in X$ and that both a and b are differentiable on X. Suppose further that f is continuous in its first argument and has a continuous partial derivative with respect to its second argument, denoted by $f_2(t, x)$, for $x \in X$ and $a(x) \leq t \leq b(x)$. Prove directly (using calculus) that g is differentiable on X and

$$g'(x) = \int_{t=a(x)}^{b(x)} f_2(t, x)dt + f(b(x), x)b'(x) - f(a(x), x)a'(x).$$

1.7   Consider the newsvendor problem (of Section 1.2).

(a) Verify that $v'(y) = p\bar{\Phi}(y) - c$. (Hint: Use Exercise 1.6.)

(b) Verify that

$$v(S) = p \int_{\xi=0}^{S} \xi\phi(\xi) \, d\xi.$$

Hint: Use (1.2) and (1.4).

1.8   Show that the following hold.

(a)
$$E(y - D)^+ = \int_{\xi=0}^{y} \Phi(\xi) \, d\xi,$$

and

(b)
$$E(D - y)^+ = \int_{\xi=y}^{\infty} \bar{\Phi}(\xi) \, d\xi.$$

Hint: Use either Lemma D.1 or integration by parts. Thus, by Exercise 1.6,

$$\frac{d}{dy}E(y - D)^+ = \Phi(y)$$

and

$$\frac{d}{dy}E(D - y)^+ = -\bar{\Phi}(y).$$

1.9   (Tunay Tunca)   (a) Show that $v(y)$ in Section 1.2 can be written as

$$v(y) = pE(D|D \leq y)\Phi(y) + py\bar{\Phi}(y) - cy.$$

(b) Using (a), show that

$$v(S) = (p - c)E(D|D \leq S).$$

(c) Interpret (b) verbally.

1.10   Some accounting systems do not charge the cost of units purchased until they are sold. The total acquisition cost is allocated across the units that are sold. In this setting, the total acquisition cost is cy, and the number of units sold is $\min(D,y)$. Thus, the per unit cost of goods sold is $cy/\min(D,y)$.

(a) Plot this cost as a function of D for the case of $c = 1$ and $y = 10$.

(b) Write down the expression for the cost of goods sold, namely, the product of the per unit cost of goods sold times the quantity sold, as a function of the initial stock level y and the quantity demanded D. Determine the expected value of this expression.

(c) Suppose the objective is to maximize the expected dollar sales less the expected cost of goods sold (instead of the cost of the goods purchased initially). Show that the optimal stock level for this case is the same as the original newsvendor solution.

1.11   Suppose, in the newsvendor model, that demand D is discrete in the sense that there exists a sequence of real numbers, $\{x_1, x_2, \ldots\}$, representing all potential demand quantities, and $0 \le x_1 \le x_2 \le \cdots$. Furthermore, suppose all these quantities are admissible stock levels. Prove that the smallest y such that

$$\Phi(y) \ge \frac{p - c}{p}$$

is an optimal stock level. (Continue to assume existence, but not necessarily uniqueness, of an optimal stock level in this problem.)

Hint: Establish the following:

(a) There exists an optimal stock level that is one of the potential demand quantities.

(b) When restricting consideration to potential demand quantities, the smallest i such that

$$\Phi(x_i) \ge \frac{p - c}{p}$$

leads to the unique optimal stock level.

(c) The smallest y such that

$$\Phi(y) \geq \frac{p - c}{p}$$

is the stock level found in (b).

1.12 Suppose, in the newsvendor model, that not all potential demand quantities are admissible stock levels. Porteus (1990:614) asserts that the smallest admissible y such that

$$\Phi(y) \geq \frac{p - c}{p}$$

is an optimal stock level. Show that this assertion is incorrect by constructing a counterexample. Hint: Let demand be continuous and uniformly distributed on $[0, 2]$. Suppose that the only admissible stock levels are integers. Select parameters such that the unique optimal stock level is 1, but the assertion leads to a stock level of 2.

1.13 Give a numerical example of a newsvendor problem in which demand is continuous and there are multiple distinct optimal stock levels. Hint: Let the demand density be strictly positive on two disjoint intervals.

1.14 Verify (1.5).

1.15 Suppose, in the newsvendor model, that demand is (approximately) normally distributed, $c = 1$, $p = 5$, $\mu = 1000$, and $\sigma = 300$. Determine the optimal stock level and the optimal expected contribution. Compute the expected contribution associated with stocking 10% less and stocking 10% more than optimal.

1.16 Suppose, in the newsvendor model, that demand is (approximately) normally distributed, that $\sigma = \mu/4$, and that the optimal stockout probability is 0.4. Calculate the optimal ratio of expected unsatisfied demand to expected total demand.

1.17 Verify in the case of normally distributed demand, that (1.7) holds and that the optimal fill rate equals

$$1 - \frac{\sigma}{\mu} I_{N}(z^{*}(\zeta)).$$

1.18   (a) Show that in the newsvendor model, the optimal expected contribution is positive (not necessarily strictly).

(b) Suppose demand is normally distributed, so, by (1.3) and (1.7), the (approximate) optimal expected contribution can be written as $(p-c)\mu-c\sigma L_{\mathbf{N}}(\zeta)$. Use this expression to derive an upper bound on the coefficient of variation of demand, σ/μ, that must hold for the expected contribution to be positive.

(c) Evaluate your upper bound for the numerical example of $c = 95$ and $p = 100$.

(d) Reconcile the apparent disagreement between parts (a) and (b).

1.19   Suppose, in the newsvendor problem, that there is an additional unit penalty π incurred for each unit short at the end of the period, so that the new expected contribution can be written as

$$v_{\mathbf{A}}(y) = v(y) - \pi E(D - y)^+.$$

(a) Show that the (new) optimal stockout probability is $\zeta = c/(p + \pi)$.

(b) Provide a numerical example for this model in which there are only two possible demand quantities and the optimal expected contribution is strictly negative.

(c) Suppose demand is normally distributed. Derive an expression analogous to that of Exercise 1.18 for the (approximate) optimal expected contribution. Use this expression to derive an upper bound on the coefficient of variation of demand, σ/μ, that must hold for the expected contribution to be positive.

(d) Evaluate your upper bound for the numerical example of $c = 100$, $p = 101$, and $\pi = 99$.

1.20   Suppose, in the newsvendor problem, that there is an additional unit holding cost h incurred for each unit leftover (unsold) at the end of the period, and each such unit is salvaged at a unit revenue of $r_{\mathbf{s}}$, so that the new expected contribution can be written as

$$v_{\mathbf{B}}(y) = v(y) + (r_{\mathbf{s}} - h)E(y - D)^+.$$

(a) What happens to the optimal solution if $r_s \geq c + h$?

(b) Assuming $r_s < c + h$, show how to redefine p and c so that one can assume without loss of generality that $r_s - h = 0$.

1.21   Consider the newsvendor model with market size n (denoting the total number of independent customers). Verify that if $p > c$ and $n > 0$, then $k := cz^* + pI_N(z^*) > 0$, where z^* satisfies $\Phi_N(z^*) = (p - c)/p$.

1.22   Consider the newsvendor model with market size n. Verify that the optimal expected contribution is $(p - c)n\mu_0 - \sigma_0 k \sqrt{n}$, where k is as given in Exercise 1.21.

1.23   Consider the newsvendor model with market size n for the case in which $c < p < 2c$.

(a) Show that it is optimal to stock nothing if $n \leq (z^* \sigma_0 / \mu_0)^2$.

(b) Show that, for $n \geq (z^* \sigma_0 / \mu_0)^2$, the expected contribution is an increasing function, and the safety stock is a decreasing function, of the market size n.

1.24   To reconcile the overage/underage cost formulation with the original formulation of the newsvendor model, we apparently must select $c_O = c$ and $c_U = p - c$. Either explain what is wrong with this selection or explain why it makes sense using the qualitative definitions of the overage and underage costs.

1.25   *(Overbooking)*   Consider a specific airline flight on a specific day with a fixed number n of seats. (You can also think of a hotel with a specific number of rooms available for a specific night.) Let p denote the return the airline receives for each seat that is occupied on that flight. (The airline receives returns only for occupied seats, not for reservations made.) If the airline overbooks the flight and m passengers show up for the flight with confirmed reservations and $m > n$, then there are $m - n$ *actual overbookings*, and the airline incurs a unit cost $\pi > 0$ (and receives no returns) for each of them, for a total actual overbooking cost of $\pi(m - n)$. The airline wishes to specify the booking level y as the number of seats that can be booked in advance for that flight. In particular, the airline plans to set y strictly greater than n: The first y requests for a reservation on the flight will be given a confirmed reservation and any after that will be told that the flight is full. Let Z denote the number of no-shows for the flight: the number of people with confirmed reservations on the flight who, for whatever reason, do not show up for it. All no-shows get their money back.

Assume that Z is statistically independent of the number of people who have confirmed reservations on the flight. For convenience, assume that Z is a continous variable with a known density ϕ and distribution Φ with $\Phi(0) = 0$ and $\Phi(n) = 1$: There is no chance that there will be zero or fewer no-shows and there is no chance of more than n no-shows.

All other costs and revenues are independent of y and Z. For example, there are no dynamic customer effects: A person's future patronage behavior is independent of (1) whether she was able to obtain a confirmed reservation or not, (2) if given a confirmed reservation, whether she shows up or not, and (3) if she shows up, whether she is able to fly on the flight or is bumped. (In practice, airlines announce how much they will offer for passengers to voluntarily get bumped, so those so volunteering are apt to feel adequately remunerated for doing so.)

(a) Derive the expression for the expected return to the airline as a function of y, assuming that (at least) y requests for a reservation are received.

(b) Derive an expression for the optimal level of y.

(c) What is the optimal probability of having empty seats on a flight?

1.26   *(Capacity Management When Producing to Order)*   An entrepreneur must set the capacity level y for her plant. Each unit of capacity costs c and is available for only a single period. A single product is produced, and once the capacity is set, the demand D will be observed. She will receive $p > c$ for each unit sold, so she will produce the feasible amount $(\leq y)$ that is as close to D as possible. Assume that there is possibly a strictly positive probability that demand will equal zero: $\Phi(0) > 0$ is allowed. Otherwise assume that our assumptions for the newsvendor model hold. For example, ϕ exists and Φ is differentiable on $(0, \infty)$.

(a) Derive the expected net contribution (sales revenues less capacity costs) as a function of y.

(b) Derive conditions for the optimal capacity level.

(c) Derive conditions under which this is an attractive business: The expected net contribution from following an optimal plan is positive.

References

Arrow, K. 1958. Historical background. K. Arrow, S. Karlin, H. Scarf (eds.). *Studies in the Mathematical Theory of Inventory and Production.* Stanford University Press, Stanford, Calif., 3–15.

Arrow, K., T. Harris, J. Marschak. 1951. Optimal inventory policy. *Econometrica.* **19** 250–72.

Edgeworth, F. 1888. The mathematical theory of banking. *J. Royal Statist. Soc.* **51** 113–27.

Harris, F. 1913. How many parts to make at once. *Factory, The Magazine of Management.* **10** 135–36, 152.

Porteus, E. 1985. Investing in reduced setups in the EOQ model. *Management Science.* **31** 998–1010.

Porteus, E., 1990. Stochastic inventory theory. D. Heyman, M. Sobel (eds.). *Handbooks in Operations Research and Management Science, Vol. 2.* Elsevier Science Publishers, Amsterdam, 605–52.

Wilson, R. 1934. A scientific routine for stock control. *Harvard Business Review.* **13** 116–34.

Table 1.1   Newsvendor Information for the Normal Distribution

Optimal Stockout Prob ζ	$z = z^*(\zeta)$	Normal Loss Function $I_N(z)$	EVPI Factor $L_N(\zeta)$	Optimal Stockout Prob ζ	$z = z^*(\zeta)$	Normal Loss Function $I_N(z)$	EVPI Factor $L_N(\zeta)$
0.95	-1.645	1.6657	0.109	0.19	0.878	0.1046	1.428
0.90	-1.282	1.3289	0.195	0.18	0.915	0.0976	1.458
0.85	-1.036	1.1141	0.274	0.17	0.954	0.0908	1.489
0.80	-0.842	0.9533	0.350	0.16	0.994	0.0842	1.521
0.75	-0.674	0.8236	0.424	0.15	1.036	0.0777	1.554
0.70	-0.524	0.7148	0.497	0.14	1.080	0.0713	1.590
0.65	-0.385	0.6209	0.570	0.13	1.126	0.0651	1.627
0.60	-0.253	0.5384	0.644	0.12	1.175	0.0590	1.667
0.55	-0.126	0.4649	0.720	0.11	1.227	0.0531	1.709
0.50	0.000	0.3989	0.798	0.10	1.282	0.0473	1.755
0.49	0.025	0.3865	0.814	0.09	1.341	0.0417	1.804
0.48	0.050	0.3744	0.830	0.08	1.405	0.0363	1.858
0.47	0.075	0.3624	0.846	0.07	1.476	0.0310	1.918
0.46	0.100	0.3507	0.863	0.06	1.555	0.0258	1.985
0.45	0.126	0.3393	0.880	0.055	1.598	0.0233	2.023
0.44	0.151	0.3280	0.896	0.050	1.645	0.0209	2.063
0.43	0.176	0.3169	0.913	0.045	1.695	0.0185	2.106
0.42	0.202	0.3061	0.931	0.040	1.751	0.0161	2.154
0.41	0.228	0.2955	0.948	0.035	1.812	0.01385	2.208
0.40	0.253	0.2850	0.966	0.030	1.881	0.01162	2.268
0.39	0.279	0.2747	0.984	0.025	1.960	0.00945	2.338
0.38	0.305	0.2647	1.002	0.020	2.054	0.00734	2.421
0.37	0.332	0.2548	1.020	0.015	2.170	0.00532	2.525
0.36	0.358	0.2451	1.039	0.014	2.197	0.00493	2.549
0.35	0.385	0.2355	1.058	0.013	2.226	0.00453	2.575
0.34	0.412	0.2262	1.078	0.012	2.257	0.00415	2.603
0.33	0.440	0.2170	1.097	0.011	2.290	0.00377	2.633
0.32	0.468	0.2079	1.118	0.010	2.326	0.00339	2.665
0.31	0.496	0.1991	1.138	0.009	2.366	0.00302	2.701
0.30	0.524	0.1904	1.159	0.008	2.409	0.00265	2.740
0.29	0.553	0.1818	1.180	0.007	2.457	0.00229	2.784
0.28	0.583	0.1734	1.202	0.006	2.512	0.00193	2.834
0.27	0.613	0.1652	1.225	0.005	2.576	0.00158	2.892
0.26	0.643	0.1571	1.248	0.004	2.652	0.00124	2.962
0.25	0.674	0.1492	1.271	0.003	2.748	0.00091	3.050
0.24	0.706	0.1414	1.295	0.002	2.878	0.00058	3.170
0.23	0.739	0.1337	1.320	0.0015	2.968	0.00043	3.253
0.22	0.772	0.1262	1.346	0.0010	3.090	0.00028	3.367
0.21	0.806	0.1189	1.372	0.0005	3.290	0.00013	3.555
0.20	0.842	0.1116	1.400	0.0001	3.719	0.00002	3.952

2

Recursion

Recursion is the philosophy that underlies the analysis of many models, particularly dynamic ones. The principle, popularized by Bellman (1957) under the label *dynamic programming*, is to decompose a complicated problem into a series of smaller, simpler problems, so that, having solved some of them, one can easily solve at least one more. In the case of dynamic models, it usually amounts to working backward. This chapter presents a variety of examples of recursions, illustrating the wide applicability of the concept. Wagner (1975) devotes several chapters to applications of recursion (dynamic programming) at a level consistent with this chapter.

2.1 Solving a Triangular System of Equations

Suppose we seek to solve a system of linear equations. That is, we are given a vector b and a matrix A, and we seek x such that

$$Ax = b.$$

If A is triangular, then the solution can be found easily by recursion. For example, suppose

$$A = \begin{pmatrix} 0.7 & 0 & 0 \\ -0.3 & 0.5 & 0 \\ -0.4 & -0.5 & 1 \end{pmatrix},$$

and

$$b = \begin{pmatrix} 0.3 \\ 0.2 \\ 0 \end{pmatrix}.$$

The first equation allows x_1 to be found easily: $0.7x_1 = 0.3$ so $x_1 = 3/7$. Once x_1 is known, it is easy to use the second equation to solve for x_2: $0.5x_2 = .2 + 0.3x_1$ so $x_2 = 0.4 + 1.8/7 = 46/70$. Finally, given x_1 and x_2, the third equation allows us to easily determine x_3: $x_3 = 0 + 0.4x_1 + 0.5x_2 = 1/2$.

This process of using backward substitution allows us to determine recursively the value of the variables, one at a time. Regardless of how many variables have been determined so far, another can easily be computed. Only one pass through the matrix is needed to solve the problem. Commercial linear equation solvers often use this approach, first converting the system into a triangular system and then back substituting.

2.2   Probabilistic Analysis of Models

Suppose that a facility is about to process a batch (lot) of Q units. The process starts in control, producing all good items, but each time a single unit is produced, the process can go out of control with probability q. Once the process is out of control, the process remains that way and only defectives are produced. No opportunity to put the process back in control, such as through inspection, arises until the entire batch is complete.

Recursion is useful in finding the expected number of defects in the batch above. Let $f(i)$ denote the expected number of defectives in a batch of i units (remaining), given that the process starts processing the first of those i units in control. Let $\bar{q} := 1 - q$, the probability that the process remains in control after processing a unit. Then the key recursive expression is

$$f(i) = qi + \bar{q}f(i - 1),$$

and $f(0) = 0$. That is, if the process goes out of control when there are i more to be produced, all i will be defective. If not, then the current unit will be good and the expected number of defectives will be the expected number in a problem with $i-1$ more to be produced. For example, suppose $q = 0.0004$. Computing recursively, we have $f(1) = 0.0004$, $f(2) = 0.0004(2) + (0.9996)(0.0004) \cong 0.0012$, and so on.

2.3   Proof by Mathematical Induction

If (1) a proposition is true for $i = 0$, and (2) given an arbitrary n, it is true for $i = n+1$ given that it is true for $i \leq n$, then (3) the proposition is true for all integers i. This principle, called *mathematical induction,* can be interpreted as another example of recursion. We now illustrate the use of mathematical induction to verify a nonrecursive formula for the expected number of defects in the simple quality control model of the previous section. (This is not the only way to prove this result.)

Lemma 2.1   *(Porteus 1986)*

$$f(i) = i - \frac{\bar{q}(1 - \bar{q}^i)}{q} \text{ for } i = 1, 2, \ldots.$$

Proof   The result is true for $i = 0$. For the inductive step:

$$f(n + 1) = q(n + 1) + \bar{q}f(n)$$
$$= q(n + 1) + \bar{q}\left(n - \frac{\bar{q}(1 - \bar{q}^n)}{q}\right)$$
$$= qn + q + n - qn - \frac{\bar{q}^2(1 - \bar{q}^n)}{q}$$
$$= n + 1 - \bar{q} - \frac{\bar{q}(\bar{q} - \bar{q}^{n+1})}{q}$$
$$= n + 1 - \frac{\bar{q}(1 - \bar{q}^{n+1})}{q}.$$

Hence, the result is true for every integer i.   □

2.4   Shortest-Route Problems

We now see how recursion can be used in optimization models. Suppose we seek the shortest route from node (state) 1 to node 16, as shown in Figure 2.1, where the distance between two nodes is shown on the arc connecting them. To

do so, we shall find the shortest route from all nodes to node 16, and we shall
do so by working backward.

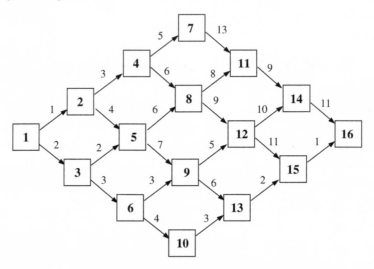

Figure 2.1   Shortest-Route Problem

We start with a mathematical form of the recursion, explain it verbally, and
end by making the computations. Let $f(i)$ denote the minimum distance from
node i to node 16, for $i = 1, 2, \ldots, 16$ and let d_{ij} denote the distance from
node i to node j for each arc leading out of node i . (In this example, there
are at most two arcs departing from any node.) Let $f(16) := 0$: The shortest
distance from node 16 to itself is zero. Then the recursion is as follows, for
$i = 1, 2, \ldots, 15$:

$$f(i) = \min_{j} \big[d_{ij} + f(j) \big].$$

Here is a verbalization of the recursion. The shortest distance from node i to
node 16 can be computed as follows. Consider the nodes that can be reached
directly from node i . For each such directly accessible node, compute the direct
distance from node i to that node, plus the shortest distance from that node
to node 16. The shortest distance from node i must be the smallest of these
computed quantities, one for each node that is directly accessible from node i .
The trick is to build up the solutions by working backward, so that at any stage
of the computation, there is always at least one node whose shortest distance
can be computed: We have already computed the shortest distance (to node
16) from each of the nodes that can be reached directly from that node.

The results of the computations are given in Figure 2.2. The shortest distance from node 15 (to node 16) is clearly 1, and that quantity is recorded above node 15. Similarly, the shortest distance from node 14 is 11. The shortest distance from node 13 is the direct distance to node 15 (2) plus the shortest distance from there (1), for a total of 3, which is recorded above node 13.

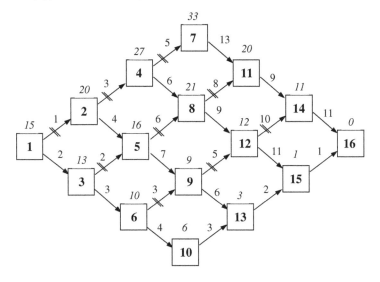

Figure 2.2   Shortest-Route Problem Solved

The essence of the recursion is illustrated with node 12. If you start in node 12, you can go directly to either node 14 or 15. If you go to node 14, you must go 10 to get there directly, plus 11 more to complete the journey optimally from there, for a total of 21. If you go to node 15, you must go 11 to get there directly, plus 1 more to complete the journey, for a total of 12. So the choice is between 21 or 12, and 12 is better, so the shortest distance from node 12 is 12, and the optimal decision, shown by the arc that is not crossed off as being nonoptimal, is to go directly to node 15. The shortest distances for the remaining nodes are computed similarly. The shortest distance from node 1 to node 16 is 15, and the shortest route is along nodes 1-3-6-10-13-15-16.

We now discuss what is called a *myopic policy*, which, in general, is shortsighted and looks only at the immediate consequences of making a decision. For example, a myopic policy in this context moves to the closest next node. In this example, this policy goes along the top nodes, 1-2-4-7-11-14-16, and the resulting total distance is 42, which is far more than the shortest distance. Indeed, in this example, this policy yields the *longest* distance from node 1 to node 16. Furthermore, regardless of the node at which you might start, it is nonoptimal to follow this policy from there. However, there are conditions under which myopic policies can be shown to be optimal. In general, they pick the decisions that optimize the immediate financial consequences, and ignore the subsequent consequences. Consequently, they are extremely easy to identify. Thus, it is of great interest if it is possible to capture the essence of the subsequent consequences of a decision by transforming the performance measurement system prior to any recursive computations. In that case, myopic policies based on the new measurement system are optimal. Chapter 6 presents conditions and examples under which this approach works.

While it may be intuitively clear why recursion can be used in this example to find the shortest route (and distance), we will examine conditions under which this approach is valid in Chapters 3–5.

2.5   Stochastic Shortest-Route Problems

Figure 2.3 below generalizes the previous example by introducing uncertainty. Decisions can be made only at the square nodes, which are called the *decision nodes*. The circle nodes are called the *chance nodes*. When you arrive at a chance node, one of the outcomes shown as an arc emanating from that node

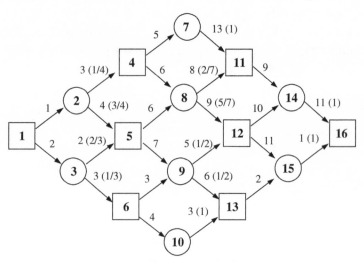

Figure 2.3   Stochastic Shortest-Route Problem

will arise, with the probability as shown in parentheses next to the distance. The distances are the same as those of the previous example, and your objective is to minimize the expected distance from node 1 to node 16. You can think of this example as traveling across country with a friend. You will alternate deciding which state (node) to visit next. Your friend has announced that he will randomly select the next state using the probabilities as shown, for each of those states (nodes) where he gets to pick the next state. (He anticipates with pleasure the surprise of the random revelation of the state to be visited next.)

The analysis proceeds as in the previous example, backward. Figure 2.4 shows the results. The analysis working back to state 10 is identical to the deterministic analysis. However, at state 9, you cannot select the next state. Your friend will pick state 12 with probability $1/2$ and state 13 with probability $1/2$. You therefore determine the expected distance from that node to node 16 by calculating

$$(5 + 12)\frac{1}{2} + (6 + 3)\frac{1}{2} = 13.$$

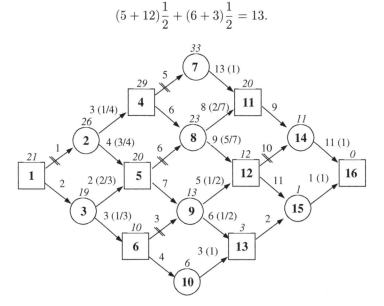

Figure 2.4   *Stochastic Shortest-Route Problem Solved*

If the next state is 12, the distance 5 will be traveled to get there, and the expected distance to complete the journey, acting optimally in the process, is 12. The 17 gets multiplied by the probability of that state being selected, and the computation is repeated for the other possible next state.

The recursion for the decision nodes is exactly as given in the previous section. The recursion for the chance nodes is as follows:

$$f(i) = \sum_j [d_{ij} + f(j)] p(j|i),$$

where the summation is over the states j that can be reached directly from node i, and $p(j|i)$ is the conditional probability that state j will be visited next given that the process is in state i.

Note that the minimum expected distance is 21 instead of the 15 found in the previous example: There are states that your friend may randomly select to visit that are not on the optimal deterministic path, namely, states 5 and 12. Thus, to implement the optimal plan in this setting, you must retain the optimal actions for these states as well as those found for the deterministic model.

2.6   Deterministic Production Planning

Consider a finite horizon, discrete time, deterministic production planning problem. Demand per month over the n month planning horizon is known and must be satisfied. There are no capacity constraints and production occurs instantaneously. Assume that production always satisfies some exact number of months' demand and that production occurs when the stock level drops to zero. (This assumption is shown to be justified for a reasonable cost structure by Wagner and Whitin, 1958.) Let c_{ij} denote the sum of production and holding costs over months i through (and including) j when producing enough to meet demand exactly for those months. In particular c_{ij} includes the cost of producing, at the beginning of month i, the sum of demands over months i through j, plus the holding costs to be incurred in those months until the production quantity is depleted to zero. Thus, a significant amount of straightforward computation may be required to obtain each c_{ij}. We seek the minimum cost production plan.

Let $f(i)$ denote the minimum cost of meeting demand over months i through n, assuming that the inventory level at the beginning of month i, before production, is zero. Then we have:

$$f(i) = \min_{j \in \{i, i+1, \cdots, n\}} [c_{ij} + f(j+1) | i \le j \le n], \qquad (2.1)$$

where $f(n + 1) := 0$. Once we find $f(1)$, we can recreate the optimal plan over time. There is so much similarity between this recursion and that of the shortest-route problem presented earlier that many say this is a variation of a shortest-route problem, with costs being substituted for distances.

2.7   Knapsack Problems

The knapsack problem is nominally the problem of maximizing the value of objects packed into a knapsack with limited capacity. Let x_i denote the number of units of object i packed, $f_i(x_i)$ the resulting value, $g_i(x_i)$ the capacity of the knapsack consumed, and b (> 0) the amount of capacity available. Let X denote the set of admissible values of each decision variable. The knapsack problem is called *discrete* or *continuous* if $X = \{0, 1, \ldots\}$ or $X = [0, \infty)$, respectively. Each g_i is assumed to be a positive and increasing function. The knapsack problem seeks to maximize a separable return subject to a single separable constraint and can be stated as a mathematical program as follows: Find a value for x_i in X for each i to

$$\max \sum_{i=1}^{n} f_i(x_i)$$

subject to

$$\sum_{i=1}^{n} g_i(x_i) \leq b.$$

Thus, the knapsack problem can represent other problems, such as selecting projects to fund under a limited budget. We are about to illustrate how recursion can be fruitfully applied to knapsack problems. It is possible to do so by working backward in the manner suggested in previous sections of this chapter. However, the sequencing of the decision variables is arbitrary, and, in particular, there is no requirement that the problem be solved by working backward. Thus, we shall illustrate the use of *forward* recursion, in which the problem is built up by working forward.

Let

$$F_i(\beta) := \max \left(\sum_{j=1}^{i} f_j(x_j) \,\middle|\, x_j \in X \text{ for } 1 \leq j \leq i \text{ and } \sum_{j=1}^{i} g_j(x_j) \leq \beta \right),$$

which is the optimal return from a knapsack of capacity β allowing only selection of objects 1 through i.

The recursion is

$$F_i(\beta) = \max_{x_i \in X} \left[f_i(x_i) + F_{i-1}(\beta - g_i(x_i)) \right],$$

which is solved in the sequence $i = 1, 2 \ldots, n$, and where $F_0(\beta)$ is defined to be zero for all $\beta \geq 0$ and $-\infty$ for all $\beta < 0$. That is, if we are limiting consideration to objects 1 through i, and we pack x_i units of object i into a knapsack of capacity β, then we will get the value of the x_i units just packed plus the optimal value of the knapsack of capacity $\beta - g_i(x_i)$ we have left over to allocate to the first $i - 1$ objects. Clearly, $F_n(b)$ is the optimal value of the objective function we seek, and, once we have it, we can recreate the optimal solution.

This approach ensures feasibility of the solution by assessing an infinite penalty if strictly more than the capacity available is allocated. It is possible to enforce feasibility directly and thereby avoid the use of such penalties by adding to each recursion the constraint $g_i(x_i) \leq \beta$ to the requirement that x_i be in X. Computational implementations of both formulations are equivalent.

Exercises

2.1   Consider the simple quality control model of Section 2.2.

(a) Assume that q is small and develop a first-order approximation of the expected number of defects (in a batch of size i).

Hint: A first-order approximation is what you get when you write down the Taylor series expansion of an expression, expanding around a pertinent value of a pertinent variable in the expression, and dropping all but the first-order terms of that expression. In this case, the pertinent variable is q, and the pertinent value is 0. Using more conventional terminology, expand around $q = 0$. Recall that the Taylor series expansion of $f(x)$ around $x = a$ is

$$f(x) = f(a) + (x - a)f'(a) + \frac{(x - a)^2}{2!}f''(a) + \cdots.$$

(b) Consider the following simple approximation of the same quantity:

$$f(i) \cong \frac{qi^2}{2}.$$

Develop conditions on i that guarantee that your approximation in (a) and that given here are no more than 1% apart.

(c) Suppose that $q = 0.0004$ and $i = 200$. Compute (i) $f(i)$ exactly, (ii) your approximation in (a), and (iii) the simple approximation in (b).

2.2   Consider the deterministic production planning problem of Section 2.6. Let D_i denote the known (deterministic) demand in month i for each i. For $x \geq 0$, let $c_i(x)$ denote the cost of producing quantity x in month i, and $h_i(x)$ the holding cost incurred in month i as a function of the ending inventory level in that month. Specify c_{ij} in terms of these parameters.

2.3   (*Discounted Deterministic Production Planning*)   (Continuation of Exercise 2.2)   Suppose, as in Appendix C, that costs are discounted using a one period discount factor of $\alpha \in (0, 1]$. That is, a cost of c incurred at the beginning of period i is equivalent to incurring a cost of $\alpha^{i-1}c$ at the beginning of period 1.

(a) Qualitatively redefine c_{ij} so that (1) continues to hold.

(b) Specify c_{ij} now in terms of the parameters specified in Exercise 2.2.

2.4   (*A Continuous Knapsack Problem*)   Consider the following specialized continuous knapsack problem, as defined in Section 2.7: $f_i(x) = f(x)$ and $g_i(x) = x$ for each $i \in \{1, 2, \ldots, n\}$ and $x \in X$ $(= [0, \infty))$. In addition, f is differentiable, strictly increasing, and concave on X, so that $f'(x)$ is decreasing in x.

(a) Use Theorem B.1 (the first theorem in Appendix B) to prove that $x_i = b/n$ is optimal for this problem.

(b) Prove that $x_i = b/n$ is optimal for this problem by proving by induction that, for $\beta \geq 0$,

$$F_i(\beta) = i f_i(\beta/i).$$

2.5 *(TV Game Show)* (Haggstrom, 1966)   You are a participant on a television game show that works as follows. Beginning the game with no accumulated winnings, you spin the wheel once, and after each spin, you are allowed to spin again if you wish. For each spin of the wheel, there are m possible strictly positive quantities, each with a known probability of arising: Amount r_i will be added to your accumulated winnings if the spinner ends up on outcome i, which will occur with probability p_i. However, all is not well in LA-LA land: There is a positive probability $p = 1 - \sum_{i=1}^{m} p_i$, where $p \in (0,1)$, that the pointer will end up on *bust:* If that happens, your accumulated winnings are lost, you win nothing, and the game is over. Otherwise, after the outcome amount r_i is added to your accumulated winnings, you must either (i) take your accumulated winnings and thereby end the game or (ii) choose to spin the wheel again. You need not decide whether to spin the wheel again until after seeing how much has been added to your accumulated winnings.

Your objective is to maximize your expected accumulated winnings from playing the game. Assume the payoffs are sorted so that $0 < r_1 < r_2 < \cdots < r_m$ and let $\mu := \sum_{i=1}^{m} p_i r_i$, the expected gain from one spin of the wheel. Consider the problem of having a maximum of n more spins, and let $f^n(x)$ denote the maximum expected accumulated winnings, when facing the decision of stopping or spinning with a current accumulation of x and with a maximum of n more spins.

(a) Write down a recursion for $f^n(x)$ in terms of $f^{n-1}(\cdot)$ and the parameters of the problem.

(b) Solve the problem numerically for the case in which $m = 3$, $p_i = 1/4$ for $i = 1, 2, 3$, $r_1 = 1$, $r_2 = 5$, $r_3 = 10$, and there are one or two more spins available. In particular, give the expected total winnings and optimal decisions as functions of the accumulated winnings x so far and the number n of spins available.

2.6 *(Optimally Selling an Asset)* (Karlin, 1962)   You have a single asset for sale. Each period a new bid for the asset is made for your asset from a new buyer. You consider this bid to be a positive random variable X described by the probability distribution Φ and density ϕ. You also consider the bids in different periods to be statistically independent. You use a single period discount factor of $\alpha \in (0,1)$. You plan to accept the first bid that exceeds *x*. Let $v(x)$ denote the expected present value of the proceeds from selling the asset, at the beginning of a period in which you still have the asset and you have not received the bid in that period yet. Assume you have an infinite period time horizon, so if the bid in a period is below x, you start over again in the next period, in the same state (still having the unsold asset and not having received the bid in that period yet).

(a) Write down a recursion for $v(x)$ and use it to find an explicit expression for $v(x)$ in terms of x, $\Phi(x)$, $I(x)$, and α, where

$$I(x) := E(X - x)^+ = \int_x^\infty (\xi - x)\phi(\xi) \, d\xi.$$

(b) Suppose that $\alpha = 0.99$ and the bids are normally distributed with a mean of 1000 and a standard deviation of 200. Furthermore, you select $x = 1200$. Evaluate $v(x)$ numerically. Hint: Use a spreadsheet program that computes the standard normal distribution function Φ_N, and apply equations (1.5) and (1.6), the latter of which says that $I(x) = \sigma I_N((x - \mu)/\sigma)$. If necessary, you may interpolate using Table 1.1.

2.7 *(Cannibals and Missionaries)* (Bellman and Dreyfus, 1962) A group consisting of three cannibals and three missionaries seeks to cross a river. A boat is available that can hold up to two people and can be navigated (over or back) by any combination of cannibals and missionaries involving one or two people. If, at any time, the missionaries on one side of the river are outnumbered by the cannibals on that side of the river, then the missionaries are toast. (Any people in the boat on that side of the river at that time are included in the comparison: It is convenient to assume that, after each crossing, everybody gets out of the boat for purposes of determining whether the missionaries remain safe.)

Let (i, j, k) denote a state of the system, where i and j denote the number of cannibals and missionaries, respectively, on the first side of the river, and $k \in \{1, 2\}$ indicates which side of the river the boat is on. (For example, $k = 1$ indicates the boat is on the first side.) Think of a state as being defined when the boat is empty, either just before commencing a crossing of the river or just after doing so. A state is *admissible* if no missionaries are outnumbered on either side of the river. That is, (i, j, k) is admissible if $i \leq j$ when $j > 0$ and $3 - i \leq 3 - j$ when $3 - j > 0$. Let Ω denote the set of admissible states.

Let S denote an arbitrary nonempty subset of Ω. Let T denote the operator such that $T(S)$ is the largest subset of Ω that can be reached in one crossing of the river from states in S. Let $S_0 := \{(3,3,1)\}$, the set consisting of the single starting state of the system. Define the recursion $S_n := T(S_{n-1})$ for $n = 1, 2, \ldots$. For example, $S_1 = \{(2,3,2), (2,2,2), (1,3,2)\}$, corresponding to who goes into the boat on the first crossing (one cannibal only, one of each, or two cannibals).

(a) Display Ω. Hint: states in Ω need not necessarily be reachable though a sequence of crossings without losing any missionaries.

(b) Find m, the smallest n such that $(0,0,2) \in S_n$. Specify, in a compact way, S_n for $n = 2, 3, \ldots, m$. Identify the sequence of states that are visited as the system moves from $(3,3,1)$ to $(0,0,2)$.

References

Bellman, R. 1957. *Dynamic Programming*. Princeton University Press, Princeton, N.J.

Bellman, R., S. Dreyfus. 1962. *Applied Dynamic Programming*. Princeton University Press, Princeton, N.J.

Haggstrom, G. 1966. Optimal stopping and experimental design. *Annals of Mathematical Statistics*. **37** 7–29.

Karlin, S. 1962. Stochastic models and optimal policy for selling an asset. K. Arrow, S. Karlin, H. Scarf (eds.). *Studies in Applied Probability and Management Science*. Stanford University Press, Stanford, Calif., 148–58.

Porteus, E. 1986. Optimal lot sizing, process quality improvement and setup cost reduction. *Operations Research*. **34** 137–44.

Wagner, H. 1975. *Principles of Operations Research*. Prentice-Hall, Englewood Cliffs, N.J.

Wagner, H., T. Whitin. 1958. Dynamic version of the economic lot size model. *Management Science*. **5** 89–96.

3

Finite-Horizon
Markov Decision Processes

In Chapter 2, we solved an example of a shortest-route problem. We also solved an example of a stochastic shortest-route problem in which there was uncertainty about the next node/state at which we might find ourselves after making an optimal decision. Thus, we needed to be prepared with a contingency plan of what to do for each possible state we might find ourselves in. Our solution approach of moving backward was very helpful in this regard: We found the optimal decision for every possible state, not just the ones that might be visited when following an optimal policy.

This book aims to prepare you to analyze dynamic models of your own choosing in which uncertainty plays an important role, and the simple idea of working backward, using recursion, and picking out the optimal decisions for each possible state is at the heart of such analyses.

This chapter continues to apply this approach on an example and uses the example to introduce the vocabulary and basic results of finite-horizon Markov decision processes. Chapter 4 shows how this approach can be used to characterize the optimal decisions in structured problems, and Chapter 5 turns to verifying formally that what we are doing is valid.

3.1   Example: e-Rite-Way

Suppose you run an Internet retailing company, e-Rite-Way, that has the e-mail addresses of its previous customers. You have tentatively categorized customers into one of two possible states: a (previous) customer is in *state 1* and is called *inactive* if s/he has not made a purchase in the last month. A customer is in *state 2* and is called *active* if s/he has made a purchase in the last month. Up to now, you have depended on the convenience of your service, including a well-designed customer user interface, to attract and retain customers. You are now considering periodically sending a modest gift/reminder, such as an animated electronic greeting card to customers to help enhance customer retention, in conjunction with either a minor or major price promotion. In particular, you are considering making one of the following three decisions for each customer each month.

Table 3.1   Options and Their Direct Costs

Decision a	Description	\$ Direct Cost $c(a)$
0	Nothing active carried out	0
1	Gift sent and minor price promotion offered	0.50
2	Gift sent and major price promotion offered	0.50

You plan to carry out an analysis of a single generic customer, with the intent of applying that analysis to all customers. At the beginning of each month, the *system*, namely the generic customer, is in one of two possible states. You want the decision you make about the customer to depend on the state of that customer at that time. For example, you want to allow the possibility that an inactive customer will be offered a major price promotion while an active one will be offered nothing.

To carry out your analysis, you must assess the probability of a customer making a purchase in response to each decision. Your assessment depends on whether the customer made a purchase in the last month or not. For example, if a gift is sent to an inactive customer with a minor price promotion, then you estimate that customer will purchase something in the next month with probability 0.0707 and will thereby become an active customer. In other words, if the state of the system is 1 and decision 1 is made, then the system will move to state 2 at the beginning of the next period with probability 0.0707. In general, p_{sj}^a denotes the probability that the system moves from state s to state j in one period if action a has been selected. The estimated parameters are shown in Table 3.2 below.

Table 3.2   Purchase Probabilities

Customer State s	Decision a	Probability of No Purchase p_{s1}^a	Probability of Purchase p_{s2}^a
1	0	0.9899	0.0101
1	1	0.9293	0.0707
1	2	0.8586	0.1414
2	0	0.8081	0.1919
2	1	0.7273	0.2727
2	2	0.5051	0.4949

Let $\alpha = 0.99$ denote the one-month discount factor, and suppose you have determined that the expected value of the contribution from purchases made over a month (valued at the end of that month) given that a purchase is made (by one customer) is $8 if no promotion is offered to that customer, is $7 if a minor promotion is offered, and is $3 if a major promotion is offered. In general, r_{sj}^a denotes the subsequent return (valued at the end of the period) if the system moves from state s to state j and action a has been made. Thus, in this case, $r_{s2}^0 = 8$, $r_{s2}^1 = 7$, $r_{s2}^2 = 3$, and the rest equal zero.

You can therefore compute the expected present value of the immediate return from each decision made for each customer type, which consists of the expected contribution from any purchases made over the next month less the direct costs:

Table 3.3   Expected Immediate Returns

Customer State s	Decision a	Direct Cost	Expected Present Value of Purchase	Immediate Return $r(s, a)$
1	0	0	$.99[(.9899)0 + (0.0101)8]$	0.08
1	1	−0.5	$.99[(.9293)0 + (0.0707)7]$	−0.01
1	2	−0.5	$.99[(.8586)0 + (0.1414)3]$	−0.08
2	0	0	$.99[0 + (0.1919)8]$	1.52
2	1	−0.5	$.99[0 + (0.2727)7]$	1.39
2	2	−0.5	$.99[0 + (0.4949)3]$	0.97

In general notation, we have the following:

$$r(s, a) := -c(a) + \alpha \sum_j p_{sj}^a r_{sj}^a$$
$$= -c(a) + \sum_j q_{sj}^a r_{sj}^a,$$

where

$$q_{sj}^a := \alpha p_{sj}^a,$$

which we call the *effective transition probability* of moving from state s to state j given action a. Effective transition probabilities can be interpreted as representing either discounted probabilities or as actual probabilities in an undiscounted problem in which there is a probability of $1 - \alpha$ that the process "stops" and no further returns are received or costs are incurred. This latter representation and interpretation is useful in general. In this example, it is also helpful in simplifying manual computations.

Table 3.4   *Effective Transition Probabilities*

Customer State s	Decision a	Effective Probability of No Purchase q_{s1}^a	Effective Probability of Purchase q_{s2}^a
1	0	0.98	0.01
1	1	0.92	0.07
1	2	0.85	0.14
2	0	0.80	0.19
2	1	0.72	0.27
2	2	0.50	0.49

You seek to maximize the expected present value of the returns you receive from your customers. As usual, we apply recursion and get started by considering the one-period problem. Assuming that a customer has no residual value at the end of the period, the policy that maximizes the expected return in a one-period problem is the one that maximizes the immediate return, and that policy can be found in Table 3.3. For example, no promotion should be offered to either customer type, because the immediate benefit of any purchases does not outweigh the cost of the gift. Because of the short time horizon, this policy ignores the value of converting inactive customers into active ones, who are more likely to buy again in the future. Put differently, this policy ignores the opportunity cost of letting customers become inactive.

Two-Period Problem

We now consider the returns over a two-month time horizon. For example, at the beginning of this horizon, consider sending an inactive customer a major promotion: Select action 2 when in state 1. The immediate return is -0.08 (a loss) over the first month. At the beginning of the next month, you will act optimally. So the optimal expected present value of the subsequent returns (over the remaining one month in this case) is $(.85)(.08)+(.14)(1.52) = 0.2808$. The total is $-.08 + .2808 = .2008$. We can now work backward to determine the optimal promotion decision for each customer state, at the beginning of a two-period problem.

Table 3.5   *Analysis of Two-Period Problem*

s	Return from Decision 0	Return from Decision 1	Return from Decision 2	Optl Decn	Optl Value
1	$.08 + (.98).08$ $+(.01)1.52$ $= .1736$	$-.01 + (.92).08$ $+(.07)1.52$ $= .17$	$-.08 + (.85).08$ $+(.14)1.52$ $= .2008$	2	.2008
2	$1.52 + (.8).08$ $+(.19)1.52$ $= 1.8728$	$1.39 + (.72).08$ $+(.27)1.52$ $= 1.858$	$0.97 + (.5).08$ $+(.49)1.52$ $= 1.7548$	0	1.8728

So, the strategy (contingency plan) you should use with a two-period (month) time horizon is as follows: At the beginning, send a major promotion to the inactive customers and nothing to the active ones. After a month, send nothing to any customer. Each inactive customer yields an expected contribution of about $0.20 over the two months, and each active customer yields about $1.87. The returns would be less with any different strategy.

Let $f^n(s)$ denote the maximum expected present value of the returns over n periods starting at state s. We computed $f^1(s)$ earlier for each state s and we have just computed $f^2(s)$ using the following recursion, called the *optimality equations:*

$$f^n(s) = \max_a \left\{ r(s,a) + \alpha \sum_j p_{sj}^a f^{n-1}(j) \right\}$$

$$= \max_a \left\{ r(s,a) + \sum_j q_{sj}^a f^{n-1}(j) \right\}.$$

The optimality equations say that the optimal return over an n-period horizon can be computed as follows. Pick an initial state s and consider an arbitrary action a. Then take the expected immediate return and add the expected present value of the optimal returns associated with each state to which the system might move by the end of this period. Call that the *conditional expected return* (for that action and state), which represents the expected present value of using that action in that state now and acting optimally thereafter. Compute the conditional expected returns for every feasible action at this state and pick the largest one. The result is the optimal value of starting in this state.

We have also been using what is called the *optimality criterion* to identify optimal actions. This criterion says that any decision that yields the largest conditional expected return for a particular state (and number of periods left) is optimal when the system is in that state. In this context, the optimality equations and the optimality criterion are almost self-evidently valid. However, as promised at the beginning of this chapter, we shall return in Chapter 5 to the question of their validity in general.

Longer-Horizon Problems

It is now straightforward to compute the optimal returns and optimal contingency plans for longer-horizon problems. Tables 3.6 and 3.7 analyze the three- and four-period problems, respectively.

Table 3.6   Analysis of Three-Period Problem

s	Conditional Exp. Return $a = 0$	Conditional Exp. Return $a = 1$	Conditional Exp. Return $a = 2$	Optl Decn	Optl Value
1	0.2955	0.3058	0.3529	2	0.3529
2	2.036	2.040	1.988	1	2.040

Table 3.7   Analysis of Four-Period Problem

s	Conditional Exp. Return $a = 0$	Conditional Exp. Return $a = 1$	Conditional Exp. Return $a = 2$	Optl Decn	Optl Value
1	0.4462	0.4575	0.5056	2	0.5056
2	2.1899	2.1949	2.1462	1	2.1949

Thus, the optimal contingency plan is as follows when there are four or fewer months in the time horizon: Send a major promotion to inactive customers each month, except in the last month, when you send nothing. Send a major promotion to active customers if there are three or four months to go, a minor promotion if there are two months to go, and nothing in the last month. Each inactive customer is worth about \$0.51 and each active customer about \$2.19 at the beginning of a four-month horizon problem.

3.2   General Vocabulary and Basic Results

We now introduce finite-horizon Markov decision processes. [Illustrations of these concepts using the e-Rite-Way example appear in square brackets.]

At the beginning of each of a given number N of periods, a process is observed to be in some *state* s, which is a member of the *state space* S. [In e-Rite-Way, there are only two states, so $S = \{1, 2\}$. We varied N from 1 to 4.] The number N is called the *planning horizon* and the *time horizon*. The process is a *chain* if S is discrete. At each such point in time, an *action* (also *decision*) a must be selected from the *set of admissible actions* $A(s)$. [There are three admissible actions for each state: $A(s) = \{0, 1, 2\}$ for $s = 1, 2$.] The process evolves probabilistically to another state, by the beginning of the next period. This evolution is Markovian in that the next state depends on the history (of past states and actions) only through the current state and action. For a chain, the probability of making a transition from state s to state j in one period, given that action a was taken, is p_{sj}^a, for each $s, j \in S$ and $a \in A(s)$. The *effective probability* is $q_{sj}^a := \alpha p_{sj}^a$, where $\alpha \in (0, 1]$ is the one-period discount factor. [$\alpha = 0.99$.] The *immediate return* resulting from action a in state s is $r(s, a)$. The *terminal value function* v_T provides a terminal value as a function of the state the process is in at the end of the planning horizon. [The terminal value function was zero, which is a common specification. We shall specify nonzero terminal value functions later.]

Decision Rules, Strategies, and Policies

A *decision rule* δ is a function defined on the state space that specifies an admissible action/decision for each state. It is used to encapsulate the decisions to be made in a given period. Formally, $\delta(s) \in A(s)$ for every $s \in S$. It can be represented as a vector when the state space is finite. [The decision rule that was found to be optimal at the beginning of a two-period problem sends a major promotion to the inactive customers and nothing to the active customers.]

The *set of admissible decision rules* Δ is the set of decision rules that are allowed. Formally, we require $\delta \in \Delta$. [Δ consists of all possible decision rules, which can be written mathematically as $\Delta = A_1 \times A_2$, which is the Cartesian product of the sets of admissible actions for each state. That is, if $\delta(s) \in A(s)$ for each s, then $\delta \in \Delta$.]

When the state space and action spaces are discrete, it is customary to let Δ consist of all possible decision rules, and there is no issue in specifying the set of admissible decision rules. However, if the state space is continuous or even more general, not all possible decision rules may be admissible. For example, if the state space is the interval $[0,1]$, and the action space is the same interval, it is possible to create a nonmeasurable decision rule, and nonmeasurable decision rules cause problems when evaluating the integrals involved in defining expected values. Thus, it is usual to require that the admissible decision rules be measurable. Sometimes they are required to have additional properties, such as being semicontinuous or even continuous. The bottom line is that what is admissible is up to the analyst: The more rules that are admissible, the more powerful the results, but perhaps the more technical the proofs must be.

A *strategy* $\pi = (\delta_1, \delta_2, \ldots, \delta_N)$ (also sometimes written as $\pi = (\pi_1, \pi_2, \ldots, \pi_N)$) gives an admissible decision rule for each period. That is, we require that $\delta_n \in \Delta$ for each n. A strategy can be thought of as a matrix when the state space is finite, a row for each state and a column for each period in the time horizon. [The optimal strategy for the four-period problem used one decision rule for the first two periods, a second for period three, and another for period four.] The *strategy space* Π is the set of admissible strategies, which is defined here to be the set of all strategies composable from admissible decision rules. That is, mathematically, Π is defined as the Cartesian product of the sets of admissible decision rules: $\Pi = \Delta \times \Delta \times \cdots \times \Delta$. ($\Delta$ appears N times.) In short, *any* combination of admissible decision rules, one for each period, forms an admissible strategy.

The literature is inconsistent in its definition of a *policy*. Some authors define a policy to be what we call a decision rule. Others use the term for what we have called a strategy. We find it convenient to use the term to refer to either a decision rule or a strategy. The exact meaning should be clear from the context. It is also convenient to use the term *contingency plan* in the same way.

Objective Function

We seek to maximize the expected present value of all returns received. Let $v_t(\pi, s)$ denote the expected present value of the returns received in periods $t, t + 1, \ldots, N$ given that the process starts period t in state s and strategy π is implemented. When working our example, we didn't need to define anything like this kind of return: We immediately applied recursion and backward optimization. However, we need notation for returns such as these to define an optimal strategy, and especially in Chapter 5 when we return to verifying that our approach is valid. Note also that we number the periods from t to N (using subscripts) rather than backward from n to 1 (using superscripts) as was done in the example. This forward numbering is particularly convenient in addressing nonstationary or infinite-horizon problems.

The present value evaluation is at the beginning of period t. We therefore have the following:

$$v_t(\pi, s) = E\left\{\sum_{i=t}^{N} \alpha^{i-t} r(s_i, \delta_i(s_i)) + \alpha^{N-t+1} v_{\mathbf{T}}(s_{N+1})\right\}, \qquad (3.1)$$

where the expectation is with respect to the random variables, namely, the random state s_i that the system is observed to be in at the beginning of period i for each i $(= t, t+1, \ldots, N)$, and the random terminal state s_{N+1} of the system (at the end of period N, which is equivalent to the beginning of period $N + 1$). Thus, the expected present value of the terminal value is included. (Of course, $s_t = s$ is fixed. In addition, recall that δ_i is the decision rule prescribed by π for period i, for each i.)

When we want to talk about the vector of present values yielded by a given strategy, we suppress s from the notation and write $v_t(\pi)$. When the state space is not discrete, we must think of $v_t(\pi)$ as a function defined on the state space rather than as a vector. When $t = 1$, we suppress the subscript and write simply $v(\pi)$.

Definition of Optimality and Optimal Value Functions

A strategy π^* is *optimal at state s for period t* if

$$v_t(\pi^*, s) \geq v_t(\pi, s) \text{ for every } \pi \in \Pi.$$

If the process starts in state s in period t, such a strategy yields the maximal return over the remainder of the planning horizon. A strategy π^* is *optimal for period t* if it is optimal at state s for period t for every state $s \in \mathcal{S}$. When $t = 1$, we suppress the period and speak of strategies that are *optimal at state s* and *optimal strategies*. We shall see in Chapter 5 that optimal strategies exist in finite state and action problems but not necessarily in more general problems.

Let

$$f_t(s) := \sup_{\pi \in \Pi} v_t(\pi, s),$$

which is called the *optimal value of starting at state s in period t*. We call the resulting function f_t the *optimal value function for period t*. Thus, a strategy π^* is optimal for period t if $v_t(\pi^*) = f_t$: $v_t(\pi^*, s) = f_t(s)$ for all s. The subscript $t = 1$ is suppressed. Thus, π^* is optimal if $v(\pi^*) = f$.

The Optimality Equations for Markov Decision Chains

We have already used the optimality equations in the e-Rite-Way example. In general, we must consider them to be a conjecture, and will see in Chapter 5 conditions under which they hold. In the more general notation presented here, they become the following for the case of a discrete state space, for each s:

$$f_t(s) = \sup_{a \in A(s)} \{r(s,a) + \alpha E f_{t+1}(s_{t+1})\}$$

$$= \sup_{a \in A(s)} \{r(s,a) + \sum_{j \in \mathcal{S}} q_{sj}^a f_{t+1}(j)\},$$

where $f_{N+1}(s) := v_{\mathrm{T}}(s)$ for every s. In words, the optimality equations say that the optimal value of starting at an arbitrary initial state can be represented as the best return over each of the immediate feasible decisions at that state, taking into account the optimal value associated with each state possibly resulting from those decisions. They therefore allow the optimal value of starting anywhere to be determined by backward recursion.

The Optimality Conditions

The *optimality conditions* consist of the following: A strategy π^* is optimal for t for every period t iff $\pi_t^*(s)$ attains the supremum in the optimality equations for every period t and state s.

The *optimality criterion* is the "if" part of this result. It says that any strategy whose decisions achieve the individual optimizations in the optimality equations for each t is optimal for every t. That is, if you optimize working backward and pick out an optimizing action for every state and period, then the resulting strategy is optimal, not only for period 1 but for every period t.

We shall see in Chapter 5 that these two conjectures hold in quite general situations. The next two subsections discuss two other plausible conjectures that deepen our understanding of optimal strategies and prepare us to discuss the famous principle of optimality.

Conjecture 1

You might conjecture that if a strategy is optimal, namely, optimal for every state at period 1, then it should be optimal for every state for every subsequent period. But you would be wrong.

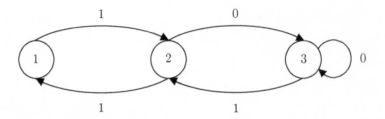

Figure 3.1   Deterministic Counterexample

Consider the deterministic problem depicted in Figure 3.1 in which the action
is the state to which you move. Each arc represents an admissible decision,
and, therefore, the corresponding transition. The resulting returns are shown
next to the arcs. There is zero terminal value, and we have a two-period time
horizon: $N = 2$. Consider the following strategy: If you are in state 1, move
to state 2, regardless of the period. Similarly, if you are in state 2, move to
state 1, regardless of the period. If you are in state 3 in period 1, move to state
2. However, if you are in state 3 in period 2, stay there. That is, $\pi = (\delta_1, \delta_2)$,
where

$$\delta_1 = \begin{pmatrix} 2 \\ 1 \\ 2 \end{pmatrix} \quad \text{and} \quad \delta_2 = \begin{pmatrix} 2 \\ 1 \\ 3 \end{pmatrix}.$$

This strategy is optimal, by our definition: It is optimal at every state for period
1. However, it is not optimal at state 3 for period 2, because a return of only
0 is received then while a return of 1 is possible. There is no chance that the
nonoptimal parts of the strategy will ever be implemented.

Conjecture 2

If you conjectured that a strategy that is optimal for a particular state for every
period should also be optimal for every other state (and period), you would also
be wrong. In the example above, the stated strategy is optimal at state 1 (and
2) for each period. It is not optimal at state 3 for period 2. If we change
the decision at state 3 to be 3 for both periods, the resulting strategy remains
optimal at states 1 and 2 for both periods yet is not optimal at state 3 for
either period. The optimality at state 1 (and 2) does not depend on optimality
of actions at state 3, because there is no chance of visiting state 3 if you start
in state 1 (or 2) and follow the stated strategy.

The Principle of Optimality

Richard Bellman (1957) introduced the following *Principle of Optimality:*

An optimal policy has the property that whatever the initial state and initial decision are, the remaining decisions must constitute an optimal policy with regard to the state resulting from the first decision.

This reads as a necessary condition for an optimal policy. That is, it says that if a policy is optimal, it must have certain properties. It turns out that the extent to which this principle holds depends on how optimality is defined and on how one interprets the "state resulting" from a decision. For instance, Hinderer (1970) verifies the principle by (roughly) requiring that there be a strictly positive probability of visiting the "resulting" states. The example given for Conjecture 1 above shows that a strategy can be optimal in one period even if it calls for clearly nonoptimal decisions in the next period at states that cannot be observed/visited/realized under that strategy. That is, the "state resulting" is a critical feature of the principle.

The following two-period example, from Porteus (1975), sheds further light on this issue. Suppose the state space is the interval $[0, 1]$ and the action space is the set $\{0, 1\}$. The immediate return is the action. Transitions are generated by a uniform distribution on the interval $[0, 1]$ regardless of the action taken. Consider a policy that selects action 1 for every state in period 1. It also selects action 1 in period 2 unless the state is one of the following eleven states: $\{0, 0.1, 0.2, \ldots, 1\}$, in which case action 0 is selected. This policy is optimal (at every state for period 1), but it is not optimal at any of the eleven designated states in period 2. The difficulty is that none of these states can arise with a positive probability. The issue deepens if you have the policy for period 2 select action 0 if the state is rational and action 1 otherwise, because there is still a zero probability that any of the rationals will arise and result in a nonoptimal action being selected.

The "only if" part of the optimality conditions could be interpreted as an alternative version of the principle of optimality: If a policy is optimal for every period, then the actions it prescribes must attain the optimum in the optimality equations for every period and state. There are two useful applications of this statement, in the context of seeking policies that are optimal for every period:

(1) You will not miss any optimal policies by forming the optimality equations and using the optimality criterion. (2) If you are able to show that any policy that attains the optimum in the optimality equations has certain properties, then you have shown that every optimal policy has these properties. In any event, the usual approach to anayzing dynamic problems is to construct the optimality equations and attempt to apply the optimality criterion to characterize the form of some optimal strategies. The next chapter emphasizes exactly this approach.

Exercises

3.1   Write a computer program (in whatever language you prefer) that recursively computes $f^n(s)$ and the corresponding optimal decisions for e-Rite-Way (as given in this chapter) for each state $s = 1, 2,$ and for $n = 1, 2, \ldots, 6$. Attach a copy of your source code and a copy of your output, which should clearly show the optimal values and decisions for each n-period problem, for $n = 1, 2, \ldots, 6$.

3.2   Suppose in e-Rite-Way that you have a nonzero terminal value function, instead of a zero valued one. In particular, at the end of the planning horizon, you will sell your business to an organization that will pay you $v_T(1)$ for each inactive customer and $v_T(2)$ for each active customer. Characterize the optimal decision rule for the one-period problem as a function of these terminal values. That is, determine all the possible optimal decision rules for this problem and the conditions that the terminal values must satisfy for each of them to be optimal.

3.3   Consider an N-period problem in which the state space differs each period. That is, the possible states in period t are in S_t for each $t = 1, 2, \ldots, N + 1$. Show how to reformulate the problem to fit the framework presented in this chapter, namely, that there is a single state space S.

3.4   *(TV Game Show)*   (Continuation of Exercise 2.5)   Suppose that you plan to follow a particular decision rule when you play the game: Spin again iff your accumulated earnings are less than S, for some S, regardless of the maximum number n of spins left in the game. Let $f^n(x|S)$ denote the expected value of your winnings from the game, using S, when you face the choice of spinning again or stopping, with an accumulated level x of winnings so far, and there is a maximum of n more spins in the game.

(a) Write down a recursion for $f^n(x|S)$ in terms of $f^{n-1}(\cdot|S)$ and the original parameters.

(b) You also assume that, at the optimal stopping threshhold, S^*, you will be indifferent between spinning again and stopping. Use your recursion in (a) for $f^n(S|S)$ to solve for S^*.

3.5 *(Optimally Selling an Asset without Recall)*   (Continuation of Exercise 2.6)   In each period in which a new bid for your asset is received, you must either accept the bid or reject it. Any rejected bid cannot be recalled later: The only bid you can accept is the latest one. Let f_n denote the optimal expected proceeds from selling your asset when there are n periods (opportunities) remaining. (Of course, once you sell the asset, all remaining opportunities are forfeited.) Because each bid is a positive random variable, $f_1 = \mu := E(X)$, the mean bid.

(a) Write a recursion for f_n in terms of f_{n-1} for $n \geq 2$.

(b) Calculate f_n for $n = 2, 3, 4$. Hint: See the hint for Exercise 2.6.

(c) Consider the infinite-horizon case in which n is arbitrarily large. Let f denote the optimal expected proceeds from selling your asset in this case. Write a recursion for f in terms of f. Show that f is the unique real number x that satisfies

$$x = \frac{I(\alpha x)}{1 - \alpha}.$$

3.6 *(Optimally Selling an Asset with Recall)*   (Continuation of Exercise 3.5) In this version of the problem, you may at any time accept any prior bid. However, you only receive the money in the period in which you accept the bid (rather than the period in which the bid was received). Let $f_n(x)$ denote the optimal expected proceeds from selling your asset when there are n periods remaining and the best bid received so far is x.

(a) Provide the intuition why it will not necessarily be optimal to wait for all bids to be received and then accept the best of them.

(b) Let $f_0(x) := 0$ for all x. Write a recursion for $f_n(x)$ in terms of $f_{n-1}(\cdot)$ for $n \geq 1$.

References

Bellman, R. 1957. *Dynamic Programming*. Princeton University Press, Princeton, N.J.

Hinderer, K. 1970. *Foundations of Non-stationary Dynamic Programming with Discrete Time Parameter*. Springer-Verlag, New York.

Porteus, E. 1975. An informal look at the principle of optimality. *Management Science*. **21** 1346–48.

4

Characterizing
the Optimal Policy

This chapter continues the analysis of finite-horizon Markov decision processes, with an emphasis on characterizing the optimal policy, which can be interpreted as either the optimal decision rules for each period or the entire strategy. In e-Rite-Way, only direct numerical computations were made and the results interpreted. Here we work with the mathematical expressions in the optimality equations and apply the optimality criterion to derive results without necessarily doing any numerical evaluations.

This chapter may be the most important in the entire book, as so much of what follows can be viewed as applying the ideas illustrated in this chapter.

4.1 Example: The Parking Problem

In this problem (MacQueen and Miller, 1960), you are driving down a one-way road toward your destination, looking for a parking space. As you drive along, you can observe only one parking space at a time, the one right next to you, noting whether or not it is vacant. If it is vacant, you may either (1) stop and park there or (2) drive on to the next space. If it is occupied (not vacant), then you must drive on to the next space. You cannot return to vacant spaces

that you have passed. Assume that vacant spaces occur independently and
that the probability that any given space is vacant is p where $0 < p < 1$. If
you have not parked by the time you reach your destination, you must park
in the pay parking lot, at a cost of c. If you park x spaces away from your
destination, then you consider that a parking cost of x has been incurred. The
closest space (before reaching the pay parking lot) to your destination is one
space away from your destination: $x = 1$. For convenience, we interpret space
$x = 0$ as existing and corresponding to having driven by the last available
space, so the only option left is the pay lot. Furthermore, $c > 1$: There are
possible spaces that are better than going straight to the pay lot. Your objective
is to minimize your total expected parking cost.

Let the state $s = (x, i)$ be defined by the number x of the space that is being
approached, and i, which is the availability of the space: $i = 0$ indicates
that the space is vacant and $i = 1$ indicates that it is occupied. For example,
if $s = (3, 0)$ then you are still looking for a space, have approached the spot
that is three spaces away from your destination, and it is vacant. Let $a = 0$
denote the decision to park and let $a = 1$ denote the decision to drive to the
next space. If you decide to park (having observed state $(3, 0)$), you incur the
cost of 3 and the process ends. (If you want to formulate the problem using
the formal framework introduced in Chapter 3, you can define an additional
trapping state to which the process moves (and stays, incurring no additional
costs) once the decision to park is made). Both options are available if the
space is vacant: $A_{(x,0)} = \{0, 1\}$, and you must drive to the next spot if the
space is occupied: $A_{(x,1)} = \{1\}$, for all x.

Optimality Equations

Let $f(s) = f(x, i)$ denote the minimum expected cost of parking, starting
in state s (space x with availability i). As usual, we work backward. In
developing the optimality equations for this problem, we do not go through
the formality of converting this minimization problem into an equivalent maximization problem for which we have presented general notation. Rather, we
formulate them directly. In particular, the optimality equations when $s = (1, i)$
are as follows:

$$f(1, i) = \begin{cases} \min(1, c) = 1 & \text{if } i = 0 \\ c & \text{if } i = 1. \end{cases}$$

That is, if $i = 0$, you have a choice of parking now (choosing $a = 0$), resulting in a cost of 1, or driving past (choosing $a = 1$), which means that you must park in the pay lot, resulting in a cost of c. Since, by assumption, $c > 1$, you prefer to park if you can.

It is convenient to define another function, which facilitates the general analysis. For $x \geq 0$, let

$$F(x) := pf(x, 0) + qf(x, 1), \tag{4.1}$$

where $q := 1 - p$ is the probability that a space is occupied. $F(x)$ is the minimum expected cost of parking, given that you are approaching space x (still looking to park) but have not yet observed its availability. If the space is vacant, which occurs with probability p, the optimal cost will be $f(x, 0)$ and if it is occupied (probability q), the cost will be $f(x, 1)$.

The optimality equations when $s = (x, i)$ and $x \geq 2$ can therefore be written as follows:

$$f(x, i) = \begin{cases} \min(x, F(x - 1)) & \text{if } i = 0 \\ F(x - 1) & \text{if } i = 1. \end{cases} \tag{4.2}$$

In words, suppose that you approach space x (still looking to park) and observe its availability. If the space is available, then you can either park there, and incur cost x, or drive on to the next space and face the optimal cost of doing so, namely, $F(x - 1)$. If $x \leq F(x - 1)$, then it is optimal to park. Otherwise it is optimal to drive on. If space x is occupied, you must drive to the next space and face the optimal expected cost, $F(x - 1)$, of doing so.

Note that, by allowing x to decrease by only one, the recursion ensures that you cannot return to spaces that you have already passed. By defining $f(0, i) := c$ for each i, the optimality equations (4.2) apply for all i and $x \geq 1$. ($F(0) = c$ then holds.)

By substituting (4.2) into (4.1), we can write

$$F(x) = p \min(x, F(x - 1)) + qF(x - 1), \tag{4.3}$$

which allows us to analyze the problem solely in terms of F, rather than f, if we like.

We now again express the optimality equations differently. Letting

$$g(x) := F(x-1) - x, \tag{4.4}$$

for $x \geq 1$, and substituting $F(x-1) = x + g(x)$ into (4.2), we can rewrite the optimality equations as

$$f(x,i) = \begin{cases} x + \min(0, g(x)) & \text{if } i = 0 \\ x + g(x) & \text{if } i = 1. \end{cases} \tag{4.5}$$

Application of the Optimality Criterion

Thus, recalling that the first term in the minimization corresponds to parking, the optimality criterion says that if $\min(0, g(x)) = 0$, then it is optimal to park in space x if it is vacant. That is, if $g(x) \geq 0$ (namely $F(x-1) \geq x$), then parking in space x is better than driving on, whereas if $g(x) < 0$, then driving on is (strictly) better. We can interpret $g(x)$ as the potential savings from finding space x vacant. (If $g(x)$ is positive and space x is vacant, parking there results in a reduction in the expected cost [of completing the process] by an amount equal to $g(x)$.) If $g(x)$ is negative, then there is no value to finding space x vacant: It is optimal to drive on to the next space regardless of its availability.

Successful analysis of a stochastic dynamic (optimization) problem usually involves establishing properties of the optimal cost/return function. In this case, if we could show that g is a decreasing function, then $g(x)$ would increase as x, the number of spaces away, gets smaller. Assuming we can later deal with the technical details (of existence and finiteness) we would have a simple cutoff point S such that $g(x) < 0$ for $x > S$ and $g(x) \geq 0$ for $x \leq S$. In particular, the optimal parking policy could be characterized as follows: Do not park at any space that is strictly farther away than S and do park at any vacant space that is closer than S. The following result is therefore of interest.

Lemma 4.1

(a) The function $F(x)$ is decreasing in x.

(b) $g(1) = c - 1 > 0$ and $g(x) \leq 0$ for all $x \geq c$.

(c) $g(x)$ is strictly decreasing in x.

Proof   (a) Since $\min\left(x, F(x-1)\right) \leq F(x-1)$ by definition, we have, by (4.3),

$$F(x) \leq pF(x-1) + qF(x-1) = F(x-1).$$

(b) Using $F(0) = c$, we get, by (4.4), that $g(1) = F(0) - 1 = c - 1 > 0$ (by assumption). By (a), F is decreasing, so, therefore, $F(x) \leq c$ for all x. Select an arbitrary $x \geq c$. Then $g(x) = F(x-1) - x \leq c - c = 0$.

(c) The function g is the sum of two decreasing functions, one of which is strictly decreasing, and is therefore also strictly decreasing.   □

Part (a) simply affirms that you can't get worse off by having more options. Part (b) merely says that you should park in space 1 if you approach it and it is vacant, and that you should purposefully drive past any space farther away than c: You would do better in the pay lot. Part (c) allows us to characterize the form of the optimal parking policy, which we will do in the next subsection. In words, it says that the potential savings from finding a space vacant strictly decreases as you get farther away from your destination.

It is often possible to obtain desired results in different ways. For example, the analysis needed to obtain part (c) can be simplified by using (4.1) and (4.4) to convert (4.5) into a recursion involving only g:

$$g(x+1) = -1 + p\min\left(0, g(x)\right) + qg(x), \qquad (4.6)$$

for $x = 1, 2, \ldots$, where $g(1) = c - 1$. Lemma 4.1(c) can then be proved directly without use of part (a):

$$\begin{aligned} g(x+1) &= -1 + p\min\left(0, g(x)\right) + qg(x) \\ &\leq -1 + pg(x) + qg(x) \\ &= -1 + g(x) \\ &< g(x). \end{aligned}$$

Form of the Optimal Policy

We now characterize the form of the optimal policy.

Lemma 4.2   There exists a cutoff point $S \geq 1$ such that it is optimal to drive straight to space S and then park in the first vacant space found.

Proof By Lemma 4.1(b) and (c), g starts strictly above zero (at $x = 1$) and decreases to zero or lower (at $x = c$). Thus, there exists a finite cutoff point $S \geq 1$ such that $g(S) \geq 0$ and $g(S + 1) < 0$. Because you should not park in space x (if it is vacant) if $g(x) < 0$, you should drive right past all spaces $x > S$. If space S is vacant, then you should park there, by the optimality criterion. If it is not vacant, you must drive on and you should park in the first vacant space you find: $g(x)$ will be positive for all $x \leq S$. □

For example, suppose $p = 0.2$ and $c = 5$. Then $g(1) = c - 1 = 4$. Using (4.6), we compute $g(x)$ for increasing values of x until $g(x) < 0$, at which point the optimal policy has been found. Here, $g(2) = -1 + .2(0) + .8(4) = 2.2$, $g(3) = -1 + 0.2(0) + 0.8(2.2) = 0.76$, and $g(4) = -1 + 0.2(0) + 0.8(.76) = -0.392$. That is, it is not optimal to park in space 4 if it is vacant, but it is optimal to park in the first vacant space found thereafter. In short, even though space 4 yields a lower cost than the parking lot, it is worth gambling and looking for a closer vacant space. However, if space 3 is vacant, it is not worth gambling: you should park in it (rather than driving past to see if space 2 is vacant). Using (4.3), the minimum expected cost of parking is $F(3)$ for all $x \geq 3$, namely, $F(3) = g(4) + 4 = 3.608$, which, as it should be, is strictly less than the cost $(c = 5)$ of driving straight to the parking lot.

Explicit Optimal Solution

Once the form of an optimal policy is identified, if that form depends on a small number of parameters, it is sometimes possible to obtain additional results by assuming a policy of that form is used and analyzing the returns as a function of those parameters. In this case, such an approach allows us to go beyond characterizing the form of the optimal policy and to derive an explicit formula for the optimal policy.

In this case, the optimal policy can be characterized by a single parameter, S, the cutoff point. We first determine the expected results as a function of this parameter, S, and then optimize over S. It is useful to move toward this goal slowly by first defining $v(x, S)$ as the expected parking cost of approaching space x (before seeing if it is vacant or not) while utilizing the cutoff point S.

Thinking recursively, we have the following.

$$v(x, S) = \begin{cases} c & \text{if } x = 0, \\ px + qv(x-1, S) & \text{if } 1 \le x \le S, \\ v(S, S) & \text{if } S < x. \end{cases}$$

That is, for any state $x > S$, we simply drive by, until we reach space S, at which point the expected cost of completing the process is $v(S, S)$. We will park in any space x between 1 and S that is vacant. Thus, the expected cost of completing the process if we approach such a space is x if it is vacant and $v(x - 1, S)$ if it is occupied. Finally, if we reach space $x = 0$, we must park in the pay lot at a cost of c.

Before starting the drive, we know we will drive directly to space S before looking for a vacant space. That is, our expected parking cost will be $v(S, S)$ if we use cutoff point S. We would therefore like to evaluate $v(S, S)$ explicitly, if possible. Again thinking recursively, we obtain the following (where $1 \le j \le S$).

$$\begin{aligned} v(S, S) &= pS + qv(S - 1, S) \\ &= pS + q[p(S-1) + qv(S-2, S)] \\ &= p[S + q(S-1) + q^2 v(S-2, S)] \\ &= \cdots = p \sum_{i=0}^{j} q^i (S-i) + q^j v(S - j, S) \qquad \text{[for } 1 \le j \le S] \\ &= p \sum_{i=0}^{S} q^i (S-i) + q^S c. \end{aligned}$$

By Exercise 4.2, this expression can be simplified as follows:

$$v(S, S) = S - \frac{q(1 - q^S)}{p} + q^S c.$$

Now that we have an explicit expression for $v(S, S)$, we can seek to minimize it over S.

Theorem 4.1   *The optimal cutoff level is the smallest integer S that satisfies*

$$q^S \le \frac{1}{(pc + q)},$$

which can be written, equivalently, as

$$S \geq \frac{\ln(pc + q)}{-\ln q}.$$

Proof By Exercise 4.3, the first forward difference, $\Delta(S) := v(S+1, S+1) - v(S, S)$, is increasing in S and can be expressed as

$$\Delta(S) = 1 - q^S(pc + q). \tag{4.7}$$

Here, $\Delta(S)$ represents the increase in expected cost from increasing the cutoff point from S to $S + 1$. Note that $\Delta(0) = 1 - (pc + q) = p(1 - c)$ is strictly negative, because $c > 1$ by assumption: Choosing $S = 1$ is strictly better than $S = 0$. Thus, Δ starts at a strictly negative value and is increasing on the positive integers. Hence, the optimal cutoff will be the smallest integer S that satisfies $\Delta(S) \geq 0$: S is better than $S + 1$ and strictly better than $S - 1$. Using (4.7), this inequality becomes $q^S \leq 1/(pc+q)$. Taking logarithms and using the facts that $\ln q < 0$ and $\ln(1/x) = -\ln(x)$ yield the equivalent inequality. □

Returning to the example in which $c = 5$ and $p = 0.2$, we see that $\ln(pc+q) = \ln(1.8) \cong 0.5878$, and $-\ln q \cong 0.2231$, so $\ln(pc + q)/[-\ln(q)] \cong 2.6$. Thus the optimal cutoff level is $S = 3$, as we had previously determined.

4.2   Dynamic Inventory Management

We now turn attention back to a dynamic version of the newsvendor problem. In the previous section, the structure of the optimal value function was important in characterizing the optimal policy. This phenomenon holds in the analysis of most dynamic problems, and our analysis of the problem in this section takes the natural next step: More work will be required to establish the properties of the optimal value function, but very strong results can then be achieved. It turns out that the terminal value function v_T plays a key role in deriving those results.

Assumptions, Notation, and Formulation

This model differs from the newsvendor problem of Chapter 1 in several ways. The biggest difference is that the model is dynamic. In particular, the system will be operated over N periods. What makes the problem more than N

copies of the original newsvendor problem is that any leftover stock at the end
of one period is retained in inventory and can be offered for sale the following
period. In this regard, each unit of positive leftover stock at the end of period
incurs a (holding) cost of c_H in that period.

This model assumes backlogging rather than lost sales. That is, demand for
the product in excess of the amount stocked will be backlogged, which means
that these customers will return the next period for the product, in addition
to the usual (random) number of customers who generate demand then. (The
newly arising [nonbacklogged] demands in different periods are assumed to be
statistically independent.) A unit penalty cost of c_P is charged for each unit
that is backlogged in each period. This penalty cost may incorporate the lost
opportunity value of the delayed revenue, the additional cost required to place
an expedited order, and/or a widely used, albeit vague, concept called lost
goodwill, which is intended to account for any resulting reduction in future
demands. (See Hall and Porteus, 2000, for conditions under which this approach
can be justified rigorously.) In particular, it is safe to ignore sales revenues and
seek to minimize the expected costs of running the system.

The remaining features of the model are either identical or analogous to those
of the newsvendor model of Section 1.2. There is only a single product in consideration. The decision of how much to order, if any, is made at the beginning
of each period and can be contingent on the amount of inventory available. A
proportional ordering cost of c per unit ordered is incurred, and orders placed
are (essentially) received immediately: They are received in time to meet demands that arise in that period. All demand is observed. Demand in a period
is continuous, strictly positive, and generically denoted by D. The one-period
demand distribution is denoted by Φ, the density by ϕ, the mean demand
per period by μ, and the one-period discount factor by α ($\in (0, 1]$). Note
that $\Phi(0) = 0$. All costs are assumed to be expressed in beginning-of-period
dollars.

The convenient way to represent the state of the system in this model is the
level x of inventory before ordering, which when positive connotes leftover
stock. When it is negative, then $-x$ indicates the backlog, the number of
units of unmet demand in the previous period. This backlog must be met first
before any future demands can be satisfied. In short, the inventory level is

defined to be the number of units of on-hand stock less the number of units backlogged. The state space is therefore the real line.

If the initial level of inventory at the end of period N is x, then the terminal cost $v_T(x)$ is incurred. We assume that v_T is convex. For example, the following is convex:

$$v_T(x) = \begin{cases} -cx & \text{if } x \leq 0 \\ 0 & \text{otherwise.} \end{cases}$$

In this example, any backlogged demands at the end of period N must be met through immediate production (at the usual unit cost), but any unsold units are valueless.

We assume that $c_P > (1 - \alpha)c$, which ensures that it is not optimal to never order anything and merely accumulate backlog penalty costs. (Deferring the purchase of a unit for a period saves $(1 - \alpha)c$, and that is outweighed by the unit backlog penalty cost.) We also assume that $c_H + (1 - \alpha)c > 0$, which will hold if $c_H > 0$, which will usually be the case in practice. This assumption ensures that it is not optimal to accumulate unbounded amounts of inventory.

It is convenient to select as the action the level y of inventory after ordering, rather than the amount ordered. The action space for state x is the set of levels above x: $A_x = [x, \infty)$. Thus, if the system begins period t with x_t units of inventory before ordering, and the decision is to have y_t units of inventory after ordering, and D_t denotes the demand during that period, then the state at the beginning of the next period, namely, the level of inventory before ordering in period $t + 1$, is $x_{t+1} = y_t - D_t$. In particular, if $D_t < y_t$, then there is positive on-hand stock at the beginning of the next period. Similarly, if $D_t > y_t$, then the level of inventory at the beginning of period $t+1$ is strictly negative, indicating the existence (and level) of the backlog (the number of unfilled orders placed in period t that are backlogged to be met in the future).

Usually, the specific period t is immaterial, so t is suppressed. Thus, we simply speak of state x and action y. As in Chapter 1, the expected one-period holding and shortage cost function can be given as a function of the action y as follows:

$$L(y) := EL(y - D) = \int_{\xi=0}^{y} c_H(y - \xi)\phi(\xi) \, d\xi + \int_{\xi=y}^{\infty} c_P(\xi - y)\phi(\xi) \, d\xi,$$

where

$$\mathcal{L}(x) := c_H x^+ + c_P(-x)^+.$$

Optimality of Base Stock Policies

Let's write out the optimality equations for this model, for $1 \le t \le N$:

$$f_t(x) = \min_{y \ge x} \left\{ c(y - x) + L(y) + \alpha \int_0^\infty f_{t+1}(y - \xi)\phi(\xi)\,d\xi \right\},$$

where $f_{N+1}(x) := v_T(x)$, for each x. In words, starting period t in state x, selecting action y, and following an optimal policy thereafter yields an expected cost equal to the sum of the cost of raising the inventory level to y plus the expected holding and shortage costs incurred in period t plus the expected present value of starting period $t + 1$ in state $y - D$ and acting optimally over the remainder of the time horizon.

The reason for selecting the level of inventory after ordering is clarified after seeing that the optimality equations can be written as

$$f_t(x) = \min_{y \ge x} \left\{ G_t(y) - cx \right\},$$

where

$$G_t(y) := cy + L(y) + \alpha \int_0^\infty f_{t+1}(y - \xi)\phi(\xi)\,d\xi. \tag{4.8}$$

Thus, the optimal decision starting with inventory level x in period t is found by minimizing $G_t(y)$ over $\{y | y \ge x\}$. This optimization is conceptually very simple: we simply minimize $G_t(y)$ looking to the right of x. Note that if G_t is as given in Figure 4.1, then, if you start below (to the left) of S_t, the minimizer of G_t, then you should move up (to the right) to it. If you start above (to the right) of S_t, you should stay where you are. This decision rule is called a *base stock policy*. Formally, a decision rule for period t is called a *base stock policy* if there exists a quantity S_t, called the *base stock level*, such that the stock level after ordering is as close to the base stock level as possible. In this context, such a policy can be represented as follows:

$$\delta(x) = \begin{cases} S_t & \text{if } x \le S_t, \\ x & \text{otherwise,} \end{cases}$$

where $\delta(x)$ is the decision made when the state is x. Note that if G_t is given as in Figure 4.2, then a base stock policy is *not* optimal in period t. In this case, a base stock policy with base stock level S_t is optimal as long as $x \leq s_t'$. However, if $x \in (s_t', S_t')$, it is optimal to order up to S_t' (ordering a strictly positive amount), which is not allowed in a base stock policy.

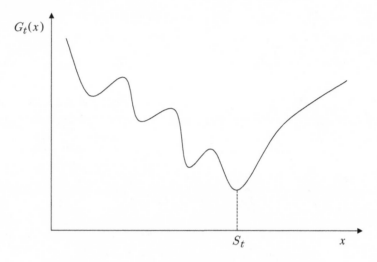

Figure 4.1   *Base Stock Policy Is Optimal*

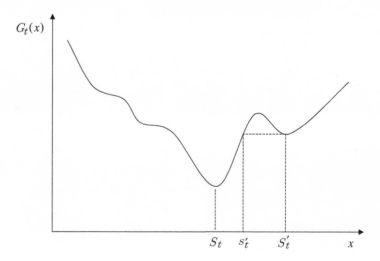

Figure 4.2   *Base Stock Policy Is Not Optimal*

The following result prepares the groundwork for showing that a base stock policy is optimal in every period.

Lemma 4.3   If f_{t+1} is convex, then the following hold.

(a) G_t is convex.

(b) A base stock policy is optimal in period t. Indeed, any minimizer of G_t is an optimal base stock level.

(c) f_t is convex.

Proof   (a) We can write G_t as

$$G_t(y) = cy + E\mathcal{L}(y - D) + \alpha E f_{t+1}(y - D).$$

Our assumptions that $c_P > (1 - \alpha)c$ and $c_H + (1 - \alpha)c > 0$ imply that $c_P + c_H > 0$. Hence, $\mathcal{L}$ is convex. Thus, by Exercise 4.7, the second and third terms are convex. G_t is therefore the sum of three convex functions and, hence, convex itself.

(b) Let S_t denote a minimizer of $G_t(y)$ over all real y. If $x < S_t$, then the minimizing $y \geq x$ is at $y = S_t$, whereas, if $x \geq S_t$, then the minimizing y is at $y = x$. That is, a base stock policy with base stock level S_t is optimal for period t.

(c) (Exercise 4.8.)   □

Theorem 4.2   A base stock policy is optimal in each period of a finite-horizon problem.

Proof   By assumption, the terminal value function is convex. Thus, by Lemma 4.3, G_N is convex and a base stock policy is optimal for period N. By Lemma 4.3(c), f_N is convex as well. Thus, the argument iterates backward through the periods in the sequence $t = N, N - 1, \ldots, 1$.   □

¿From the practical perspective of a researcher, a certain amount of trial and error is often needed to settle on the right mathematical form for the optimal value functions and the right form for the optimal policies. A common approach is first to solve the one-period problem, and, possibly, the two-period problem, to gain inspiration regarding the possible form of the optimal policy for a general multiperiod problem. One then examines the optimality equations for the general multiperiod problem and attempts to discover what mathematical form (structure) for the optimal value function will be sufficient to guarantee that the postulated form (structure) for the policy will indeed be optimal. In general, this step is called *attainment:* If the optimal value function (for starting the next period) has a certain mathematical form (or structure), then there exists an optimal policy for this period (an optimizer of the optimality equations) that has the desired form/properties/structure. The final step is to show that f_t will have the requisite mathematical form (structure) if f_{t+1} does. This step is called *preservation:* The desired mathematical form of the optimal value function is preserved as the optimization is carried out for another period.

Explicit Optimal Base Stock Level

While we have already illustrated that a base stock policy is optimal in every period of a finite-horizon problem, and that the optimal value function is convex, there is a very interesting special case that leads to an extemely tractable solution. This case involves a special assumption on the terminal (salvage) value function:

$$v_T(x) = -cx.$$

This case arises when, at the end of the last period, we can obtain reimbursement of the unit (ordering) cost for each leftover unit and must incur the unit cost for each unit backlogged (on top of any unit shortage penalty incurred in the previous period).

Let's examine the one-period problem at the end of the time horizon. The expected ordering, holding, and shortage cost, less any expected salvage value, in that period, starting with zero inventory and ordering y units can be written as

$$cy + L(y) - \alpha \int_{\xi=0}^{\infty} c(y - \xi)\phi(\xi)\,d\xi = c(1 - \alpha)y + L(y) + \alpha c\mu$$

$$= g(y) + \alpha c\mu,$$

where

$$g(y) := c(1 - \alpha)y + L(y). \tag{4.9}$$

This one-period problem is another variation of a newsvendor problem. Let S denote a solution to

$$g'(S) = 0. \tag{4.10}$$

Thus, S is a minimizer of g and can be easily found (Exercise 4.9) as the following critical fractile solution:

$$\Phi(S) = \frac{c_P - (1 - \alpha)c}{c_P + c_H}. \tag{4.11}$$

We would like the fractile in (4.11) to be strictly between 0 and 1, so that S would be finite. This explains why we have assumed that $c_P > (1 - \alpha)c$ and $c_H + (1 - \alpha)c > 0$, because they are sufficient to do the job.

Reexamination of the preceding steps reveals that, if the terminal value function has a slope of $-c$, then the optimal base stock level in the last period (N) will be given explicitly by (4.11). If we could show that all the optimal value functions had a slope of $-c$, then (4.11) would give the optimal base stock level for every period. Let's examine f_N, by plugging in the optimal decision for each state:

$$f_N(x) = \begin{cases} G_N(S) - cx & \text{if } x \le S, \\ G_N(x) - cx & \text{otherwise.} \end{cases}$$

Therefore,

$$f'_N(x) = \begin{cases} -c & \text{if } x \le S, \\ G'_N(x) - c & \text{otherwise.} \end{cases} \tag{4.12}$$

That is, $f_N(x)$ has a slope of $-c$ for $x \le S$. Its slope is not $-c$ for bigger arguments, so our initial hope is ruined. However, if you go back to the derivation of S, you will see that it depended only on the slope of the terminal value function being $-c$ for arguments less than S. The following result formalizes the consequences of this observation.

Lemma 4.4   *If f_{t+1} is convex and $f'_{t+1}(x) = -c$ for $x < S$, where S is as defined in (4.11), then the following hold.*

(a) *S minimizes $G_t(y)$ over all real y.*

(b) *The optimal base stock level in period t is also S.*

(c) *f_t is convex and $f'(x) = -c$ for $x < S$.*

Proof   (a) As in Lemma 4.3, G_t is convex. To see that S is a minimizer of G_t,

$$G'_t(S) = c + L'(S) + \alpha \int_0^\infty f'_{t+1}(S - \xi)\phi(\xi)\, d\xi \qquad \text{[by (4.8)]}$$

$$= \alpha c + \alpha \int_0^\infty (-c)\phi(\xi)\, d\xi \qquad \text{[(4.9), (4.10), and assumption]}$$

$$= 0.$$

Hence, S must be a minimizer of G_t, and, therefore, by Lemma 4.3, part (b) must also hold.

(c) Lemma 4.3 ensures that f_t is convex. By calculating the consequences of using the optimal base stock level in period t, as was done in (4.12) for period N, we get:

$$f_t'(x) = \begin{cases} -c & \text{if } x \le S, \\ G_t'(x) - c & \text{otherwise.} \end{cases}$$

□

The consequence is therefore the following result, which is due to Veinott (1965), who used a different proof.

Theorem 4.3   (Veinott 1965)   *If the terminal value function v_T has a slope of $-c$, then a base stock policy with base stock level defined by (4.11) is optimal for t for every t.*

Proof   The recursive argument used for Theorem 4.2 applies here as well. In other words, the initial step of a proof by induction was demonstrated in the process of defining S, and Lemma 4.4 verifies the inductive step.   □

Proving that f_t is convex in Lemma 4.3 did not depend on the fact that a base stock policy was optimal for that period. However, in this section, proving that the slope of f_t was $-c$ to the left of S did use the fact that the base stock level was S in period t. Thus, as is typical of many other analyses, the form (structure) of the optimal decision rule for a period plays an intimate role in verifying that f_t has the form desired.

In summary, provided the terminal value function has a slope of $-c$, what is called a *myopic policy* (as it looks myopically only at a single period problem) is optimal in every period, regardless of the time horizon N. Furthermore, the optimal policy is completely determined by a single parameter, the optimal base stock level S, which is an easily computed critical fractile solution. Chapter 6 addresses the question of conditions under which myopic policies are optimal in more general settings.

4.3   Preservation and Attainment

In the dynamic inventory problem, we identified specific properties (structure) of the optimal value functions that were needed to verify that the optimal policy had a specific desired characteristic (structure). It will be useful to have some general notation in this regard. Let V^* denote the (nonempty) class of functions that possess the desired properties of the optimal value functions, and let Δ^* denote the (nonempty) subset of the decision rules that have the characteristics that are desired of the optimal policy. In our latest example, V^* denotes the set of convex functions defined on $\mathbf{R}$ that have a slope of $-c$ to the left of S as defined by (4.11). Similarly, Δ^* denotes the set of base stock policies with a base stock level of S, again as defined by (4.11).

We then used two properties, preservation and attainment. The *preservation* property is that if $f_{t+1} \in V^*$, then $f_t \in V^*$. The *attainment* property is that if $f_{t+1} \in V^*$, then there exists a decision rule $\delta \in \Delta^*$ that attains the optimization in the optimality equations. In words, if the optimal value function for period $t+1$ has the postulated structure, then preservation says that the optimal value function for period t will have that structure as well. And attainment says that, by virtue of the optimality criterion, the optimal decision rule for that period will have the desired structure. This formalization can be considered to be merely convenient vocabulary in the finite-horizon problem. It will be more than that in the infinite-horizon case as can be seen in Porteus (1975, 1982) and in Chapter 11.

Exercises

4.1 Suppose that $a \neq 1$. Prove by induction that

$$\sum_{i=0}^{n} i a^i = \frac{a[1 + na^{n+1} - (n+1)a^n]}{(1-a)^2}.$$

4.2 Suppose that $0 < p < 1$. Let $q := 1 - p$. Use Exercise 4.1 to prove that

$$p \sum_{i=0}^{n} q^i (n - i) = n - \frac{q(1 - q^n)}{p}.$$

4.3 Define the function f on the positive integers as:

$$f(x) := x - \frac{q(1 - q^x)}{p} + q^x c.$$

Let $\Delta(x) := f(x + 1) - f(x)$, the first forward difference. Show that

$$\Delta(x) = 1 - q^x (pc + q),$$

and that $\Delta(x)$ is increasing in x. (Thus, by Exercise A.10, f is [discretely] convex.)

4.4   This is a variation of the parking problem of Section 4.1. You now realize that instead of being required to use the pay parking lot, you can continue driving along the road past your destination until you find an unoccupied space. Make the same probabilistic assumptions about this stretch of road as you did on the approaching stretch of road. It still costs you s if you park s spaces away from the destination. Show how to transform this problem into one that is equivalent to the original formulation.

Hint: Use Exercise 4.1 to simplify your answer.

4.5   *(TV Game Show)*   (Continuation of Exercises 3.4 and 2.5)   Prove that the form of the decision rule that you decided to follow in Exercise 3.4 is indeed optimal in any finite-horizon problem. (Thus, the optimal value of S that you found there characterizes an optimal policy.)

Hint: Define $G^n(x) := -x + \sum_{i=1}^{m} f^{n-1}(x + r_i)p_i$ and show that $G^n(x)$ is decreasing in x for each n.

4.6   *(Equipment Replacement)*   (Derman, 1963)   A piece of equipment (machine) is observed to be in some state i at the beginning of each of N periods. Let α denote the one-period discount factor. State 1 corresponds to a new machine, while state n corresponds to an inoperable machine. Intermediate states represent gradual states of breakdown and inefficiency. There are two decisions possible: Decision "0" corresponds to "doing nothing" and just continuing to operate the existing machine. Decision "1" corresponds to replacing the machine, which costs c_R and occurs instantaneously: You can think of the machine making an immediate transition to state "1." The resulting, possibly unchanged, machine is then operated for the period, incurring a cost of $c(i)$ during that period as a function of the state the machine is in at the beginning of the period (after replacement, if any). Assume that $c(i)$ increases in i and that the state space is the set of integers $1, 2, \ldots, n$. Let p_{ij} denote the probability that a machine that starts a period in state i makes a transition to state j by the end of the period. Your objective is to minimize the expected present value of the costs of managing the machine over the finite time horizon, assuming $v_T(i) = 0$ for each i.

(a) Assume henceforth in this problem that $\sum_{j=k}^{n} p_{ij}$ is an increasing function of i, for each $k \leq n$. Interpret this assumption from a managerial perspective.

(b) A *control limit* policy for period t is a decision rule δ_t for that period that can be characterized by a single critical number a_t such that δ_t replaces the machine if the state i of the machine (in that period) is above a_t and does nothing otherwise. Prove that the optimal value function in each period is increasing (in the state) and that a control limit policy is optimal. (Present your proof.)

4.7 Suppose that g is a convex function defined on $\mathbf{R}$ and the real valued function G is defined on $\mathbf{R}$ by $G(y) := E_D g(y - D)$, where D is a random variable with a density ϕ. Prove, without assuming that g is differentiable everywhere, that G is convex on $\mathbf{R}$.

4.8 Prove Lemma 4.3(c).

Hint: Use Theorem A.4.

4.9 Show that $L'(y) = -c_P + (c_H + c_P)\Phi(y)$, where L is as defined in Section 4.2. Thus, (4.11) does indeed yield a minimizer of g.

4.10 Define S as the following fractile:

$$\Phi(S) = \frac{c_P - c}{c_P + c_H - \alpha c},$$

where Φ is the distribution for a random variable D. Assume that the fractile is strictly between 0 and 1. Let $g_t(x) := \mathcal{L}(x) + \alpha f_{t+1}(x^+)$, where $0 < \alpha \leq 1$, $\mathcal{L}$ is as defined in Section 4.2, and, as usual, $x^+ = \max(0, x)$. In addition, let $G_t(y) := cy + Eg_t(y - D)$. Show that if f_{t+1} has a slope of $-c$ between 0 and S, then G_t is convex and is minimized at S.

Hint: Use Exercise 4.7.

4.11 The dynamic inventory problem of Section 4.2 assumed that all shortages were backlogged. Assume now that units sold yield a unit revenue of p and all shortages now become lost sales. (Backlogging is no longer possible.) Assume that the only consequence of a lost sale is the lost revenue: There is no lost goodwill or other costs. Note that the salvage value function $v_{\mathrm{T}}(x) = -cx$

is now defined only for $x \geq 0$. The objective is to maximize the expected present value of the returns less costs incurred in operating over N periods. All other aspects of the problem remain unchanged.

Write down the optimality equations for this problem. Show how to convert the maximization problem into an equivalent minimization problem whose optimality equations can be written as follows:

$$f_t(x) = \min_{y \geq x^+} \left\{ G_t(y) - cx^+ \right\},$$

where $G_t(y) := cy + Eg_t(y - D)$, $g_t(x) := \mathcal{L}(x) + \alpha f_{t+1}(x)$, and $c_P = p$ is used in defining $\mathcal{L}$.

4.12   (Continuation of Exercise 4.11)   Suppose that $c_P = p$, $p + c_H > \alpha c$, and S is defined as in Exercise 4.10. Show that if the terminal value function has a slope of $-c$ between 0 and S, then a base stock policy with base stock level of S is optimal in each period.

Hint: Use Exercises 4.10 and 4.11.

References

Derman, C. 1963. On optimal replacement rules when changes of state are Markovian. R. Bellman (ed.) *Mathematical Optimization Techniques*. University of California Press, Berkeley. 201–10.

Hall, J., E. Porteus. 2000. Customer service competition in capacitated systems. *Manufacturing and Service Operations Management*. **2** 144–65.

MacQueen, J., R. Miller, Jr. 1960. Optimal persistence policies. *Operations Research*. **8** 362–80.

Porteus, E. 1975. On the optimality of structured policies in countable stage decision processes. *Management Science*. **22** 148–57.

Porteus, E. 1982. Conditions for characterizing the structure of optimal strategies in infinite horizon dynamic programs. *Journal of Optimization Theory and Applications*. **37** 419–32.

Veinott, A., Jr. 1965. Optimal policy for a multi-product, dynamic, nonstationary inventory problem. *Management Science*. **12** 206–22.

5

Finite-Horizon Theory

This chapter verifies that the optimality equations and the optimality conditions hold. Its approach is to develop abstract notation for the quantities of interest and to obtain relatively simple proofs. In short, the mathematical notation may be difficult for you if you are unfamiliar with this level of abstraction, but, once you digest the notation, you will find the proofs almost trivial.

5.1 Finite-State and -Action Theory

In this section, the state space S is a finite set $\{1, 2, \ldots, S\}$. The symbols i and j are commonly used to denote states as well as s. The set of admissible actions $A(s)$ is a finite set for each state s. The set Δ of admissible decision rules consists of *all* decision rules and a generic decision rule is denoted by δ. Thus, every admissible decision is represented by at least one admissible decision rule: For every s and $a \in A(s)$, there exists $\delta \in \Delta$ such that $\delta(s) = a$. All strategies are admissible and π denotes a generic one. For convenience, we now denote a strategy by $\pi = (\pi_1, \pi_2, \ldots, \pi_N)$, so that π_t denotes the decision rule for period t. (In Chapter 3, we let δ_t denote the decision rule for period t.) The time horizon (last period) is N, and the terminal value function for a finite-horizon problem is $v_{\mathbf{T}}$.

Recall from Chapter 3 that $v_t(\pi, s)$ is defined as the expected present value of starting period t in state s when following strategy π. Recall also that the optimal value function f_t is defined, for each t $(\in \{1, 2, \ldots, N\})$ and each s $(\in \mathcal{S})$, by

$$f_t(s) := \sup_{\pi} v_t(\pi, s).$$

We seek to verify the optimality equations (OE), which can be written in this setting, for each t and s, as

$$f_t(s) = \max_{a \in A(s)} \left\{ r(s, a) + \sum_{j \in \mathcal{S}} q_{sj}^a f_{t+1}(j) \right\},$$

where $f_{N+1}(j) := v_{\mathbf{T}}(j)$ for all $j \in \mathcal{S}$. That is, we must show that the optimal value of starting in period t in state s can be found by solving a one-period problem, using $f_{t+1}(j)$ as the value of arriving in each possible state j at the beginning of the next period. Furthermore, we seek to verify the optimality criterion, which says that an optimal decision for that one-period problem will be optimal in the dynamic problem.

To verify these, we establish that $v_t(\pi, s)$ can be computed recursively. We use this recursion as a building block in our proofs in Section 5.2. Later, in Section 5.3, we consider the general case, where the state and action spaces need not be finite or even denumerable, and assume that the analogous value functions can be computed recursively. Assume henceforth in this and the next section that the state and action spaces are finite.

For convenience, let

$$v_{N+1}(\pi, s) := v_{\mathbf{T}}(s),$$

for every strategy π and state s: In words, we assume that, for every strategy, there is a value of starting period $N+1$, which is considered equivalent to the end of period N, in each state, and that this value equals the (exogenously given) terminal value function.

The recursion is, for each t, s, and π, as follows:

$$v_t(\pi, s) = r(s, \pi_t(s)) + \sum_{j \in \mathcal{S}} q_{sj}^{\pi_t(s)} v_{t+1}(\pi, j). \tag{5.1}$$

We derive the recursion in words. Suppose the system starts period t in state s and strategy π is being implemented. Thus, $a = \pi_t(s)$ is the feasible action called for by this strategy under this contingency. The expected present value of the returns received over the remainder of the planning horizon consists of $r(s, a)$, the expected present value of the (net) returns received in this period, plus the expected present value of the returns over the remaining periods. Now suppose that the system moves to state j by the end of this period. The expected present value of the returns received under this strategy over the rest of the periods under this outcome is $v_{t+1}(\pi, j)$. This outcome arises with probability p_{sj}^a, so the expected value of these returns, evaluated at the beginning of period $t+1$, is $\sum_j p_{sj}^a v_{t+1}(\pi, j)$. Multiplying that by α gives the expected value, evaluated at the beginning of period t. Finally, recognizing that $q_{sj}^a = \alpha p_{sj}^a$ leads to the recursion.

Denardo (1967, 1982) pioneered the use of what he calls the *local income function* $h(s, a, v)$, also written as $h_s^a v$, which is defined in this case as follows:

$$h(s, a, v) := r(s, a) + \sum_j q_{sj}^a v_j.$$

Note that the three arguments of the local income function $h(s, a, v)$, are the state $s \in S$, the action $a \in A(s)$, and the arrival value function v, which gives a value for arriving at each state in S. (In this case, v is a real S-vector.) Furthermore, the local income function can be interpreted as the expected present value in a one-period problem starting in state s and making decision a if v_j is received at the end of that period if the system makes a transition to state j, for each j.

Equation (5.1), which we have established, can therefore be expressed equivalently as

$$v_t(\pi, s) = h\big(s, \pi_t(s), v_{t+1}(\pi)\big), \tag{5.2}$$

and the optimality equations, which we seek to establish, can be compactly written as

$$f_t(s) = \max_{a \in A(s)} h(s, a, f_{t+1}).$$

In words, the optimal value of starting period t in state s equals the optimal value in the corresponding one-period problem using the optimal value of starting period $t + 1$ as the arrival value function.

Formulation in Vector and Matrix Notation

The next step is to express (5.1) in vector and matrix notation. Let $r(\delta)$, also written as r_δ, denote the vector of expected immediate returns (from a single period) resulting from using decision rule δ. Its value at state (component/point) s is therefore $r(s, \delta(s))$. Thus, $r(\pi_t)$ is the vector of expected returns in period t when strategy π is implemented, as a function of the state at which that period is begun.

Let P_δ, also written as $P(\delta)$, denote the S by S matrix of one-period transition probabilities when decision rule δ is implemented in that period. That is, the ijth element of P_δ is

$$[P_\delta]_{ij} = p_{ij}^{\delta(i)}.$$

Let Q_δ, also written as $Q(\delta)$, denote the *effective transition matrix:*

$$Q_\delta := \alpha P_\delta,$$

which can be written pointwise as

$$[Q_\delta]_{ij} = q_{ij}^{\delta(i)} = \alpha p_{ij}^{\delta(i)}.$$

As before, the discount factor is built into the effective transition matrix. Technically, the discount factor α can be any positive real number, but in most applications $\alpha \leq 1$ will hold and we usually require that $\alpha < 1$ in the infinite-horizon case we consider later. Note that $Q(\pi_t)$ therefore denotes the effective transition matrix (into period $t + 1$ from period t).

Different problem formulations lead to different forms of Q_δ: In undiscounted problems in which there is a fixed probability of $1 - \alpha$ of the process stopping at the end of any stage and stopping the flow of any additional costs and/or revenues, we obtain exactly the same effective transition matrix. With discounted semi-Markov decision chains, in which there is continuous discounting with a strictly positive interest rate, and a random time that elapses from the point of one decision (action) until the next, the effective transition matrix Q_δ has unequal row sums, all of which are less than or equal to one. Chapter 14 analyzes a contextual example of such a problem.

We can now express (5.1) in vector and matrix notation:

$$v_t(\pi) = r(\pi_t) + Q(\pi_t)v_{t+1}(\pi). \tag{5.3}$$

That is, the vector of present values of starting period t, as a function of the state, equals the vector of immediate returns plus the vector of present values of starting the next period premultiplied by the effective transition matrix.

Recall that in Chapter 3, we defined an optimal strategy π^* for period t as satisfying $v_t(\pi^*, s) \geq v_t(\pi, s)$ for all π and s. Now, we can equivalently define such a strategy as satisfying $v_t(\pi^*) \geq v_t(\pi)$ for all π.

Operator Notation

There is one final level of abstraction in the notation that will facilitate the analysis, and it involves the use of operator notation. An operator is also called a *map*, a *mapping*, and a *function*. The notation $H : U \to V$ means that H is an operator that takes an arbitrary element of the set U and converts it into an element of V. That is, if $u \in U$, then $Hu \in V$. One also says that U is the *domain* of H and that V is the *range* of H. For the purposes of this section, let $V := \mathbf{R}^S$, the set of real S-vectors, which we call the set of *admissible vectors* and the set of *admissible value functions*. Assume henceforth that u and v are always elements of (vectors in) V.

Let the operator H_δ, also written as $H(\delta)$, be defined by

$$H_\delta v := r_\delta + Q_\delta v.$$

Think of v as the vector that gives the value of starting the next period in every possible state, perhaps as the salvage value function for a one-period problem. Then $H_\delta v$ is the expected present value of using decision rule δ for a one-period problem with v given as the value (function) of arriving at every possible state. Formally, H_δ is an *affine operator* because it is the sum of a linear operator Q_δ and a constant r_δ. In addition, $H_\delta : V \to V$: If v is an S-vector, then $H_\delta v$ is an S-vector. In other words, if v is an arrival value vector for next period, then $H_\delta v$ is an arrival value vector for this period.

Another way to think of $H_\delta v$ is as a generalization of the local income function: The pointwise expression of $H_\delta v$ is its value at state s, which we write as $[H_\delta v]_s$

and $[H_\delta v](s)$, and which can be written as

$$[H_\delta v]_s = [H_\delta v](s) = h(s, \delta(s), v).$$

The following lemma formalizes the results of putting the value functions into operator notation and summarizes one of their essential properties.

Lemma 5.1   *(Exercise 5.1)*
(a) *The value functions for a given strategy π can be expressed as follows:*

$$v_t(\pi) = H(\pi_t)v_{t+1}(\pi). \qquad (5.4)$$

(b) *The value of using strategy π when starting period t in state s depends at most on $\pi_t(s)$, the decision called for at that point, and π_τ for $\tau = t + 1, t + 2, \ldots, N$, the decision rules to be used in the remaining periods.*

Optimal Value Operator

Define the *optimal value (return) operator A* as follows:

$$Av := \sup_{\delta \in \Delta} H_\delta v.$$

In words, if v is the arrival value (terminal return) function for a one-period problem, Av gives the vector of optimal values of starting that one-period problem, as a function of the starting state. That is, the optimal value operator converts a vector of arrival values for the next period into a vector of values of starting this period (arrival values for this period).

Its pointwise expression (value at state s), also written as $[Av](s)$, is

$$
\begin{aligned}
[Av]_s &= \sup_{\delta \in \Delta} [H_\delta v]_s \\
&= \sup_{\delta \in \Delta} h(s, \delta(s), v) \\
&= \sup_{a \in A(s)} h(s, a, v).
\end{aligned}
$$

The last equality reveals an important subtlety that arises in our representation of optimization in vector notation. Our vector notation, which optimizes over decision rules, allows a different decision rule to be selected for each state s. However, because of the structure of this problem, the only part of the decision rule that matters when the state is s is the action selected in that state, namely $\delta(s)$. This reveals why, in the general case, we must assume that all admissible decisions are represented by at least one admissible decision rule, so that the optimization can be simplified to considering only the admissible decisions when the state is s.

The *optimality equations* can now be stated in operator notation:

$$f_t = A f_{t+1} \quad \text{for every } t.$$

In operator vocabulary, the (OE) say that the optimal value function for a period can be obtained by applying the optimal value operator to the optimal value function for the next period. From a procedural perspective, one starts with $f_{N+1} = v_{\mathrm{T}}$, the terminal value function, and applies the optimal value operator to it to get $f_N = A f_{N+1}$. The process is repeated recursively to obtain f_t for $t = N, N - 1, \ldots, 1$.

5.2   Proofs for the Finite-State and -Action Case

With the use of operator notation, the proofs in this section are nearly identical for the general case as for the finite-state and -action case. Thus, rather modest changes are required to make them apply in more general settings.

An operator H is *isotone* on V if $u, v \in V$ and $u \le v$ imply that $Hu \le Hv$. This property is a simple generalization of an increasing function defined on the real line. The terminology comes from functional analysis.

Lemma 5.2

(a) *Every H_δ is isotone on V.*

(b) *A is isotone on V.*

Proof   (a) Exercise 5.2.

(b) (Denardo, 1967) By definition, $H_\delta v \le Av$. Suppose $u \le v$. Then, since H_δ is isotone, $H_\delta u \le H_\delta v$. That is, $H_\delta u \le Av$ for every δ. Hence, $Au \le Av$. (Otherwise, a contradiction would arise.)   □

These properties are fundamental in proving that the optimality equations hold, and they have a simple economic interpretation: Suppose u and v are two arrival value functions for the next period and $u \leq v$, which can be written as $u(s) \leq v(s)$ for every state $s \in S$. Then, from the perspective of starting the next period, you prefer v to u: The value of v at every state s is greater than the value at u. Since H_δ is isotone, $H_\delta u \leq H_\delta v$, which means that from the perspective of starting this period with any fixed decision rule, you still prefer v to u. In the vocabulary of preference theory, the induced utility defined through the value functions $v_t(\pi)$ exhibits temporal consistency of preference: Suppose we have two strategies π and π' that call for the same decision rule in period t: $\pi_t = \pi'_t$. Suppose further that the value of starting period $t+1$ is uniformly better with strategy π: $v_{t+1}(\pi) \geq v_{t+1}(\pi')$. Then, using the fact that $H(\pi_t)$ is isotone, we get

$$
\begin{aligned}
v_t(\pi) &= H(\pi_t)v_{t+1}(\pi) &&\text{[by (5.4)]}\\
&\geq H(\pi_t)v_{t+1}(\pi') &&\text{[H is isotone]}\\
&= H(\pi'_t)v_{t+1}(\pi') &&\text{[$\pi_t = \pi'_t$]}\\
&= v_t(\pi') &&\text{[by (5.4)]}
\end{aligned}
$$

Here is another interpretation. By Lemma 5.1(b), the return from period t through the end of the horizon depends only on the decision rules selected for those periods. Thus, if one collection of decision rules for each of those periods yields a higher value at every state than does another collection, then, regardless of the decision rule selected for period t, the value at t is better with the former collection of decision rules.

The interpretation for A being isotone is similar. If you prefer v over u next period, then you prefer the best you can do this period with v as the arrival value function to the best you can do this period with u as the arrival value function.

Lemma 5.3 (Exercise 5.3) *For any $v \in V$, there exists a $\delta^* \in \Delta$ such that $H_{\delta^*} v = Av$.*

The proof of this result amounts to selecting an optimal action for each state and composing the results into a decision rule, which is admissible, because all decision rules are admissible, by assumption. (In a more general case, such as when the state space is continuous and admissible decision rules must be measurable, this result does not hold without adding further conditions.) Note that, even in this case, the optimal decision rule may not be unique, because there may be ties for the optimal decision for one or more states.

Theorem 5.1   *The following hold (for this, the finite-state and -action case).*

(a) The optimal value functions, $f_1, f_2, \ldots, f_N$, exist.

(b) There exists a strategy that is optimal for every t.

(c) The optimality equations hold:

$$f_t = A f_{t+1} \quad \text{for every } t.$$

(d) The optimality conditions hold: A strategy $\pi = (\pi_1, \pi_2, \ldots, \pi_N)$, is optimal for t for every period t if and only if $\pi_t(s)$ attains the optimum in the optimality equations for every period t and state s.

Proof   We prove parts (a)–(c) simultaneously, by backward induction. The inductive step is demonstrated here, as the initial step is a specialization of it. Suppose (a)–(c) hold for $i \geq t + 1$. We use the fact that if we can find a vector v that satisfies $v \geq v_t(\pi)$ for every π and there exists π^* such that $v = v_t(\pi^*)$, then f_t exists and equals v. Furthermore, π^* is optimal for t. $A f_{t+1}$ will play the role of v, so (a)–(c) will therefore hold for $i \geq t$.

Pick arbitrary π. Then, by definition, $f_{t+1} \geq v_{t+1}(\pi)$.

Thus,

$$
\begin{aligned}
A f_{t+1} &\geq A v_{t+1}(\pi) && \text{[A is isotone]} \\
&\geq H(\pi_t) v_{t+1}(\pi) && \text{[definition of A]} \\
&= v_t(\pi). && \text{[by (5.4)]}
\end{aligned}
$$

By the inductive assumption, there exists a strategy π^* that is optimal for period $t + 1$. By Lemma 5.1 (b), that strategy is independent of the decision rules for periods 1 through t. Suppose we now require that the decision rule π_t^* specified for period t satisfy

$$H(\pi_t^*) f_{t+1} = A f_{t+1},$$

which is justifiable by Lemma 5.3. Thus,

$$
\begin{aligned}
A f_{t+1} &= H(\pi_t^*) f_{t+1} && \text{[construction]} \\
&= H(\pi_t^*) v_{t+1}(\pi^*) && \text{[inductive assumption]} \\
&= v_t(\pi^*). && \text{[by (5.4)]}
\end{aligned}
$$

(d) Suppose first that π^* attains the optimum in the (OE) for each period:

$$H(\pi_t^*) f_{t+1} = A f_{t+1} \quad \text{for every } t.$$

Suppose inductively that π^* is optimal for $t+1$: $v_{t+1}(\pi^*) = f_{t+1}$. Select an arbitrary strategy π. Then

$$
\begin{aligned}
v_t(\pi^*) &= H(\pi_t^*)v_{t+1}(\pi^*) &&\text{[by (5.4)]} \\
&= H(\pi_t^*)f_{t+1} &&\text{[inductive assumption]} \\
&= Af_{t+1} &&\text{[assumed condition]} \\
&\geq Av_{t+1}(\pi) &&\text{[definition and A isotone]} \\
&\geq H(\pi_t)v_{t+1}(\pi) &&\text{[definition of A]} \\
&= v_t(\pi). &&\text{[by (5.4)]}
\end{aligned}
$$

Hence, π^* is optimal for t as well.

Now suppose that π^* is optimal for every t: $v_t(\pi^*) = f_t$ for every t. Then

$$
\begin{aligned}
H(\pi_t^*)v_{t+1}(\pi^*) &= v_t(\pi^*) &&\text{[by (5.4)]} \\
&= f_t &&\text{[inductive assumption]} \\
&= Af_{t+1} &&\text{[by (c)]}
\end{aligned}
$$

That is, π^* attains the optimum in the (OE) for each period t.   □

5.3   Generalizations

The proof of the optimality equations and the optimality conditions depends only on the operator form of the recursion given in (5.1) and therefore, does not depend on $H(\pi_t)$ being affine. What matters is that $H(\pi_t)$ be isotone. Thus, the optimality equations and criterion also hold in more general dynamic problems in which the criterion can be expressed recursively with an operator having such properties. Examples of such formulations can be found in Porteus (1975) and Kreps and Porteus (1978, 1979).

The optimality equations and criterion hold under other generalizations as well. Neither the state space nor the action space need be finite. Returns and transition probabilities need not be stationary. The following is an example of more general results that can be obtained.

Theorem 5.2   *If the conditions below hold for a finite-horizon problem, then the optimal value functions exist, an optimal strategy exists, and the optimality equations and conditions hold.*

(a) Every admissible decision is represented by at least one admissible decision rule.

(b) *Any collection of admissible decision rules for each period comprises an admissible strategy: If $\pi_t \in \Delta$ for each t, then $\pi = (\pi_1, \pi_2, \ldots, \pi_N)$ is admissible.*

(c) $v_{N+1}(\pi) = v_\mathbf{T} \in V$.

(d) *There exists an operator $H_t(\delta)$ for every t and $\delta \in \Delta$ such that, for each t and π, $v_t(\pi) = H_t(\pi_t)v_{t+1}(\pi)$.*

(e) $H_t(\delta): V \to V$ *for every t and $\delta \in \Delta$.*

(f) $H_t(\delta)$ *is isotone on V for every t and $\delta \in \Delta$.*

(g) *The optimal value operator A_t, defined for each t by*

$$A_t v := \sup_{\delta \in \Delta} H_t(\delta)v, \text{ for } v \in V,$$

satisfies $A_t : V \to V$.

(h) *For each t and $v \in V$, there exists $\delta \in \Delta$ such that $H_t(\delta)v = A_t v$.*

5.4   Optimality of Structured Policies

In Chapter 4, we explored the process of characterizing the form of the optimal policies. This section formalizes that process.

Let Δ_t^* denote the (nonempty) set of *structured decision rules* for period t. As indicated earlier, we sometimes call them structured policies as well. As researchers, we specify Δ_t^* to suit our needs and intuition. The idea is to have Δ_t^* far simpler than the set of admissible decision rules. Let Π^* denote the set of *structured strategies*, which we assume here is the Cartesian product of the sets of structured decision rules. We seek to show that there is an optimal strategy that is structured. The key to the approach presented here is to identify a nonempty set V^* of *structured value functions* that, together with Δ_t^*, allows conditions (a)–(c) of the following theorem to be verified, for each t.

Theorem 5.3   (*Porteus, 1975, 1982*)   *Consider a finite-horizon problem in which the optimality equations and conditions hold. If*

(a)   (*Preservation*) $A_t : V^* \to V^*$,

(b)   (*Attainment*)   *if $v \in V^*$, then there exists $\delta^* \in \Delta_t^*$ such that $H_t(\delta^*)v = A_t v$, and*

(c) $v_\mathbf{T} \in V^*$, *then*

(d) *the optimal value function f_t is structured ($f_t \in V^*$) for every t, and*

(e) *there exists a structured strategy ($\pi^* \in \Pi^*$) that is optimal for every t.*

Proof   Suppose that $f_{t+1} \in V^*$, so, by (b), we can select a structured decision rule for period t that attains the optimum in the optimality equations: $\pi_t \in \Delta_t^*$ and $H(\pi_t)f_{t+1} = A_t f_{t+1}$. By the optimality equations, $f_t = A_t f_{t+1}$, so, by (a), f_t is structured ($f_t \in V^*$). Since f_{N+1} is defined to be v_T, which by (c), is in V^*, we can initiate the recursion. We thereby recursively construct a structured strategy that, by the optimality criterion, is optimal for every period and verify that the optimal value functions are all structured in the process.   □

Attainment can also be written as follows: For every $v \in V^*$, there exists a $\delta \in \Delta_t^*$ such that

$$h(s, \delta(s), v) = [A_t v](s).$$

Exercises

5.1   Prove Lemma 5.1.

5.2   Prove Lemma 5.2(a).

5.3   Prove Lemma 5.3.

5.4   A strategy π is *conserving* if

$$f_t = H(\pi_t)f_{t+1} \quad \text{for every } t \quad (1 \leq t \leq N).$$

A conserving strategy has the following property: Suppose you select an arbitrary period t. You consider the one-period problem, starting at the beginning of period t and using as the salvage value the optimal value function for the next period $(t + 1)$. You then implement the decision rule called for by that strategy in that one-period problem. The resulting vector of expected present values is the optimal value function for period t. Prove that if the optimality equations and the optimality conditions hold, then any conserving strategy is optimal for t, for every t.

5.5   A strategy π is *unimprovable* if

$$v_t(\pi) = Av_{t+1}(\pi) \quad \text{for every } t.$$

Suppose the results of Theorem 5.1 hold. Prove that an unimprovable strategy is optimal for every t.

5.6   Fix N and suppose that $v_\mathbf{T} = 0$. Prove that if the immediate returns are positive and uniformly bounded (that is, there exists a real number M such that $0 \leq r(s,a) \leq M$ for every s and a) then the following vector inequalities hold

$$f_1 \geq f_2 \geq \cdots \geq f_{N+1} \quad (= 0)$$

and that, independent of N,

$$f(s) = f_1(s) \leq \frac{M}{1-\alpha} \quad \text{for every } s.$$

5.7   Fix a time horizon N and a strategy π. Suppose that $v_\mathbf{T}(s) = 0$ for every s (there is no salvage value) and that $r(s,a)$ is deterministic (all uncertainty arises in the transition probabilities). Suppress π and let X_{ts} denote the present value of the returns over periods t through N, given that the process starts period t in state s (and strategy π is implemented). The evaluation is in beginning of period t dollars. Let X_t denote the vector of those values, each component corresponding to a different state. Our focus has been on expected values so far. That is, we denote EX_t by $v_t(\pi)$, and, when fully suppressing π, by v_t. We denote EX_{ts} by v_{ts}. Thus, we have the recursions $v_t = H_t v_{t+1}$, where $v_{N+1} := 0$, and $v_{ts} = h(s, \delta_t(s), v_{t+1})$.

(a) Let F_{ts} denote the distribution function of X_{ts}. That is,

$$F_{ts}(x) = P\{X_{ts} \leq x\}.$$

Show that

$$F_{ts}(x) = \sum_j p_{sj}^{\delta_t(s)} F_{t+1,j}\left(\frac{x - r(s, \delta_t(s))}{\alpha}\right).$$

(b) Let $\hat{v}_{ts}$ denote the variance of X_{ts}. That is,

$$\hat{v}_{ts} := E[(X_{ts} - v_{ts})^2].$$

Show that

$$\hat{v}_{ts} = \alpha^2 \sum_j p_{sj}^{\delta_t(s)} \hat{v}_{t+1,j} + \sum_j p_{sj}^{\delta_t(s)} [r(s, \delta_t(s)) + \alpha v_{t+1,j}]^2 - (v_{ts})^2.$$

5.8   Suppose $\mathcal{S} = [0,1]$ and $A(s) = [0,1]$ for every $s \in \mathcal{S}$, so we have continuous-state and -action spaces. If the system starts period t in state $s_t = s$

and decision $a_t = a \in A(s)$ is made, $r(s, a)$ continues to denote the immediate return and $\Phi(x|s, a) = P\{s_{t+1} \leq x | s_t = s, a_t = a\}$ denotes the conditional probability distribution of the state of the system at the beginning of the next period.

(a) How would you define Δ, V, and $H_t(\delta)$ for each t and $\delta \in \Delta$?

(b) What conditions would you impose on $r(\cdot, \cdot)$ so that conditions (e), (g), and (h) of Theorem 5.2 would hold?

References

Denardo, E. 1967. Contraction mappings in the theory underlying dynamic programming. *SIAM Review.* **9** 165–77.

Denardo, E. 1982. *Dynamic Programming: Models and Applications.* Prentice-Hall, Englewood Cliffs, N.J.

Kreps, D., E. Porteus. 1978. Temporal resolution of uncertainty and dynamic choice theory. *Econometrica.* **46** 185–200.

Kreps, D., E. Porteus. 1979. Dynamic programming and dynamic choice theory. *Econometrica.* **47** 91–100.

Porteus, E. 1975. On the optimality of structured policies in countable stage decision processes. *Management Science.* **22** 148–57.

Porteus, E. 1982. Conditions for characterizing the structure of optimal strategies in infinite horizon dynamic programs. *Journal of Optimization Theory and Applications.* **37** 419–32.

6

Myopic Policies

We have already discussed myopic policies: In Chapter 2, we saw that a myopic policy can lead to very poor results, whereas in Chapter 4, we found that a myopic policy is optimal in every finite-horizon stochastic demand problem, provided that certain conditions are satisfied. This chapter focuses on more general conditions under which a myopic policy is optimal. We first put the idea into a more general framework by discussing the general motivation for efficiently finding solutions to dynamic problems.

Most practical dynamic inventory problems have long planning horizons, are nonstationary (in the sense that economic and/or distributional parameters change over time), provide better information about the near term than the long term, and are too big to solve by enumeration, even with current computers. For example, suppose we have a 20 product inventory problem, with 10 different stock levels for each product, so there are 10^{20} states. If there are 10 different decisions for each state, and 10 computer ops (operations) are required to evaluate each decision, 10^{22} ops are needed per period to compute the optimal decision rule. If we have a 10-period problem, then 10^{23} ops are required to solve the problem. Suppose we have a computer that can carry out an average of 500 million ops per second. Even if we assume that the computer operates continuously without any breakdowns or maintenance required, it would take more than 6 million years to solve this problem by enumeration.

Note the key role of the number of products in the example. Each different product adds another dimension to the state space. In general, the size of the state space grows exponentially in the number of dimensions. As the number of dimensions gets large, the problem becomes intractable. Bellman (1957) calls this phenomenon the *curse of dimensionality*. The next section touchs on some general approaches for dealing with this curse.

6.1   General Approaches to Finding Solutions

Aggregation

One approach is to aggregate the problem into a relatively small number of similar products, which reduces the problem complexity drastically. In general, aggregation partitions the state space into a smaller number of blocks of states. The aggregation need not be simply to combine several different products into a common representative product. A literature exists on this topic.

Planning Horizons

This approach develops bounds that can be used to identify the solution to a short finite-horizon problem as optimal for a longer, possibly infinite-horizon problem. Theory exists primarily for deterministic problems, although they can be nonstationary. How long the finite-horizon problem must be depends on the problem data and is determined by working on the problem. The curse of dimensionality is the primary computational problem, not the number of periods.

Simplified Modeling Assumptions

This approach makes assumptions that aren't correct, but simplifies the problem and its solution. This is the essence of the challenge to any analytical manager or analyst. One must map the solution of the simplified model back to the solution of the real problem and somehow assess the effect of the missing ingredients.

Exploit Special Structure

This approach attempts to prove the form of the optimal policy is simple. The problem of searching over a huge number of decision rules for each period reduces to the problem of finding a small number of parameters, such as the base stock level S of an optimal base stock policy.

One of the most important, practical subapproaches is to attempt to prove that a *myopic* policy is optimal: the decision rule that optimizes the return in a single-period problem with an easily identifiable arrival (terminal) value function for that period is optimal. This subapproach is the focus of this chapter.

6.2   Development

As indicated in Chapter 2, myopic means near sighted, which, in this context, means looking only at the "current" one-period problem. What we seek is a form of a planning-horizon theorem: You need only to solve a one-period problem (possibly modified in some way) to know you have the optimal decision rule for that period, regardless of the planning horizon of the actual problem. This result can be valid for both deterministic and stochastic problems, stationary and nonstationary.

The result that we shall examine in this chapter involves the existence of an optimal *action* for the single-period problem, rather than the more general case of an optimal decision rule. However, this action need not be optimal for every state: There will exist a set of states, which we will call *consistent states*, such that if you start a period in that set, then the designated action will be both admissible and optimal. Furthermore, you are assured of ending up in the same set at the start of the next period. Thus, the same action is optimal in every subsequent period.

We assume that the immediate return is additively separable:

$$r(s, a) = r_{\mathbf{s}}(s) + r_{\mathbf{A}}(a), \tag{6.1}$$

for all s and a. We also assume there exists a sequence $\{X_t\}$ of i.i.d. random variables, one for each period $t = 1, 2, \ldots, N$, such that the state of the system at the beginning of period $t+1$ depends only on the action in period t and X_t: Suppose the system starts period t in state s, and action a is selected. Then the system will start period $t+1$ in state

$$s_{t+1} = z(a, X_t), \tag{6.2}$$

for every a. In particular, the next period's state is a random variable that can depend on the current action a but not on the current state. Furthermore, it must be statistically independent of the random variables for the other periods. Let Φ denote the common distribution of each X_t, and let X denote a generic random variable with that distribution.

In this case, the optimality equations can be written as follows:

$$f_t(s) = \max_a \left\{ r_s(s) + r_A(a) + \alpha E f_{t+1}(z(a, X)) \right\}$$
$$= \max_a h(s, a, f_{t+1}),$$

where, as in Chapter 5, $h(s, a, v) := r_s(s) + r_A(a) + \alpha E v(z(a, X))$ for each admissible real valued function v defined on S.

Let $A_* := \bigcup_{s \in S} A(s)$, which is the union of all feasible decisions. For each $a \in A_*$, let $S(a) := \{s \in S \,|\, a \in A(s)\}$, which is the set of states for which action a is admissible. Let $\gamma(a)$ be defined, for each $a \in A_*$, by

$$\gamma(a) := r_A(a) + \alpha E r_s(z(a, X)), \tag{6.3}$$

which we interpret as the immediate return from decision a plus the discounted expected value of the return associated with the next state we visit. Let a^* denote a maximizer of $\gamma(\cdot)$ over A_*. Consider a^* to be fixed henceforth in this section.

Assumption (a) below is that, if the system starts in $S(a^*)$ and the admissible decision a^* is made, then the next state visited will be in $S(a^*)$. For this reason, $S(a^*)$ is called the set of *consistent states*.

Theorem 6.1   *(Veinott, 1965; Sobel, 1981)   If, in addition to the assumptions stated above (namely, (6.1), (6.2), and $\{X_t\}$ being i.i.d.),*

(a) $z(a^*, X) \in S(a^*)$ for every realization of X, and

(b) $v_T(s) = r_s(s)$ for all s, then

(c) there exists an optimal policy that selects action a^* *whenever a consistent state is visited. In particular, action* a^* *is optimal at state* s *for all* $s \in S(a^*)$. *Furthermore, once a consistent state is visited, then only consistent states will be visited thereafter.*

Proof   We verify the conditions of Theorem 5.3. Let the structured decision rules be those that always implement decision a^* when in a state in $S(a^*)$:

$$\Delta^* := \{\delta | \delta(s) = a^* \text{ for every } s \in S(a^*)\}.$$

Let $V^* := \{v | \text{ there exists } b \in \mathbf{R} \text{ such that } v(s) \leq b + r_{\mathbf{s}}(s) \text{ for all } s$ and $v(s) = b + r_{\mathbf{s}}(s) \text{ for } s \in S(a^*)\}$. Thus, each structured value function is, in general, bounded above by a translation of the immediate return associated with the state and equals that tranlsation when in a consistent state. Given $v \in V^*$, and arbitrary s, note that

$$
\begin{aligned}
h(s, a, v) &= r_{\mathbf{s}}(s) + r_{\mathbf{A}}(a) + \alpha E v(z(a, X)) \\
&\leq r_{\mathbf{s}}(s) + r_{\mathbf{A}}(a) + \alpha E[b + r_{\mathbf{s}}(z(a, X))] && [v \in V^*] \\
&= r_{\mathbf{s}}(s) + \alpha b + \gamma(a) && [\text{definition of } \gamma] \\
&\leq r_{\mathbf{s}}(s) + \alpha b + \gamma(a^*). && (6.4)
\end{aligned}
$$

For attainment, suppose $s \in S(a^*)$. Then the quantity in (6.4) is attained by $h(s, a^*, v)$: The first inequality above is an equality because, by (a), $z(a^*, X) \in S(a^*)$ and, therefore, since $v \in V^*$, $v(z(a, X)) = b + r_{\mathbf{s}}(z(a, X))$. That is, action a^* attains the one-period optimization for such starting states.

For preservation, we have, from (6.4), that

$$[Av](s) \leq r_{\mathbf{s}}(s) + \alpha b + \gamma(a^*),$$

and if $s \in S(a^*)$, then equality holds. That is, $\alpha b + \gamma(a^*)$ plays the role of the constant b in the definition of structured value functions. By (b), $v_{\mathbf{T}} \in V^*$. Thus, the result holds by Theorem 5.3. $\square$

The version of Theorem 6.1 for the cost minimization case is analogous, using an additively separable cost function $c(s, a) = c_{\mathbf{s}}(s) + c_{\mathbf{A}}(a)$.

There is an interesting application of the results of this section to managerial incentives. Different people can be given responsibility for the performance of the organization in different periods: If manager t is given responsibility for the performance in period t and that performance is measured as $\gamma(\cdot)$, then, provided there are no hidden effects, such as costs of managerial effort, each manager will select the myopically optimal action for that period, which is optimal for the organization. Such a structure is particularly desirable for an

organization that has high employee turnover: There are no end game effects
that will induce a manager, who is planning to leave the job soon, to act in a
way that is counter to the long-run objectives of the organization. In this case,
Theorem 6.1 says how to design myopic performance measures that will lead to
optimal decision making in a dynamic environment.

6.3   Application to Inventory Theory

Consider the following generalization of the single product inventory model
of Section 4.2, where state x is the stock level before ordering, action y is
the stock level after ordering, and c is the unit ordering cost. The random
variable is the demand D in the period, with generic outcome ξ. As usual,
the immediate cost is

$$c(x, y) = cy - cx + L(y),$$

where, as in Section 4.2, $L(y) := E\mathcal{L}(y - D)$ and $\mathcal{L}(x) := c_{\mathrm{H}}x^+ + c_{\mathrm{P}}(-x)^+$.

The generalization introduced here is that there can be proportional deterministic deterioration of positive stock and proportional partial backlogging. In
particular, the transition function is

$$z(y, \xi) = \begin{cases} \beta_{\mathrm{R}}(y - \xi) & \text{if } \xi \leq y \\ \beta_{\mathrm{B}}(y - \xi) & \text{if } \xi > y, \end{cases}$$

where β_{R} is the (constant) fraction of positive leftover stock at the end of the
period that remains usable the next period, and β_{B} is the (constant) fraction
of unsatisfied demand during a period that is backlogged. Both fractions are
between 0 and 1.

Theorem 6.2   *If the terminal value function is given by* $v_{\mathrm{T}}(x) = -cx$, *and*
S *is defined as the following critical fractile,*

$$\Phi(S) = \frac{c_{\mathrm{P}} - c(1 - \alpha\beta_{\mathrm{B}})}{c_{\mathrm{P}} + c_{\mathrm{H}} + \alpha c(\beta_{\mathrm{B}} - \beta_{\mathrm{R}})}, \tag{6.5}$$

then it is optimal to order up to S *if the inital stock level is below* S.

Proof   The immediate cost is additively separable: we can represent it as

$$c(x, y) = c_S(x) + c_A(y),$$

where $c_S(x) := -cx$ and $c_A(y) := cy + L(y)$. Thus,

$$\gamma(y) := cy + L(y) + \alpha \int_0^y [-c\beta_R(y - \xi)]\phi(\xi)\,d\xi + \alpha \int_y^\infty [c\beta_B(\xi - y)]\phi(\xi)\,d\xi,$$

which is the objective function for a newsvendor problem. Exercise 6.3 demonstrates that if S satisfies (6.5), then S minimizes γ over $\mathbf{R}$. Let $a^* = S$. The set of consistent states is $S(a^*) = (-\infty, a^*]$. Clearly, once we start below S, and order up to S, we remain at or below S thereafter. Since $v_T(x) = c_S(x)$, Theorem 6.1 applies.   ☐

This proof is simpler than the one given in Chapter 4. While we have not shown here that it is optimal to order nothing for stock levels above S, there are ways to prove that result using this approach. Furthermore, in many practical settings, it is not important to determine the optimal actions for transient states that will, at most, be visited only during the early stages of the process.

6.4   Application to Reservoir Management

This section addresses a simple water reservoir management problem. This problem is similar to a single product inventory model, except that (a) the decision is how much to subtract from the amount available, rather than add, and (b) the random variable during the period is added to the amount available rather than subtracted.

The state x is the amount of water in the reservoir at the beginning of the period, action a is the amount to be released during the period, and D denotes the random (positive) inflow of water during the period, assumed to have distribution Φ and density ϕ, with $\Phi(0) = 0$. Inflows are assumed to be i.i.d. random variables.

It is convenient to let $y := x - a$ denote the worst-case ending level, which is the water level at the end of the period should there be no inflow during the period.

Each unit of water released yields a commercial benefit of r. A public (recreational) benefit of $B(x)$ is enjoyed at the beginning of each period, as a function of the level x of water in the reservoir at that time. Thus, the immediate return from carrying out decision $a = x - y$ in a period that begins with level x is $ra + B(x) = rx - ry + B(x)$, which is additively separable as required by (6.1). Management of the reservoir is charged with maximizing the expected present value of the benefits enjoyed over a finite horizon, using a one-period discount factor of α.

It is convenient to work with an equivalent formulation of the problem, in which the set of feasible actions y for each initial state x is given as $A(x) = [0, x]$: only a positive amount can be discharged, and the worst-case ending level cannot be strictly negative.

The reservoir has a fixed capacity of C units of water. Thus, assuming the outflow occurs essentially instantaneously at the beginning of the period, the level of water at the beginning of the next period can be written as

$$z(x, y, D) = z(y, D) = \min\{y + D, C\},$$

which is independent of x as required by (6.2).

Theorem 6.3   *If the terminal value function is given by* $v_\mathrm{T}(x) = rx + B(x)$, *and* S *is a maximizer of* γ *over* $[0, C]$, *where*

$$\gamma(y) := -ry + \alpha \int_{\xi=0}^{C-y} \Big[r(y + \xi) + B(y + \xi) \Big] \phi(\xi)\, d\xi$$
$$+ \alpha \big[rC + B(C) \big] \big[1 - \Phi(C - y) \big], \tag{6.6}$$

then it is optimal to bring the level down to S *(release* $x - S$ *whenever the initial water level is above* S*).*

Proof   Let $r_\mathbf{S}(x) := rx + B(x)$ and $r_\mathbf{A}(y) := -ry$, so that (6.1) holds. Thus, (6.6) follows from (6.3). The set of consistent states is $S(a^*) = [S, C]$: Once we start with at least an amount S of water available, we remain at that level or higher thereafter. Theorem 6.1 again applies.   □

6.5   Extensions

Nonstationary problems can be dealt with analogously: Suppose that $\{X_t\}$ remain statistically independent but are not necessarily identically distributed.

Furthermore, assume that the immediate return in period t is now given by

$$r_t(s, a) = r_t^{\mathrm{S}}(s) + r_t^{\mathrm{A}}(a), \tag{6.7}$$

and the next state by

$$s_{t+1} = z_t(a, X_t). \tag{6.8}$$

Let

$$\gamma_t(a) := \begin{cases} r_t^{\mathrm{A}}(a) + \alpha E r_{t+1}^{\mathrm{S}}(z_t(a, X_t)) & \text{if } t \in \{1, 2, \ldots, N-1\}, \\ r_N^{\mathrm{A}}(a) + \alpha E v_{\mathrm{T}}(z_N(a, X_N)) & \text{if } t = N, \end{cases}$$

and let a_t^* denote a maximizer of γ_t over $\mathbf{R}$ for each t. Then define, for each t, $S_t^* := S(a_t^*)$, the set of states for which (the intended myopically optimal decision for period t) a_t^* is feasible.

Theorem 6.4 *Suppose that (6.7) and (6.8) hold, and $\{X_t\}$ are independent. If*

(a) the initial state is consistent $(s_1 \in S_1^*)$, and

(b) $z_t(a_t^*, X_t) \in S_{t+1}^*$ for every realization of X_t and each $t = 1, 2, \ldots, N-1$, then

(c) it is optimal to implement decision a_t^* in period t for each t.

Proof Exercise 6.8. □

Given part (a), part (b) ensures that, after making the myopically optimal decision in one period, the myopically optimal decision for the next period will be feasible. Exercise 6.9 explores the application of this result to the stochastic inventory problem. In particular, if the optimal base stock levels increase over time, then it is easy to verify that (c) holds.

By contrast, we may know by the natural generalization of Theorem 2.2 that a base stock policy is optimal in each period of a nonstationary problem. However, if the optimal base stock levels can decrease from one period to the next, then it is possible for the system to end up above the optimal base stock level at the beginning of some period, which means that the conditions of Theorem 6.4 no longer hold.

As pointed out in Section 6.3, the theory presented here says nothing about the optimal decisions for states that are not consistent (with respect to the defined optimal solution to the myopic objective function). Heyman and Sobel (1984) present conditions under which the optimal policy selects the "closest" action to a^* that is admissible. They also give a good introduction to the literature, list of pertinent references, and numerous other applications of myopic theory, including fishery harvesting and reservoir management. Some interesting applications to fishery management can be found in Lovejoy (1986, 1988).

Exercises

6.1   *(Inverse Distributions)*   This exercise and the next show that, without loss of generality, each X_t used in (6.2) may be assumed to be uniformly distributed on $(0, 1)$.

Suppose that X is a random variable with distribution function Φ and density function such that Φ is strictly increasing on $(-\infty, \infty)$. In addition, suppose that f and g are real valued functions defined on $\mathbf{R}$, and Y is a random variable that is uniformly distributed on $(0, 1)$. Let $h(y) := g(\Phi^{-1}(y))$ for $y \in (0, 1)$. Show that

$$Ef(g(X)) = Ef(h(Y)). \tag{6.9}$$

6.2   *(Inverse Distributions, continued)*   Show that the result of Exercise 6.1 holds if the assumptions therein are generalized in the following two ways.

Hint: In each case, identify a real valued function G defined on $(0, 1)$, to take the place of Φ^{-1}, let $h(y) := g(G(y))$, and show that (6.9) holds.

(a) *(Impossible Outcomes)*   There exist real numbers $x_1 < x_2$ such that $\Phi(x_2) = \Phi(x_1)$. Φ is strictly increasing on $(-\infty, x_1)$ and on (x_2, ∞).

Hint: Define $G(y) := \Phi^{-1}(y)$ for $y \neq \Phi(x_1)$ and define $G(\Phi(x_1))$ arbitrarily, such as equal to x_1.

(b) *(Discrete Outcome)*   There exists a real number x_1 such that

$$\lim_{x \uparrow x_1} \Phi(x) < \Phi(x_1).$$

(Prove this case independently of (a) rather than cumulatively.)

Hint: Define $G(y) := x_1$ for $y \in [\lim_{x \uparrow x_1} \Phi(x), \Phi(x_1)]$.

6.3 Show that γ as defined in the proof of Theorem 6.2 is convex and that any solution to (6.5) minimizes γ over **R**.

6.4 *(Inventory Disposal)* Consider the following generalization of the in-ventory model of Section 6.3. Some realizations of demand can be negative, which can be interpreted as having more units returned during the period than newly sold. It is also possible to return stock to the supplier at the beginning of each period. In particular, not only does it cost c per unit to purchase new units, but old ones can be sent back to the supplier and a credit of c for each such unit will be given. Show that the optimal policy in each period is a base stock policy with base stock level S as given in Theorem 6.2. That is, if you begin a period at a stock level below S, then bring the stock level up to S. If you begin above S, then bring the stock level down to S.

6.5 *(Reservoir Management, continued)* Suppose that the B of Section 6.4 is differentiable, concave, and increasing on $[0, C]$. Show that if there exists $S \in [0, C]$ such that

$$\alpha r \Phi(C - S) + \alpha \int_{\xi=0}^{C-S} B'(S + \xi)\phi(\xi)\, d\xi = r$$

then S is an optimal decision (as used in Theorem 6.3).

6.6 *(Equipment Maintenance)* You have m machines that can be operated during each period. Let the state x at the beginning of a period be the (integer) number of machines that are operating then. Thus, $0 \le x \le m$. You may repair any number of the currently nonoperating machines at a cost of c_R each. It takes virtually no time to repair a machine, so the number y of operating machines that you select to have at the beginning of a period ($x \le y \le m$), yields an expected return of $R(y)$ due to the output that can be produced with these machines during the period. Let q denote the probability that a machine that is operating at the beginning of a period (after all repairs for the period are complete) breaks down by the end of the period. Let p_{xj}^y denote the probability of moving from state x at the beginning of a period to state j at the beginning of the next period when decision y has been made. Find p_{xj}^y explicitly.

6.7   (Continuation of Exercise 6.6)   Assuming the objective is to maximize
the net present value of the returns received over a finite horizon, using a one-
period discount factor of α, identify the set of terminal value functions such
that a myopic policy is optimal in each period and characterize that policy as
fully as you can.

6.8   Prove Theorem 6.4.

6.9   Consider the following nonstationary (Section 6.5) version of the inventory problem of Section 6.3: In each period t, the unit order cost is c_t, the unit
holding cost is c_t^H, the unit shortage cost is c_t^P, and the demand distribution
is Φ_t. Furthermore, there exists c such that $v_T(x) = -cx$.

(a) Generalize (6.5) for this case. (Characterize the intended myopically optimal
base stock level as a critical fractile.)

(b) Derive as general a set of conditions as you can on the parameters and
probabilities distributions of demand that are sufficient to show that a myopic
policy is optimal in each period.

Hint: Show that the base stock levels in part (a) increase over time.

References

Bellman, R. 1957. *Dynamic Programming*. Princeton University Press, Princeton, N.J.

Heyman, D., M. Sobel. 1984. *Stochastic Models in Operations Research, Volume II*. McGraw-Hill, New York.

Lovejoy, W. 1986. Bounds on the optimal age-at-first-capture for stochastic,
age-structured fisheries. *Canadian Journal of Fisheries and Aquatic Sciences.*
43 101–7.

Lovejoy, W. 1988. Effect of stochasticity on optimal harvesting strategies in
some lumped-parameter fishery models. *Canadian Journal of Fisheries and
Aquatic Sciences.* **45** 1789–800.

Sobel, M. 1981. Myopic solutions of Markovian decision processes and stochastic games. *Operations Research.* **26** 995–1009.

Veinott, A., Jr. 1965. Optimal policy for a multi-product, dynamic, nonstationary, inventory problem. *Management Science.* **12** 206–22.

7

Dynamic Inventory Models

We consider two classical inventory models in this chapter. The first is the stochastic inventory (s, S) model in which the objective function is neither convex nor concave, yet the form of the optimal policy can still be established. The second is a linear-quadratic production planning model in which the objective function is shown to be convex, and it is possible to show that the optimal decision rule is linear in the state and independent of the demand variability.

7.1   Optimality of (s, S) Inventory Policies

We return to the dynamic inventory model of Section 4.2, introducing a strictly positive setup cost (as in the EOQ model of Chapter 1) to the ordering cost function. The objective function in the optimality equations now consists of a concave ordering cost function plus a convex holding and shortage cost function, plus the expected value of continuing (from the arrival value function). Researchers in the 1950s presumed that the optimal policy in each period would be as depicted in Figure 7.1, where an arrow's base indicates the level of inventory before ordering and its point indicates the level after ordering. This policy, called an (s, S) policy, brings the level of inventory after ordering up to some level S if the initial inventory level x is below some level s (where $s \leq S$), and orders nothing otherwise. The idea is to defer an order if only a small amount is needed, so that the setup cost will be incurred only when a substantial amount (at least $S - s$) is ordered. It is customary to say that an (s, S) policy is optimal even in nonstationary problems where the two parameters may differ from period to period. It turned out to be quite difficult to prove that such a policy was optimal, because the pertinent objective function was neither convex nor concave. Scarf (1960) cracked the problem by introducing a new class of functions, K-convex functions.

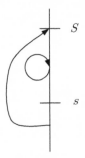

Figure 7.1   Workings of an (s, S) Policy

Assumptions and Notation

Let K denote the setup/fixed cost, which is incurred if an order is placed (for a strictly positive amount), regardless of its size. (If no order is placed, no setup cost is incurred.) The remaining assumptions and symbols are as they were defined in Section 4.2: Unmet demands are backlogged, to be met as soon as sufficient stock is available, c is the unit ordering/production cost, Φ is the one-period demand distribution, ϕ is the density, D is the generic random variable representing demand in a period, μ is the mean demand per period, c_{H} is the unit holding cost, charged against positive ending inventory, c_{P} is the unit shortage penalty cost, charged against any shortages at the end of a period, and α is the one-period discount factor. The expected one-period holding and shortage cost function of the level y of inventory after ordering remains

$$L(y) := E\big(c_{\mathrm{H}}(y - D)^+ + c_{\mathrm{P}}(D - y)^+\big)$$
$$= E\mathcal{L}(y - D),$$

where, as usual, $\mathcal{L}(x) := c_{\mathrm{H}}x^+ + c_{\mathrm{P}}(-x)^+$.

Formulation

As in the dynamic inventory model of Section 4.2, the state space is the real line, a state x is the level x of inventory before ordering, an action y is the level y of inventory after ordering, and the (admissible) action space is $A(x) = [x, \infty)$. As in Section 4.2, let

$$G_t(y) := cy + L(y) + \alpha \int_0^\infty f_{t+1}(y - \xi)\phi(\xi)\,d\xi, \qquad (7.1)$$

so that the optimality equations (OE) can be written as

$$f_t(x) = -cx + \min\left\{ G_t(x), \min_{y \geq x}\left[K + G_t(y) \right] \right\}.$$

That is, we either order nothing, or we plan to order something, which requires incurring the setup cost K in addition to the usual costs.

Starting at state x, we wish to minimize G_t looking to the right. If the resulting minimal value is more than K below where we are now, we should move (order up to that point). Otherwise, we should stay put.

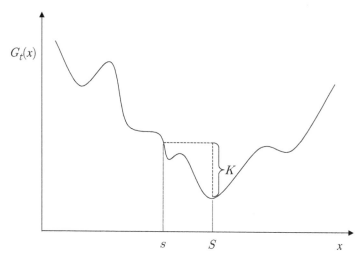

Figure 7.2   Example in Which an (s, S) Policy Is Optimal

In Figure 7.2, if $x < s$, it is optimal to move up to S, because the savings exceed the fixed cost K incurred when a change is made. In addition, if $x \geq s$, it is optimal to order nothing.

Letting

$$G_t^*(x) := \min\Big\{G_t(x), \min_{y \geq x}[K + G_t(y)]\Big\},$$

the (OE) can be rewritten as

$$f_t(x) = -cx + G_t^*(x). \tag{7.2}$$

K-Convex Functions

A function $f : \mathbf{R} \to \mathbf{R}$ (a real valued function of a single real variable) is
K-convex if $K \geq 0$, and for each $x \leq y$, $0 \leq \theta \leq 1$, and $\bar{\theta} := 1 - \theta$,

$$f(\theta x + \bar{\theta}y) \leq \theta f(x) + \bar{\theta}[K + f(y)]. \tag{7.3}$$

Scarf (1960) invented the notion of K-convex functions for the explicit purpose
of analyzing this inventory model. For a function f to be K-convex, it must
lie below the line segment connecting $(x, f(x))$ and $(y, K + f(y))$, for all real
numbers x and y such that $x \leq y$. Figure 7.3 shows that a K-convex function,
namely, f_1, need not be continuous. However, it can be shown that a K-convex
function cannot have a positive jump at a discontinuity, as illustrated by f_2.
Furthermore, a negative jump cannot be too large, as illustrated by f_3.

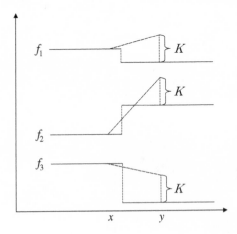

Figure 7.3   One K-Convex Function and Two That Are Not

We shall see that if G_t is K-convex, where K is the setup cost, then an
(s, S) policy is optimal in period t. However, it is not necessary that G_t be

K-convex for an (s, S) policy to be optimal: An (s, S) policy is optimal for the G_t in Figure 7.2, yet that function is shown in Figure 7.4 to violate the requirements of a *K*-convex function.

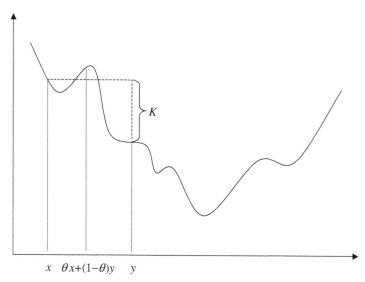

x $\theta x + (1-\theta)y$ *y*

Figure 7.4   *Another Function That Is Not K-Convex*

Figure 7.5 provides an example of a *K*-convex G_t such that an (s, S) policy is optimal in period t. A possible selection of y is shown along with several

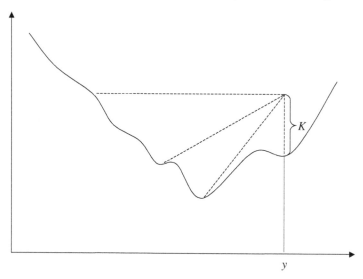

y

Figure 7.5   *A K-Convex Function*

possible selections of x. Note that a K-convex function need not be convex or even quasi-convex: This function has three distinct local minima.

For real valued functions of a single real variable, K-convexity is a simple generalization of convexity: f is convex iff f is 0-convex, and any function that is convex is K-convex for all $K \geq 0$. However, K-convexity is only defined for functions of a single real variable, while convexity is defined for functions of many real variables.

The next result presents some useful properties of K-convex functions.

Lemma 7.1   *(Scarf, 1960) (Exercise 7.1)*

(a) If f is K-convex and a is a positive scalar, then af is k-convex for all $k \geq aK$.

(b) The sum of a K-convex function and a k-convex function is $(K+k)$-convex.

(c) If v is K-convex, ϕ is the probability density of a positive random variable, and $G(y) := Ev(y - D) = \int_0^\infty v(y - \xi)\phi(\xi)\,d\xi$, then G is K-convex.

(d) If f is K-convex, $x < y$, and $f(x) = K + f(y)$, then $f(z) \leq K + f(y)$ for all $z \in [x, y]$.

Part (d) says that a K-convex function f can cross the value $K + f(y)$ at most once on $(-\infty, y)$ for each real y. In Figure 7.4, three such crossings occur for the value of y illustrated, confirming that the function shown is not K-convex.

We now see that the definition of K-convexity in (7.3), which was introduced by Porteus (1971), is equivalent to the original definitions, which were introduced by Scarf (1960) and appear in parts (a) and (b) of the following result.

Lemma 7.2

(a) (Porteus, 1971) (Exercise 7.2)   A function $f : \mathbf{R} \to \mathbf{R}$ is K-convex iff

$$K + f(x + a) \geq f(x) + \frac{a}{b}[f(x) - f(x - b)]$$

for all $x \in \mathbf{R}$, $a \geq 0$, and $b > 0$.

(b) (Exercise 7.3)   Among differentiable functions defined on $\mathbf{R}$, f is K-convex iff

$$K + f(y) \geq f(x) + f'(x)(y - x)$$

for all (scalars) $x \leq y$.

Definition of Structure

Henceforth in this section, K will refer specifically to the setup cost. Let V^* denote the set of continuous K-convex functions, and let Δ^* denote the set of (s, S) policies: As in Figure 7.1, there exist parameters s and S such that $s \leq S$ and the policy δ orders up to S if the stock level is strictly below s and orders nothing otherwise:

$$\delta(x) = \begin{cases} S & \text{if } x < s \\ x & \text{otherwise.} \end{cases}$$

Lemma 7.3 (*Scarf, 1960*) *If* $G_t \in V^*$, *then there exists* $\delta \in \Delta^*$ *that is optimal for period* t.

Proof Let S denote a minimizer of G_t. (Follow along with Figure 7.6.)

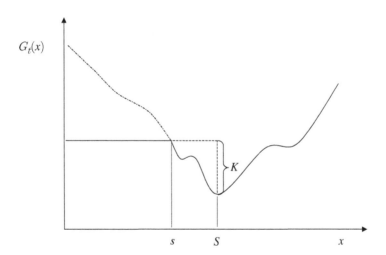

Figure 7.6 *Determining* s *and* S

To avoid some technical details, we assume henceforth that $\liminf_{x \to -\infty} G_t(x) > G_t(S) + K$. (Exercise 7.4 addresses these details.) Let s denote the smallest value of x such that $G_t(x) = K + G_t(S)$. Thus, s is guaranteed to exist. If $x < s$, then $G_t(x) > K + G_t(S)$, and, therefore, it is optimal to order up to S. If $s \leq x \leq S$, then, by Lemma 7.1(d), $G_t(x) \leq K + G_t(S)$, so it is optimal not to order. If $x > S$, it is also optimal not to order: Suppose to the contrary that there exists $y > x$ such that $G_t(x) > K + G_t(y)$.

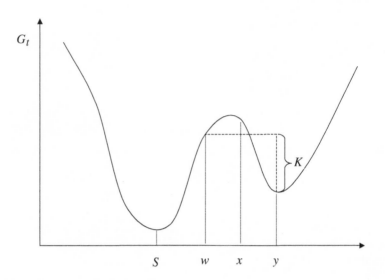

Figure 7.7   A Case Ruled Out

Because G_t is continuous, there must exist w between S and x such that $G_t(w) = K + G_t(y)$, as illustrated in Figure 7.7. By Lemma 7.1(d), $G_t(x)$ must lie below $K + G_t(y)$ between w and y, which is a contradiction. Hence, it is optimal to order up to S if $x < s$ and not to order otherwise.   □

Lemma 7.4   (Scarf, 1960)   If $G_t \in V^*$, then $G_t^* \in V^*$.

Proof   By Lemma 7.3, we have

$$G_t^*(x) = \begin{cases} K + G_t(S) & \text{for } x < s \\ G_t(x) & \text{otherwise.} \end{cases}$$

where S is a minimizer of G_t. (See Figure 7.6 again.) G_t^* is clearly continuous. Select arbitrary $x < y$ and $\theta \in [0, 1]$. We seek to show that G_t^* satisfies (7.3). If $x \geq s$, then $G_t^* = G_t$, which is K-convex, so (7.3) holds. Similarly, if $y \leq s$, then G_t^* is a constant and (7.3) holds. Finally, suppose that $x < s < y$. Let $w = \theta x + \bar{\theta} y$.

(The remainder of this proof uses Figure 7.8 informally, to set the ideas. Exercise 7.5 addresses the formal details.) We seek to show that, on $[x, y]$, G_t^* is below the line segment connecting $\big(x, G_t^*(x)\big)$ and $\big(y, K + G_t^*(y)\big)$. Note that because S minimizes G_t, $K + G_t(y) \geq K + G_t(S) = G_t^*(x)$, so the line segment of interest is increasing. Thus, if $w \leq s$, then (7.3) holds. Finally, if $s < w \leq y$, then, because G_t is K-convex, G_t is below the line segment connecting $\big(s, G_t(s)\big)$ and

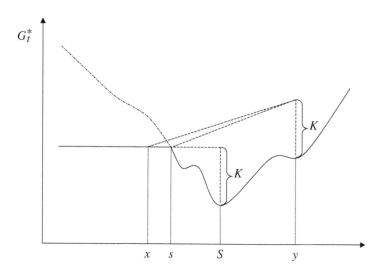

Figure 7.8   Verification of K-Convexity

$(y, K + G_t(y))$. It is straightforward to show that this line segment is below the line segment of interest, which completes the proof.   □

Lemma 7.5   *(Scarf, 1960)   Preservation and attainment hold.*

Proof   Suppose that $f_{t+1} \in V^*$. (7.1) then reveals that G_t is the sum of two convex functions and a function that, by Lemma 7.1(c) and (a), is αK-convex. Therefore, by Lemma 7.1(b), G_t is αK-convex, and hence, K-convex by Lemma 7.1(a), because $\alpha \leq 1$. It is straightforward to show that G_t is continuous. Thus, $G_t \in V^*$, and, therefore, by Lemma 7.3, attainment follows.

Hence, by Lemma 7.4, G_t^* is K-convex. By (7.2) and Lemma 7.1(b), f_t is also K-convex and continuous, which verifies preservation.   □

Theorem 7.1   *If v_T is continuous and K-convex, then, for each period, the optimal return function is K-convex and there exists an optimal (s, S) policy, where the two parameters of the policy may depend on the period.*

Proof   A direct application of Theorem 5.3, using Lemma 7.5.   □

7.2   Linear-Quadratic Model

This is a famous model presented by Holt, Modigliani, Muth, and Simon (HMMS) (1960). Its fame arises from the simple form of the optimal policy, the fact that it does not depend on the demand variability, and the ease with which an optimal policy can be computed. Indeed, we shall see that, in this finite-horizon, dynamic problem, there exists an optimal linear decision rule: The optimal decision is an affine function of the state variable in each period. The weakness of this model lies in the difficulty of fitting its parameters to the cost functions observed in practice and in the fact that it must allow for redemptions of excess stock as well as replenishment of low stock levels.

Formulation

We examine only the single product problem, for clarity and convenience. Excess demand is backlogged. The state space is the real line, and we interpret a state x as the level of inventory at the beginning of the period. The action space is also the real line, and we interpret the action y as the number of units of the product ordered, added, and/or manufactured, instead of the level of inventory after ordering (manufacturing), as in the dynamic inventory model of Section 4.2. (Henceforth in this section x and y are assumed to be real numbers.) An important consequence of this formulation is that y is allowed to be negative: Reductions in the stock level are allowed. Furthermore, we assume that the immediate costs $c(x, y)$ (incurred in this period) are quadratic and convex in (x, y) and strictly convex in y. For example, if we were to formulate the inventory model of Section 4.2 in this notation, we would have $c(x, y) = cy + L(x + y)$, which can be interpreted as approximating the convex holding and shortage cost function by a (convex) quadratic function and allowing excess stock to be redeemed at full unit purchase value: If $y > 0$, we want to purchase y units and it will cost us cy. If $y < 0$, then we want to redeem $-y$ units and we will receive $-cy$ for doing so. (It will cost us $cy < 0$.) Exercise 6.4 characterizes the optimal policy for a generalization of this model, without requiring a quadratic approximation of L. In other words, this model is not the appropriate approach to studying the model of Exercise 6.4. In particular, it is better suited to an environment in which the ordering/production cost function can be reasonably approximated by a *nonlinear* quadratic (convex) function (that is defined for negative arguments as well as positive ones).

Because excess demand is backlogged, the transition structure is linear with additive uncertainty: The next state is a linear function of the current state and action plus a random variable. In particular, if x_t denotes the state at time period t and y_t the action taken (the amount added), then the state at the beginning of the next period is given by

$$x_{t+1} = x_t + y_t - D_t,$$

where D_t is the demand in period t. We assume that $D_1, D_2, \cdots, D_N$ are i.i.d. and that D denotes a generic random variable with the same distribution. Let $\mu := E(D)$ and $\mu_2 := E(D^2)$.

Thus, the optimality equations can be written as

$$f_t(x) = \min_y \left[c(x, y) + \alpha E f_{t+1}(x + y - D) \right]$$
$$= \min_y G_t(x, y),$$

where y need not be positive, and

$$G_t(x, y) := c(x, y) + \alpha E f_{t+1}(x + y - D). \tag{7.4}$$

Preliminary Results

The *high-order coefficients* of a quadratic function are the coefficients of its variable terms (that is, all coefficients except the constant). For example, if $g : \mathbf{R} \to \mathbf{R}$ is quadratic, so it can be expressed as $g(x) = a + bx + cx^2$, the high-order coefficients of g are b and c.

Lemma 7.6   (*Exercise 7.9*)   *If $g(x, y)$ is quadratic and convex in (x, y) and strictly convex in y, then the following hold.*

(a) $f(x) := \inf_y g(x, y)$ is quadratic and convex in x.

(b) For each $x \in \mathbf{R}$, there is a unique minimizer, say $y(x)$, of $g(x, y)$ over $y \in \mathbf{R}$, that is affine in x : there exist real numbers a and b such that $y(x) = a + bx$.

(c) $y(x)$ and the high-order coefficients of $f(x)$ depend only on the high-order coefficients of $g(x, y)$.

Lemma 7.7   *If f is a convex function of a single real variable, then $g(x, y) := f(x + y)$ is jointly convex in (x, y).*

Proof   Every term in the Hessian of g is $f''(x + y)$. Thus, by Theorem A.6(a) and corollary A.1, g is jointly convex.   □

Lemma 7.8   If $f_{t+1}(x)$ is a convex quadratic function of x whose high-order coefficients depend on the distribution of D at most through μ, then $g(x,y) := Ef_{t+1}(x + y - D)$ is a convex quadratic function of (x,y) whose high-order coefficients depend on the distribution of D at most through μ.

Proof   Let $F(x) := Ef_{t+1}(x - D)$. By Exercise 4.7, F is convex. Therefore, by Lemma 7.7, g is (jointly) convex. Here, f_{t+1} has the representation

$$f_{t+1}(x) = a + bx + cx^2,$$

where $a, b, c \in \mathbf{R}$, $c \geq 0$, and b and c depend on the distribution of D at most through μ. Therefore,

$$
\begin{aligned}
Ef_{t+1}&(x + y - D) \\
&= E[a + b(x + y - D) + c(x + y - D)^2] \\
&= a + bx + by - b\mu + cE[x^2 + 2xy + y^2 - 2(x + y)D + D^2] \\
&= (a - b\mu + c\mu_2) + (b - 2c\mu)x + (b - 2c\mu)y + 2cxy + cx^2 + cy^2.
\end{aligned}
$$

Thus, g is indeed quadratic. In addition, the high-order coefficients are functions only of the parameters b, c, and μ, so they depend on the distribution of D at most through μ. (The constant term $a - b\mu + c\mu_2$ can depend on higher moments of D.)   □

Definition of Structure

Let V^* denote the convex quadratic functions defined on $\mathbf{R}$ whose high-order coefficients depend on the distribution of D at most through μ. Let Δ^* denote the linear decision rules that depend on the distribution of D only through its mean μ.

Lemma 7.9   (HMMS, 1960)

(a) Attainment holds.

(b) Preservation holds.

Proof   Given $f_{t+1} \in V^*$, we have by Lemma 7.8 and (7.4) that $G_t(x,y)$ is quadratic and convex in (x,y) with high-order coefficients that depend on D at most through μ. Since $c(x,y)$ is strictly convex in y, $G_t(x,y)$ is also strictly convex in y. Thus, (a) holds by Lemma 7.6.

Part (b) also holds by Lemma 7.6: The high-order coefficients of $f_t(x)$ depend only on the high-order coefficients of $G_t(x,y)$, and those depend on D at most through μ.   □

Theorem 7.2 (*HMMS, 1960*) *If v_T is quadratic and convex, then the optimal return functions are quadratic and convex, and, for each period, there exists an optimal linear decision rule that does not depend on the demand variability.*

Proof Using Lemma 7.9, this is a direct application of Theorem 5.3. □

Exercises

7.1 Prove Lemma 7.1.

7.2 Prove Lemma 7.2(a).

7.3 Prove Lemma 7.2(b).

7.4 (*Example Approach to Addressing Technical Details of the* (*s, S*) *Model*) Let V^* denote the set of continuous K-convex functions v such that there exists $a, b \in \mathbf{R}$ such that v is differentiable on $(-\infty, b)$, $v'(x) = -a$ for $x < b$, and $a \geq c$.

(a) Show that if $f_{t+1} \in V^*$, then

$$\liminf_{x \to -\infty} G_t(x) > G_t(S) + K,$$

where, as in the proof of Lemma 7.3, S is a minimizer of G_t.

(b) Show that if $f_{t+1} \in V^*$, then $f_t \in V^*$.

7.5 Complete the formal proof of Lemma 7.4. (Operationalize the details of the ideas used in the informal proof.)

7.6 Suppose that f_1 and f_2 are both differentiable functions defined on $\mathbf{R}$ that have finite minimizers, S_1 and S_2, respectively, and that $f_1' \leq f_2'$.

(a) Show that if S_1 and S_2 are unique minimizers, then $S_1 \geq S_2$.

(b) Show that, in general, there exist minimizers, say S_1^* and S_2^*, of f_1 and f_2, respectively, that are finite and satisfy $S_1^* \geq S_2^*$.

7.7 (*Inventory Disposal*) (*Continuation of Exercise 6.4*) Suppose in contrast to Exercise 6.4, that each unit of inventory that is disposed yields a unit return/credit of d and that $d < c$: Only partial credit is obtained on returns. At the end of the planning horizon, units of positive stock are redeemed for d each and any outstanding backlog must be removed:

$$v_{\mathrm{T}}(x) = \begin{cases} -cx & \text{if } x \le 0 \\ -dx & \text{otherwise.} \end{cases}$$

Define G_t and g_t as follows:

$$G_t(y) := cy + L(y) + \alpha \int_0^\infty f_{t+1}(y - \xi)\phi(\xi)\,d\xi, \text{ and}$$

$$g_t(y) := dy + L(y) + \alpha \int_0^\infty f_{t+1}(y - \xi)\phi(\xi)\,d\xi.$$

(a) Verify that the optimality equations can be written as

$$f_t(x) = \min\left[-cx + \min_{y \ge x} G_t(y), -dx + \min_{y \le x} g_t(y)\right].$$

(b) Let Δ^* denote the set of decision rules δ such that there exist two parameters $\underline{S} \le \bar{S}$ that represent δ in the following way:

$$\delta(x) = \begin{cases} \underline{S} & \text{if } x \le \underline{S} \\ x & \text{if } \underline{S} < x \le \bar{S} \\ \bar{S} & \text{otherwise.} \end{cases}$$

Let's call such a decision rule a *target interval policy*. Such a rule specifies a *target interval* $[\underline{S}, \bar{S}]$ such that the inventory level is moved as little as possible to bring it into the target interval: it brings the level up to $\underline{S}$ if the level at the beginning of the period is below $\underline{S}$, it leaves the level alone if it is between $\underline{S}$ and $\bar{S}$, and it brings it down, through disposal, to $\bar{S}$ otherwise. (Note that the limits $\underline{S}$ and $\bar{S}$ of the optimal target interval may depend on t.)

Prove that there exists an optimal target interval policy in each period.

Hint: Define V^* as the set of convex functions defined on $\mathbf{R}$ and use Exercise 7.6.

7.8   *(Stochastic Cash Management)*   A cash account is to be maintained over N periods. At the beginning of each period, the cash balance is observed, and a decision is made whether to add to the account or withdraw funds. (The balance cannot be drawn down below zero.) Let $c(z)$ denote the transaction costs incurred when the level of the account is increased by z. (Withdrawals correspond to z being negative.) In particular, $c(z)$ has the following form:

$$c(z) = \begin{cases} c_U z & \text{if } z \geq 0 \\ -c_D z & \text{if } z < 0, \end{cases}$$

where c_U and c_D are positive constants. Thus, there are proportional transactions costs assessed on the changes: c_U is assessed on each dollar added to the account, and c_D is assessed on each dollar withdrawn.

The opportunity cost of capital per period is i, so that the one-period discount factor is $\alpha = 1/(1+i)$. Let D_t denote the "demand" on the account during period t, which consists of obligations paid less funds received. Assume that the demands are i.i.d. random variables with common probability distribution Φ and density ϕ. Note that the "demand" in a period can be negative, which corresponds to receiving more funds than were paid out that period. If insufficient funds were placed in the account at the beginning of the period to cover the realized demand, a shortage occurs. The bank will cover all such obligations as they arise with the requirement that you pay the bank back at the end of the period plus a proportional service (penalty) fee of c_P ($> i$) per dollar short. At the end of N periods, any leftover cash is withdrawn from the account, and any shortages must be paid off to the bank, including the service fee. The objective is to find the cash management policy that minimizes the expected present value of the costs of managing the account over the planning horizon.

Define G_t and g_t as follows:

$$G_t(y) := (1 + c_U)y + L(y) + \alpha \int_{-\infty}^{\infty} f_{t+1}(y - \xi)\phi(\xi)\,d\xi, \text{ and}$$

$$g_t(y) := (1 - c_D)y + L(y) + \alpha \int_{-\infty}^{\infty} f_{t+1}(y - \xi)\phi(\xi)\,d\xi,$$

where

$$L(y) := \int_{y}^{\infty} c_P(\xi - y)\phi(\xi)\,d\xi$$

is the expected service fee at the end of the period as a function of the level y of cash in the account at the beginning of the period. The salvage value function is

$$v_T(x) = -x \quad \text{for every } x.$$

(a) Verify that the optimality equations can be written as

$$f_t(x) = \min\left[-(1 + c_U)x + \min_{y \geq x} G_t(y), -(1 - c_D)x + \min_{y \leq x} g_t(y)\right].$$

In this formulation, not only are the transactions costs and service charges paid, but the funds for the account are accounted for directly. The opportunity cost of capital will be charged implicitly against funds that are kept in the cash account (because they earn no interest) and are not otherwise invested. (The formulation can be derived starting at a more primitive level, assuming that there are two accounts, the cash account identified here and an unlimited investment account that yields a return of i per period for funds in it. A transformation can be carried out that reduces the problem to consideration of solely the cash account, with the formulation given here.)

(b) Apply Exercise 7.7 to prove that an optimal target interval policy is optimal in each period of a finite-horizon problem.

7.9   Prove Lemma 7.6.

References

Holt, C., F. Modigliani, J. Muth, H. Simon. 1960. *Planning Production, Inventories, and Work Force.* Prentice-Hall, Englewood Cliffs, N.J.

Porteus, E. 1971. On the optimality of generalized (s, S) policies. *Management Science.* **17** 411–26.

Scarf, H. 1960. The optimality of (S, s) policies in the dynamic inventory problem. K. Arrow, S. Karlin, H. Scarf (eds.) *Mathematical Methods in the Social Sciences, 1959.* Stanford University Press, Stanford, Calif. 196–202.

Zangwill, W. 1969. *Nonlinear Programming: A Unified Approach,* Prentice-Hall, Englewood Cliffs, N.J.

8

Monotone Optimal Policies

This chapter deals with the question of when optimal policies are *monotone* (either increasing or decreasing) functions of the state. We just saw a special case in Section 7.2 in which the optimal policy was not only monotone but linear as well. The conditions required to prove that optimal policies are monotone depend on properties of functions that were introduced in the literature by Topkis (1978), namely submodularity and/or supermodularity, rather than convexity and/or concavity as has usually been the case in models analyzed in earlier chapters. It turns out that our analysis in Section 8.3 uses both submodularity and concavity, whereas our analysis in Section 8.4 uses supermodularity and convexity. Albright and Winston (1979) present an interesting application to optimal advertising and pricing, and submodularity plays a central role in the important work by Milgrom and Roberts (1992). See Topkis (1998) for a comprehensive presentation.

8.1   Intuition

Consider the single-stage optimization problem in which we seek to minimize a function $g(s, a)$ over a for each state s. Suppose, in this section, that both the state and action spaces are single dimensional. In particular, suppose that $\mathcal{S} = \mathbf{R}$ and that $A(s) = \mathbf{R}$ for each s: Every real number is a feasible decision. Suppose, in addition, that g is twice differentiable. Since we wish to minimize $g(s, a)$ over a, we examine the first-order condition

$$g_2(s, a) := \frac{\partial g(s, a)}{\partial a} = 0.$$

Suppose that the cross partials of g are negative: for all s and a,

$$g_{12}(s, a) := \frac{\partial^2 g(s, a)}{\partial s \partial a} \leq 0,$$

and that the minimization is attained: for each s, there exists a minimizer $a^*(s)$: $g(s, a^*(s)) \leq g(s, a)$ for all admissible actions a.

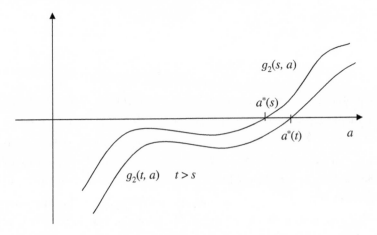

Figure 8.1   *Illustration of Minimizers Increasing in the State*

Lemma 8.1   *Suppose $g_{12} \leq 0$, g_{12} is continuous, $g_2(s, \cdot)$ is continuous, and, for each s, there is a unique $a^*(s)$ such that $g_2(s, a) \leq 0$ for $a \leq a^*(s)$ and $g_2(s, a) \geq 0$ for $a \geq a^*(s)$. Then a^* is an increasing function.*

Proof   Considered as a function of a for fixed s, $g(s, a)$ must be decreasing for $a \leq a^*(s)$ and increasing for $a \geq a^*(s)$. Hence, as illustrated in Figure 8.1, the minimizer can be seen to be the point at which $g_2(s, a)$ crosses zero, as a function of a. Pick $t > s$ and arbitrary a. By the fundamental theorem of integral calculus, we have

$$g_2(t, a) = g_2(s, a) + \int_{x=s}^{t} g_{12}(x, a)\, dx$$

$$\leq g_2(s, a) \qquad\qquad\qquad\qquad [g_{12} \leq 0]$$

Thus, $g_2(t, a^*(s)) \leq 0$, so $g(t, a)$ is still decreasing in a when $a = a^*(s)$. Therefore, the minimizer for t, $a^*(t)$, must be at least as large as the minimizer for s.   □

Intuitively, as seen in Figure 8.1, the minimizer $a^*(s)$ occurs where $g_2(s, \cdot)$ crosses zero, and since $g_2(t, \cdot)$ lies below $g_2(s, \cdot)$, $g_2(t, \cdot)$ must cross zero to the right of where $g_2(s, \cdot)$ does.

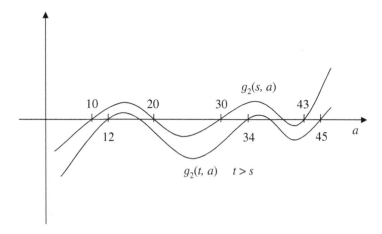

Figure 8.2   *A Case in Which There Is a Tie for the Optimal Solution*

What happens if $a^*(s)$ is not unique for all s? For example, note that in Figure 8.2, $g(s, \cdot)$ has three local minima, at 10, 30, and 43, where $g_2(s, \cdot)$ crosses zero from below. Suppose that the integral of $g_2(s, \cdot)$ between 10 and 30 is zero: The area under $g_2(s, \cdot)$ between 10 and 20 is the same as the corresponding area above it between 20 and 30. By another application of the fundamental theorem of integral calculus,

$$g(s, 30) = g(s, 10) + \int_{a=10}^{30} g_2(s, a)\, da = g(s, 10).$$

In this case, the decrease in the function between 20 and 30 equals exactly the increase between 10 and 20. Thus, there are alternative optimal solutions. In this case, it can be seen by inspection in Figure 8.2 that the global minimum of $g(t, \cdot)$ occurs at $a^*(t) = 45$. We shall see that for every global minimizer for a state s, there exists a larger global minimizer for every larger state. In other words, we shall see below that there exists an optimal solution that is an increasing function of the state.

8.2   Lattices and Submodular Functions

Suppose that X is a subset of $\mathbf{R}^m$ for some (strictly positive integer) m and that x and y are arbitrary members of X. The pointwise minimum of x and y is called the *meet* of x and y and is denoted by

$$x \wedge y := \big(\min(x_1, y_1), \min(x_2, y_2), \ldots, \min(x_m, y_m)\big).$$

Similarly, the pointwise maximum is called the *join* of x and y and is denoted by

$$x \vee y := \big(\max(x_1, y_1), \max(x_2, y_2), \ldots, \max(x_m, y_m)\big).$$

The set X is a *lattice* if both $x \wedge y$ and $x \vee y$ are elements of X. If $m = 1$, then X must be a lattice, because then either $x \leq y$ or $x > y$, and, therefore, $x \wedge y$ and $x \vee y$ will be either x or y, which are clearly in X. However, if $m > 1$, then verification is required. For example, if $m = 2$ and $X = \{(x_1, x_2)|x_1 + x_2 \leq 1\}$, then X is *not* a lattice: Let $x = (0, 1)$ and $y = (1, 0)$. Then $x \vee y = (1, 1)$, which clearly is not a member of X. It is straightforward to show that if $X = \mathbf{R}^m$, then X is a lattice. More generally, if X is the Cartesian product of m subsets of the real line, then X is a lattice. Exercise 8.1 shows that $X = \{(x_1, x_2)|x_1 \leq x_2\}$ is a lattice.

A function $g : X \to \mathbf{R}$ is *submodular* if

$$g(x \wedge y) + g(x \vee y) \leq g(x) + g(y) \tag{8.1}$$

whenever $x \wedge y \in X$ and $x \vee y \in X$. A function $g : X \to \mathbf{R}$ is *supermodular* if $-g$ is submodular.

Lemma 8.2   *(Topkis, 1978)   Suppose g is twice partially differentiable. Then submodularity is equivalent to negative cross partials.*

For example, if g is separable (of the form $g(x) = \sum_{i=1}^{m} g_i(x_i)$) then g is submodular (and supermodular) because the cross partials all vanish.

Submodularity is a more general concept than negative cross partials, as a function can be submodular but not differentiable. The proofs are more elegant using submodularity, but the concept isn't as intuitive, at first exposure. Hence, we shall often focus on the less general case to emphasize the intuition.

Lemma 8.3   *(Exercise 8.2)   If f and g are submodular [supermodular], then the following are submodular [supermodular]: (a) af for each positive scalar a, (b) $f + g$, and (c) $h(y) := Ef(y - D)$, where D is a random variable.*

Adding Optimization

Suppose, for each state $s \in \mathcal{S}$, we seek to minimize $g(s, a)$ over $a \in A(s)$. Assume henceforth that the state space $\mathcal{S}$ is a lattice subset of $\mathbf{R}^m$ for some m and that each action space $A(s)$ is also finite dimensional. Let $\mathcal{C}$ denote the set of feasible states and actions:

$$\mathcal{C} := \{(s, a) \mid s \in \mathcal{S} \text{ and } a \in A(s)\}. \tag{8.2}$$

For example, if $A(s)$ is independent of s, then $\mathcal{C}$ is a lattice. Furthermore, Exercise 8.1 shows that if $\mathcal{S} = \mathbf{R}$ and $A(s) = [s, \infty)$ for each $s \in \mathcal{S}$, then $\mathcal{C}$ is a lattice.

Suppose that g is submodular, so, by Lemma 8.2, its cross partial with respect to an arbitrary state/action pair is negative. In words, the marginal cost of increasing the action decreases in the state. Equivalently, the marginal cost of an increase in the state decreases in the action. Having more of one thing (the state) induces you to want more of the other (the action). That's a conventional definition of *economic complements*.

Similarly, if g is supermodular, then the states and actions are economic substitutes (in the minimization problems we consider).

Ascending Set Functions

We now present the formal concepts needed to show there exists an optimal decision rule that is increasing in the state. Recall that $A(s)$ denotes the set of admissible actions when the state is s and, hence, $A(\cdot)$ can be called a *set function*. Suppose that s and t are arbitrary states such that $s \leq t$ and

a and b are corresponding feasible actions: $a \in A(s)$ and $b \in A(t)$. $A(\cdot)$
is called *ascending* if $a \wedge b \in A(s)$ and $a \vee b \in A(t)$ for all such s, t, a, b.
Intuitively, if we have a small state and a large one and feasible decisions for
each state, then the meet of the feasible decisions, which is smaller than both,
is feasible for the small state and the join is feasible for the large state. For
example, if $S = \mathbf{R}$ and $A(s) = [s, \infty)$ as in an inventory problem, it is
straightforward to show that $A(\cdot)$ is ascending: If $s \leq t$, $a \in A(s)$, and
$b \in A(t)$, then $a \wedge b \geq s$ so $a \wedge b \in A(s)$, and $a \vee b \geq t$ so $a \vee b \in A(t)$.

If there are possibly alternative optima for a particular state, then the optimal
action for a given state is a *set* of actions. Let $A^*(s)$ denote the set of optimal
actions for state s, in this case, the set of minimizers of $g(s, \cdot)$ over $A(s)$.
The following result provides conditions that guarantee that there exists an
optimal decision rule that is increasing in the state.

Theorem 8.1   *(Topkis, 1978)   If (a) g is submodular on C, (b) $A(\cdot)$ is
ascending on S, and (c) $A^*(s)$ is nonempty for every s, then (d) $A^*(\cdot)$ is
ascending on S.*

Proof Suppose s and t are states such that $s \leq t$. Suppose $a \in A^*(s)$
and $b \in A^*(t)$. Let $x := (s, a)$, and $y := (t, b)$. Since $A(s)$ is ascending,
$a \wedge b \in A(s)$, and $a \vee b \in A(t)$. Thus, $x \wedge y := (s, a \wedge b)$ and $x \vee y := (t, a \vee b)$
are both in C. Therefore, since g is submodular on C, we can rewrite (8.1)
as

$$g(x \wedge y) - g(x) \leq g(y) - g(x \vee y). \tag{8.3}$$

Therefore,

$$
\begin{aligned}
0 &\leq g(s, a \wedge b) - g(s, a) && [a \in A^*(s)] \\
&\leq g(t, b) - g(t, a \vee b) && [\text{by (8.3)}] \\
&\leq 0, && [b \in A^*(t)]
\end{aligned}
$$

so the inequalities must all be equalities, and, therefore, $a \wedge b \in A^*(s)$ and
$a \vee b \in A^*(t)$.   □

If $A^*(s)$ is nonempty for every s and $A^*(\cdot)$ is ascending on S, then there
exists an optimal decision rule that is increasing in the state. For example,
suppose that the state and action spaces are single dimensional. Then we can
optimize conceptually in the order of increasing states. At an arbitrary state
s, we select an optimal action $\delta(s)$. For $t > s$, we can restrict our choice
to actions at least as large as $\delta(s)$: If $a \in A^*(t)$ and $a < \delta(s)$, then, since

$A^*(s)$ is ascending, $a \vee \delta(s) \in A^*(t)$, and, therefore, $\delta(s) = a \vee \delta(s)$ will also be optimal at t. No loss of optimality arises from the restriction. The resulting selection will clearly be increasing. In general, an optimal decision rule that is increasing in the state can, at least conceptually, be constructed from an arbitrary optimal decision rule: if δ is optimal, then, for any s and t such that $s < t$ and $\delta(s) \not\leq \delta(t)$, we can replace $\delta(s)$ by $\delta(s) \wedge \delta(t)$, and $\delta(t)$ by $\delta(s) \vee \delta(t)$. Since $A(\cdot)$ is ascending, these actions are feasible for s and t, respectively. By definition, $\delta(s) \wedge \delta(t) \leq \delta(s) \vee \delta(t)$. Finally, because $A^*(\cdot)$ is ascending, these actions are optimal for s and t, respectively.

Returning to Figure 8.2, where $A^*(s) = \{10, 30\}$, Theorem 8.1 guarantees that 12, which is a local minimizer of $g(t, \cdot)$, cannot be an element of $A^*(t)$: Because $s \leq t$ and $30 \in A^*(s)$, if $12 \in A^*(t)$, then Theorem 8.1(d) says that $A^*(\cdot)$ is ascending, which implies that $12 \wedge 30 = 12 \in A^*(s)$, which clearly is not the case.

Lemma 8.4   *If C is a lattice, then $A(\cdot)$ is ascending.*

Proof   Suppose $s, t \in S$, $s \leq t$, $a \in A(s)$, and $b \in A(t)$. Then, by definition, $(s, a), (t, b) \in C$. Thus, $(s, a) \wedge (t, b) = (s, a \wedge b) \in C$, so that $a \wedge b \in A(s)$. Similarly, $a \vee b \in A(t)$.   □

Preservation of Submodularity

The next result gives quite general conditions under which submodularity is preserved under minimization.

Theorem 8.2   *(Submodularity Preservation under Minimization)*   *(Topkis, 1978:314)   If S and C are lattices, $g(s, a)$ is submodular for $(s, a) \in C$, and $f(s) := \inf_{a \in A(s)} g(s, a)$, then f is submodular on S.*

Proof   We prove the case in which the minimization is always attained. (The general case is addressed in Exercise 8.7.) Pick arbitrary $s_1, s_2 \in S$. Let a_1 and a_2 denote the respective minimizers: $f(s_i) = g(s_i, a_i)$ for $i = 1, 2$. Here

$$
\begin{aligned}
f(s_1) + f(s_2) &= g(s_1, a_1) + g(s_2, a_2) \\
&\geq g\big((s_1, a_1) \wedge (s_2, a_2)\big) + g\big((s_1, a_1) \vee (s_2, a_2)\big) && [g \text{ is submodular}] \\
&= g(s_1 \wedge s_2, a_1 \wedge a_2) + g(s_1 \vee s_2, a_1 \vee a_2) && [\text{definitions}] \\
&\geq f(s_1 \wedge s_2) + f(s_1 \vee s_2) && [C \text{ is a lattice}]
\end{aligned}
$$

In the last inequality, the fact that $\mathcal{C}$ is a lattice implies that $(a_1 \wedge a_2) \in A(s_1 \wedge s_2)$ and $(a_1 \vee a_2) \in A(s_1 \vee s_2)$, so these actions are feasible for their states, yielding values that cannot be smaller than the optimal ones. □

It is worth noting that, if $A^*(s)$ is nonempty for each s and the conditions of Theorem 8.2 hold, then $A^*(\cdot)$ is ascending, by Lemma 8.4 and Theorem 8.1. Furthermore, Theorem 8.2 is trivial whenever the state space $\mathcal{S}$ is a single dimensional lattice, because any real valued function of a single real variable is submodular.

8.3　A Dynamic Case

We now apply the theory developed so far to a dynamic cost minimization model in which the state and action spaces are single dimensional. (In particular, $\mathcal{S}$ is a subset of $\mathbf{R}$.) The model here is similar to that of Section 6.2, with some differences: A minor difference is that we minimize rather than maximize here. (We seek to minimize the expected discounted cost over a finite horizon.) Importantly, we do not assume that (6.1) and (6.2) hold, and myopic policies play no role in the solution to this problem. In particular, we assume there exists a sequence $\{X_t\}$ of i.i.d. random variables such that, if the system starts period t in state s and action $a \in A(s)$ is selected, then the state at the beginning of period $t+1$ is $s_{t+1} = z(s, a, X_t)$. Letting X denote a generic random variable with the same distribution as each X_t, we can, using Exercises 6.1 and 6.2, assume without loss of generality that X is uniformly distributed on $(0, 1)$. We can then write the optimality equations in the following convenient form, for $t = 1, 2, \ldots, N$:

$$f_t(s) = \min_a \left(c(s, a) + \alpha \int_{\xi=0}^{1} f_{t+1}(z(s, a, \xi)) \, d\xi \right)$$
$$= \min_a G_t(s, a),$$

where

$$G_t(s, a) := c(s, a) + \alpha \int_{\xi=0}^{1} f_{t+1}(z(s, a, \xi)) \, d\xi,$$

and $f_{N+1}(s) := v_{\mathbf{T}}(s)$.

In this notation, $z(s, a, \xi)$ is the next state of the system, given that the current state (in period t) is s, the current action is a, and the realization of X_t is ξ. Thus, for example, if $z(s, a, \xi)$ is increasing in s for each a and ξ, the next state of the system (a random variable) becomes, in the language of Appendix D, first-order stochastically larger as s increases.

Assumptions

The approach given here is original and does not follow Topkis (1978).

(A1) $z(s, a, \xi)$ is submodular and increasing in (s, a) for each ξ.
(A2) $z(s, a, \xi)$ is concave in s for each $a \in A(s)$ and ξ.
(A3) $c(s, a)$ is submodular in (s, a).
(A4) $c(s, a)$ is concave increasing in s for each $a \in A(s)$.
(A5) $A(s)$ is independent of the state s.

In words, (A1) and (A2) say that the next state is stochastically larger if the current state or action is increased, and that the amount of the increase due to a larger initial state decreases as the state and/or action is increased. (A3) and (A4) say that immediate costs increase as the state increases and that the increase in costs due to a larger initial state decreases as the state and/or action is increased.

Definition of Structure

Let V^* denote the increasing, concave functions defined on $\mathcal{S}$, and let Δ^* denote the decision rules that are increasing in the state. Note that since $A(\cdot)$ is independent of the state, it is ascending.

Theorem 8.3   *Suppose that (A1)–(A5) hold. If an optimizing action exists for each state and period, and v_{T} is increasing and concave, then, for each period, the optimal cost functions will be concave increasing functions of the state and there exists an optimal strategy that is increasing in the state.*

Proof (Attainment) Suppose $f_{t+1} \in V^*$. Assume for convenience that f_{t+1} is twice differentiable. Thus, $f'_{t+1}(s) \geq 0$, and $f''_{t+1}(s) \leq 0$ for all s. For convenience, we use subscripts on c and z and superscripts on G_t to denote partial derivatives. For example, $z_1(s, a, \xi)$ is the partial derivative of z with respect to its first argument, evaluated at the point (s, a, ξ). By (A1), it is positive. Hence,

$$G_t^1(s, a) = c_1(s, a) + \alpha \int_{\xi=0}^1 f'_{t+1}\big(z(s, a, \xi)\big) z_1(s, a, \xi) \, d\xi \qquad (8.4)$$

and

$$G_t^{12}(s, a) = c_{12}(s, a) + \alpha \int_{\xi=0}^1 f''_{t+1}\big(z(s, a, \xi)\big) z_1(s, a, \xi) z_2(s, a, \xi) \, d\xi$$

$$+ \alpha \int_{\xi=0}^1 f'_{t+1}\big(z(s, a, \xi)\big) z_{12}(s, a, \xi) \, d\xi. \qquad (8.5)$$

By virtue of the assumptions, each of the stated terms on the right-hand side of (8.5) is negative, and, therefore, by Lemma 8.2, G_t is submodular. Hence, by Theorem 8.1, there exists an optimal decision rule in Δ^* that attains the minimum.

(Preservation) We first prove that concavity is preserved. Suppose $f_{t+1} \in V^*$.

$$G_t^{11}(s, a) = c_{11}(s, a) + \alpha \int_{\xi=0}^1 f''_{t+1}\big(z(s, a, \xi)\big) \big(z_1(s, a, \xi)\big)^2 \, d\xi$$

$$+ \alpha \int_{\xi=0}^1 f'_{t+1}\big(z(s, a, \xi)\big) z_{11}(s, a, \xi) \, d\xi.$$

Each term is negative, so $G_t(\cdot, a)$ is concave for each fixed a. Thus, since $A(s)$ is independent of s, Theorem A.3 guarantees that f_t is concave.

We now prove that increasingness is preserved. Suppose $f_{t+1} \in V^*$ and $s \leq x$. Let $a(x)$ be optimal for x. First, each of the two terms in (8.4) above are positive, so $G_t(\cdot, a)$ is increasing. Then,

$$
\begin{aligned}
f_t(x) &= G_t(x, a(x)) \\
&\geq G_t(s, a(x)) && [G_t(\cdot, a) \text{ is increasing}] \\
&\geq f_t(s). && [a(x) \in A(s) \text{ and (OE)}]
\end{aligned}
$$

The result therefore follows from Theorem 5.3.   □

Note that whereas Theorem 8.3 says that the optimal cost functions will be concave increasing functions of the state at each period, nothing is said about whether the minimizations arising at each period and state involve convex functions, concave functions, or something more general. It should be clear that variations of assumptions (A1)–(A5) can lead to other analogous results.

8.4   Capacitated Inventory Management

Consider the stochastic inventory model of Section 4.2 with one change: There is a capacity level $Q > 0$ such that no more than Q units can be ordered/added in any given period. The optimality equations become

$$f_t(x, Q) = \min_{y \in A(x)} \Big\{ G_t(y, Q) - cx \Big\} \quad \text{for } 1 \le t \le N,$$

and $f_{N+1}(x, Q) := v_\mathsf{T}(x)$, where

$$G_t(y, Q) := cy + L(y) + \alpha E f_{t+1}(y - D, Q),$$

$A(x) = [x, x + Q]$, c is the unit procurement cost, L is the (convex) expected holding and shortage cost function, and α is the one-period discount factor. We explicitly indicate the dependence on Q because we wish to examine the ramifications of the solution of the problem as a function of this parameter.

Exercise 8.1 shows that $A(\cdot)$ is ascending. However, we will see that there does not exist an optimal policy that is increasing in the capacity level Q. Rather, we will show that a base stock policy is optimal and the base stock level $S(Q)$ is *decreasing* in Q.

Let $\mathcal{S} := \{(x, Q) | x \in \mathbf{R} \text{ and } Q > 0\}$, which is a convex set. Let V^* denote the set of functions that are supermodular and convex on $\mathcal{S}$, and let Δ^* denote the base stock policies characterized by a base stock level $S(Q)$ that is decreasing in Q for $Q \ge 0$. Under such a policy, given the initial inventory level x in period t, the level of inventory after ordering is as close to $S(Q)$ as possible, within the feasible interval $[x, x + Q]$. In particular, an arbitrary $\delta \in \Delta^*$ has the following form:

$$\delta(x) = \begin{cases} x + Q & \text{if } x \le S(Q) - Q, \\ S(Q) & \text{if } S(Q) - Q \le x \le S(Q), \\ x & \text{otherwise.} \end{cases}$$

Assume, for convenience, that $G_t(\cdot, Q)$ has a unique finite minimizer $S_t(Q)$ over $\mathbf{R}$ for each $Q > 0$.

Lemma 8.5   If $f_{t+1} \in V^*$, then (a) $S_t(Q)$ is a decreasing function of Q, (b) the optimal policy in period t is a base stock policy with base stock level $S_t(Q)$, (c) the optimal value of starting period t can be written as

$$
f_t(x, Q) = \begin{cases} G_t(x + Q, Q) - cx & \text{if } x \leq S_t(Q) - Q, \\ G_t(S_t(Q), Q) - cx & \text{if } S_t(Q) - Q \leq x \leq S_t(Q), \\ G_t(x, Q) - cx & \text{if } S_t(Q) \leq x, \end{cases}
$$

and (d) $f_t \in V^*$.

Proof By Lemma 8.3, G_t is supermodular because f_{t+1} is. Part (a) then follows, as in Lemmas 8.1 and 8.2, because $S_t(Q)$ is found by minimizing $G_t(\cdot, Q)$ over $\mathbf{R}$ for a fixed $Q > 0$. Parts (b) and (c) follow from Exercise A.8. Convexity of f_t follows from Theorem A.4, by Exercise 8.1. We prove the rest of (d) for the case in which G_t is partially differentiable. In particular, we examine the partial derivative of f_t with respect to its second argument:

$$
f_t^2(x, Q) = \begin{cases} G_t^1(x + Q, Q) + G_t^2(x + Q, Q) & \text{if } x \leq S_t(Q) - Q, \\ G_t^2(S_t(Q), Q) & \text{if } S_t(Q) - Q \leq x \leq S_t(Q), \\ G_t^2(x, Q) & \text{if } S_t(Q) \leq x, \end{cases}
$$

where we have used the fact that $G_t^1(S_t(Q), Q) = 0$ because $S_t(Q)$ is the minimizer. It is straightforward to show that f_t is supermodular within any of the three regions. It follows immediately from $G_t^1(S_t(Q), Q) = 0$ that $f_t^2(x, Q)$ is continuous at the two boundaries, and, hence, f_t is supermodular on S.   □

Theorem 8.4   If v_T is convex and supermodular on S, then the optimal policy in period t is a base stock policy with base stock level $S_t(Q)$, which is a decreasing function of Q, and f_t is convex and supermodular on S, for each t.

Proof Preservation and attainment follow from Lemma 8.5.   □

Note that we cannot say that the optimal level of inventory after ordering is either an increasing or a decreasing function of the capacity level Q: If we start period t with a sufficiently small initial inventory level x, then adding a little to Q will increase the amount ordered and, thus, the level after ordering. However, if we start that period with a moderate amount of inventory, so that it is optimal to order up to $S_t(Q)$, then adding a little to Q will decrease $S_t(Q)$ and the level after ordering will decrease!

Exercises

8.1 Suppose that $S = \mathbf{R}$. Prove that C, as defined in (8.2), is a convex lattice (both a convex set and a lattice) if either (a) $S = \mathbf{R}$ and $A(x) = [x, \infty)$, or (b) $S = \{(x, Q) | x \in \mathbf{R} \text{ and } Q > 0\}$ and $A(x) = [x, x + Q]$, where $Q > 0$.

8.2 Prove Lemma 8.3.

8.3 Prove that if $g : \mathbf{R} \to \mathbf{R}$ is convex and $f : \mathbf{R}^2 \to \mathbf{R}$ is defined by $f(x, y) := g(x - y)$, then f is submodular.

8.4 Provide an example of a convex function $g : \mathbf{R} \to \mathbf{R}$ such that if $f : \mathbf{R}^3 \to \mathbf{R}$ is defined by $f(x, y, z) := g(x + y - z)$, then f is neither submodular nor supermodular.

8.5 Suppose X is a lattice subset of $\mathbf{R}^n$, $g : X \to \mathbf{R}$, and $f : \mathbf{R} \to \mathbf{R}$ are given, and that $h : X \to \mathbf{R}$ is defined by $h(x) := f(g(x))$ for each $x \in X$. The function h is the *composition* of f and g and is denoted by $h = f \circ g$. Show that if either (a) f is concave increasing and g is submodular and *monotone* (either increasing or decreasing), or (b) f is concave decreasing and g is supermodular and monotone, then h is submodular. (Assume as much differentiability as you wish.)

8.6 Suppose

$$C = \{(s, a) | s \in \mathbf{R}, a \in \{0, 1\}\}.$$

Prove that g is submodular on C if and only if

$$g(s, 0) + g(t, 1) \le g(s, 1) + g(t, 0)$$

for every $s, t \in \mathbf{R}$ such that $s \le t$.

8.7 Complete the proof of Theorem 8.2 by providing the proof for the case in which the minima are not necessarily attained.

8.8 (*Binary Decision Processes*) Consider the model of Section 8.3 in which there are only two admissible decisions in each period, denoted "0" and "1." That is, $A(s) = \{0, 1\}$ for each $s \in S$. Consider the following additional assumptions:

(B1) $z(s,0,\xi)$ is increasing in s for every ξ.
(B2) $z(s,1,\xi)$ is independent of s for every ξ.
(B3) $c(s,a)$ is increasing in s for each $a \in A(s)$.
(B4) $c(s,a)$ is submodular in (s,a).

Prove that if the terminal value function is increasing and if assumptions (B1)–(B4) hold, then there exists an optimal increasing policy.

8.9   *(Equipment Replacement)*   A piece of equipment is observed to be in some state s at the beginning of each of N periods. The one-period discount factor is α. State 0 corresponds to a new machine. State S corresponds to an inoperable machine. Intermediate states represent gradual states of breakdown and inefficiency. Let $\mathcal{S} = [0, S]$ denote the state space. There are two decisions possible: "0" corresponds to "doing nothing" and just continuing to operate the existing machine. Decision "1" corresponds to replacing the machine, which costs $c_\mathbf{R}$ and takes an entire period to achieve. During the intervening period, the existing machine is operated. The cost of operating a machine that starts the period in state s is given by $c(s)$, which is an increasing function of s. Let Φ_s denote the distribution function of the state at the beginning of the next period given that the equipment is operated during this period beginning in state s. Assume that $\Phi_s(x)$ is decreasing in s for every $x \in \mathcal{S}$. Also assume that $v_\mathbf{T}(s)$ is increasing in s. Your objective is to minimize the expected present value of the costs of managing the machine over the finite time horizon. Prove that, under these assumptions, a control limit policy is optimal. That is, for each period t, there exists a single critical number a_t such that it is optimal to replace the machine if the state s of the machine is above a_t and to do nothing otherwise. (Hint: Apply Exercise 8.8.)

References

Albright, C., W. Winston. 1979. Markov models of advertising and pricing decisions. *Operations Research.* **27** 668–81.

Milgrom, P., J. Roberts. 1992. *Economics, Organization, and Management.* Prentice-Hall, Englewood Cliffs, N.J.

Topkis, D. M. 1978. Minimizing a submodular function on a lattice. *Operations Research.* **26** 305–21.

Topkis, D. M. 1998. *Supermodularity and Complementarity.* Princeton University Press, Princeton, N.J.

9

Structured
Probability Distributions

This chapter focuses on some special probability distributions, their properties, and two closely related applications to inventory theory. Most of the definitions and results on probability distributions come from Barlow and Proschan (1965), whereas the applications come from Porteus (1971).

9.1 Some Interesting Distributions

IFR and DFR Distributions

The *failure rate*, also called the *hazard rate* of a probability distribution Φ (and its associated random variable X) is defined, when a density function ϕ exists, by

$$r(x) := \frac{\phi(x)}{1 - \Phi(x)},$$

on $\{x | \Phi(x) < 1\}$. In the discrete (integer) case, we have

$$r(i) := \frac{\phi_i}{\sum_{j=i}^{\infty} \phi_j},$$

where ϕ_i is the probability $P(X = i)$ for each i. The vocabulary comes from reliability usage in which the random variable of interest is the lifetime of a component, and the failure rate gives (in the discrete case) the conditional probability that the component will fail at a given point in time given that it lasts at least that long.

A probability distribution Φ is *IFR* (has an *increasing failure rate*) if r is an increasing function (on its domain). Distributions such as the uniform, Erlang, normal, and truncated normal (if X is normal, then $\{X|X \geq 0\}$ is truncated normal) are IFR.

A probability distribution Φ is *DFR* (has a *decreasing failure rate*) if r is a decreasing function. The lognormal distribution is an example of a DFR distribution. The exponential distribution in the continuous case, and the geometric distribution in the discrete case, have constant failure rates, and are therefore both IFR and DFR.

Random variables possess the properties of their distributions. For example, an *IFR random variable* is a random variable with an IFR distribution.

Lemma 9.1   *(Barlow and Proschan, 1965)*

(a) The distribution of a sum of independent IFR random variables is IFR.

(b) A mixture (convex combination) of DFR distributions is DFR: If $\Phi_1, \Phi_2,$ $\cdots, \Phi_n$ are DFR distributions, and $p_1, p_2, \cdots, p_n$ are probabilities, then $\Phi = p_1\Phi_1 + p_2\Phi_2 + \cdots + p_n\Phi_n$ is DFR.

Part (a) says that if demands in different periods are independent IFR random variables, then the total demand over a fixed number of periods will also be IFR. Suppose X_1 and X_2 are independent random variables with distributions Φ_1 and Φ_2 and densities ϕ_1 and ϕ_2, respectively. It is standard (for example, Feller, 1968) that the distribution of the sum of X_1 and X_2 is given by the *convolution* of Φ_1 and Φ_2, which is defined, for each $x \in \mathbf{R}$, as

$$\Phi(x) := \int_{\xi=-\infty}^{\infty} \Phi_1(x - \xi)\phi_2(\xi)\,d\xi.$$

Part (a) therefore can be stated as follows: The convolution of IFR distributions is IFR.

Similarly, it is possible to express part (b) in terms of random variables instead of distributions: If $X_1, X_2, \cdots, X_n$ are DFR random variables, $p_1, p_2, \cdots, p_n$ are probabilities, and X is the random variable formed by selecting X_i with probability p_i, for $i = 1, 2, \cdots, n$, then X is DFR. For example, suppose that there are n different underlying states of the economy and that the probability that the economy will be in state i during a period is p_i for each i. If the conditional demand during the period is DFR for each given underlying state, then the (unconditional) demand during the period is DFR.

PF$_n$ Distributions

Barlow and Proschan (1965) and Karlin (1968) define what are called *Pólya frequency functions of order n* and *PF_n distributions* for short. These definitions are elaborate and difficult to understand intuitively. Thus, we discuss only their equivalent characterizations, which can be considered to be their definitions for our purposes. We also identify examples, to help develop the reader's intuition.

A distribution Φ and its density ϕ is *PF_2* (a *Pólya frequency function of order 2*) if

$$\frac{\phi(x)}{\Phi(x+y) - \Phi(x)}$$

is increasing in x for every fixed $y > 0$. By (essentially) selecting $y = \infty$, it is clear that a PF$_2$ distribution is IFR. The following distributions are PF$_2$: the exponential, the reflected exponential (if X is exponential, then $-X$ is reflected exponential), the uniform, the Erlang, the normal, the truncated normal, and all translations ($a + X$ is a translation of X for each scalar a) and convolutions of such distributions.

A density function $f : \mathbf{R} \to \mathbf{R}$ is *unimodal* and *quasi-concave* if $-f$ is quasi-convex, as defined in Appendix A. For each such density, we may assume without loss of generality that there exists a scalar a such that f is increasing on $(-\infty, a]$ and decreasing on $[a, \infty)$.

Lemma 9.2   *(Barlow and Proschan, 1965)*   PF$_2$ *densities are unimodal.*

A PF$_\infty$ distribution is called a *Pólya distribution*, and a *Pólya random variable* is a random variable with a Pólya distribution.

Lemma 9.3   *(Schoenberg, 1951)   A Pólya distribution consists solely of translations and convolutions of exponentials, reflected exponentials, and normals. A Pólya random variable consists of the sum of a translated normal, exponentials, and reflected exponentials. A positive Pólya random variable consists of a positive translation of the sum of exponentials.*

We shall see that PF_n distributions have useful smoothing properties. The *number of sign changes* of a real valued function f is the supremum of the number of sign changes of the sequence $f(x_1), f(x_2), \ldots, f(x_n)$, with zero values discarded and the supremum being taken over all possible finite sequences of points with $x_1 < x_2 < \cdots < x_n$, and n any finite integer. Before examining the smoothing properties of PF_n distributions, let's examine a special case.

Lemma 9.4   *If $f : \mathbf{R} \to \mathbf{R}$ is continuous, $g : \mathbf{R} \to \mathbf{R}$ exists and is defined by $g(x) := Ef(x - X)$, where X is an exponential random variable with mean $1/\lambda$, then g is continuously differentiable and*

$$g'(x) = \lambda[f(x) - g(x)].$$

Proof   Write $g(x)$ in the form

$$g(x) := \int_{\xi=0}^{\infty} f(x - \xi)\lambda e^{-\lambda \xi} \, d\xi = \int_{z=-\infty}^{x} f(z)\lambda e^{-\lambda(x-z)} dz$$

and then apply Leibnitz's rule (Exercise 1.8).   □

We first give an interpretation of f and g in the context of a single product dynamic inventory problem with backlogging. If $f(x)$ is the optimal value of starting the next period in state x and the demand D is exponentially distributed with mean $1/\lambda$ (having hazard rate λ) then $g(y) = Ef(y - D)$ is the resulting expected value (of starting the next period) as a function of the level y of inventory after ordering in the current period.

Lemma 9.4 has powerful smoothing implications that can be seen in Figure 9.1: The derivative of g is proportional to the difference between f and itself. If g is below f, then g is increasing (tries to get close to f). The more g is below f, the faster g increases. In general, g is a lot smoother than f. In particular, it is clear that the number of sign changes of g must be less than the number of sign changes of f. We now present a general result.

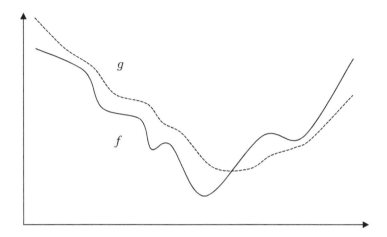

Figure 9.1   *A Convolution with the Exponential Distribution*

Theorem 9.1   *(Schoenberg, 1951)   If $f : \mathbf{R} \to \mathbf{R}$ changes sign $j < n$ times, X is a PF_n random variable, and $g(x) := Ef(x - X)$, then g also changes sign at most j times. If g changes sign exactly j times, then the changes must occur in exactly the same order as f.*

9.2   Quasi-K-Convexity

This section develops the foundations that will be used in the next two sections to address two variations of Scarf's (s, S) inventory model of Section 7.1. These models will be more general in some ways but less general in another.

A function $f : \mathbf{R} \to \mathbf{R}$ is *non-K-decreasing* if $x \leq y$ implies that

$$f(x) \leq K + f(y).$$

Clearly, K must be positive. A function $f : \mathbf{R} \to \mathbf{R}$ is *quasi-K-convex* if $x \leq y$ and $0 \leq \theta \leq 1$ imply that

$$f(\theta x + (1 - \theta)y) \leq \max[f(x), K + f(y)].$$

Note that if $K = 0$, then a quasi-K-convex function is quasi-convex on $\mathbf{R}$. A function $f : \mathbf{R} \to \mathbf{R}$ is *quasi-K-convex with changeover at a* if f is decreasing on $(-\infty, a]$ and non-K-decreasing on $[a, \infty)$. A function f is *nontrivially* *quasi-K-convex* if there exists a scalar a such that f is quasi-K-convex with changeover at a. Figure 9.2 illustrates a function that is quasi-K-convex with changeover at a. Note that the changeover point is not unique: in this case any point in the interval $[s, b]$ qualifies as a changeover point.

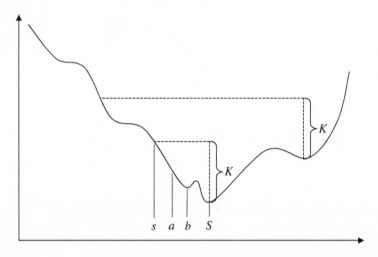

Figure 9.2   *A Function That Is quasi-K-convex with Changeover at a*

Lemma 9.5   *(Exercise 9.3)*   (a) *If f is K-convex, then f is quasi-K-convex, (b) if f is either decreasing, non-K-decreasing, or nontrivially quasi-K-convex, then f is quasi-k-convex, (c) if f is quasi-K-convex and $\gamma > 0$, then γf is quasi-(γK)-convex and (d) the sum of a quasi-K-convex function with changeover at a and a quasi-k-convex function with changeover at a is quasi-$(k+K)$-convex with changeover at a.*

Lemma 9.6   *If f is quasi-K-convex with changeover at a and X is a positive Pólya random variable, then there exists $b \geq a$ such that $g(x) := Ef(x - X)$ is quasi-K-convex with changeover at b.*

Proof   By Lemma 9.3, X can be represented as a positive translation of the sum of exponentially distributed random variables. Therefore, its density can be represented recursively as a sequence of convolutions. Thus, we can apply Lemma 9.4 recursively: Each time we compute the expectation with respect to one of the terms of the sum representing X, we smooth the output function of the previous expectation a little more and the changeover point can be taken to increase: If $g(x) = Ef(x - D)$, D is a positive random variable, and f is decreasing on $(-\infty, a]$, then g is clearly also decreasing on $(-\infty, a]$.   □

The following is a variation of Lemma 9.6 to cover the case when X is a uniformly distributed random variable.

Lemma 9.7 *(Porteus, 1972) If f is quasi-K-convex with changeover at a and X is a positive, uniformly distributed random variable, then there exists $b \geq a$ such that $g(x) := Ef(x - X)$ is quasi-K-convex with changeover at b.*

9.3   A Variation of the (s, S) Inventory Model

In many of our stochastic inventory models, $\mathcal{L}$ is the holding and shortage cost function of the ending inventory level: $\mathcal{L}(x)$ is the holding cost incurred at the end of the period if $x \geq 0$ and is the shortage cost incurred then if $x < 0$. Thus, the expected holding and shortage cost, as a function of the level y of inventory after ordering, is $L(y) := E\mathcal{L}(y - D_t)$. In our treatment of Scarf's stochastic (s, S) inventory model in Section 7.1, we specified that

$$\mathcal{L}(x) = \begin{cases} -c_{\mathrm{P}}x & \text{for } x \leq 0 \\ c_{\mathrm{H}}x & \text{otherwise.} \end{cases}$$

In general, the results of Section 7.1 go through if L is convex, which will be the case if $\mathcal{L}$ is convex. We now do not require that L be convex. In particular, we make the following, less restrictive, assumption.

(A1) $(1 - \alpha)cx + \mathcal{L}(x)$ is quasi-$(1 - \alpha)K$-convex with changeover at 0.

For example, a lump sum cost of incurring any shortages can be incorporated in the shortage cost function, and the holding cost function can incorporate economies of scale and can even be decreasing over certain intervals. (See Exercise 9.5 for a qualifying example in which $\mathcal{L}$ exhibits numerous discontinuities and is not quasi-convex.)

We also make the following less general assumption.

(A2) The demands $\{D_t\}$ are i.i.d. random variables, each of which has the distribution of the sum of a positive Pólya random variable and a finite number of positive, uniformly distributed random variables.

By Lemma 9.3, demand in a period has the distribution of a positive constant plus the sum of exponentially and uniformly distributed (positive) random variables, each of which can have different parameters. The sum can be partially degenerate. For example, if demand is either exponentially or uniformly distributed, then (A2) holds. Finally, we make the following technical assumptions.

(A3) $\mathcal{L}$ gets sufficiently large for large absolute arguments so that it is not optimal either never to order or to order an infinite amount.

(A4) L is continuous.

For example, (A4) will hold if $L(y)$ exists for every y, and $\mathcal{L}$ is piecewise continuous. We assume that (A1)–(A4) hold henceforth in this section and include a formal acknowledgment in the final theorem of this section.

This section continues to assume that the ordering cost function C has the following form, as a function of the amount z ordered:

$$C(z) = \begin{cases} 0 & \text{if } z = 0 \\ K + cz & \text{if } z > 0, \end{cases} \tag{9.1}$$

where K is the setup cost and c is the unit purchase cost, both of which are positive constants. In both this section and the next, where the ordering cost function will be considerably generalized, the optimality equations can be expressed as follows, for each $x \, (\in \mathbf{R})$ and each $t \, (\in \{1, 2, \ldots, N\})$:

$$f_t(x) = \min_{y \geq x}\{C(y - x) + L(y) + \alpha E f_{t+1}(y - D_t)\},$$

where $f_{N+1}(x) := v_{\mathrm{T}}(x)$.

It is convenient to present a foundational result from Lippman (1969) here that will be useful in both this section and the next. A function $C \colon [0, \infty) \to \mathbf{R}$ is *subadditive* if $C(a + b) \leq C(a) + C(b)$ for $a, b \geq 0$. Such a function captures an important feature of an economy of scale: It is cheaper to order an entire quantity from a single supplier than to order pieces from different suppliers. In manufacturing vocabulary, it is cheaper to produce the entire quantity in a single batch than to produce it in smaller batches. The next result shows that our ordering cost function is subadditive.

Lemma 9.8   *(Exercise 9.6)   If C is concave on $[0, \infty)$ and $C(0) = 0$, then C is subadditive.*

Lemma 9.9   (Lippman, 1969)   If $x \leq y$, then $f_t(x) \leq f_t(y) + C(y - x)$, for each t.

Proof   For convenience, let $w_t(y) := L(y) + \alpha E f_{t+1}(y - D_t)$ for all $y \in \mathbf{R}$. Then, given t and $x \leq y$, we have

$$
\begin{aligned}
f_t(x) &= \inf_{z \geq x}\left[C(z - x) + w_t(z)\right] && \text{[optimality equation]} \\
&\leq \inf_{z \geq y}\left[C(z - x) + w_t(z)\right] && \text{[fewer choices]} \\
&\leq \inf_{z \geq y}\left[C(z - y) + w_t(z) + C(y - x)\right] && \text{[subadditive]} \\
&= f_t(y) + C(y - x). && \text{[optimality equation]}
\end{aligned}
$$

$\square$

Lemma 9.9 says that, starting period t at state x, it is cheaper to make a single decision about the optimal level of inventory after ordering, compared to ordering some amount $y - x$ first and then deciding what additional amount to order from there.

Lemma 9.10   The function $cx + f_t(x)$ is non-K-decreasing in x for each t.

Proof   Fix $x \leq y$. By Lemma 9.9 and (9.1), $f_t(x) \leq f_t(y) + C(y - x) \leq f_t(y) + K + c(y - x)$. Rearranging terms completes the proof. $\square$

Given $f_{t+1} : \mathbf{R} \to \mathbf{R}$, define $G_t : \mathbf{R} \to \mathbf{R}$ by

$$
G_t(y) := E g_t(y - D_t) = \int_{\xi = 0}^{\infty} g_t(y - \xi)\phi(\xi)\, d\xi, \tag{9.2}
$$

where

$$
g_t(x) := cx + c\mu + \mathcal{L}(x) + \alpha f_{t+1}(x),
$$

μ is the mean demand per period, and α is the discount factor. Exercise 9.7 demonstrates that

$$
G_t(y) = cy + L(y) + \alpha E f_{t+1}(y - D_t). \tag{9.3}
$$

As in Section 7.1, let

$$
G_t^*(x) := \min\left\{G_t(x), \inf_{y \geq x}\left[K + G_t(y)\right]\right\}, \tag{9.4}
$$

where the two choices correspond to not ordering and ordering, respectively. (It is convenient to allow ordering zero in the latter case, although, of course, that selection will never be optimal if $K > 0$.) Thus, the optimality equations can be written, for each t, as

$$f_t(x) = -cx + G_t^*(x). \tag{9.5}$$

Lemma 9.11   *Given t, suppose that G_t is continuous and quasi-K-convex with changeover at a. There exist s and S such that $s \leq a \leq S$ and an (s, S) policy is optimal in period t.*

Proof   Since G_t is quasi-K-convex with changeover at a, G_t is decreasing on $(\infty, a]$ and non-K-decreasing on $[a, \infty)$. (Figure 9.2 can be helpful.) Thus, let S be any minimizer of G_t. We may assume without loss that $S \geq a$, because a is at least as good as anything smaller, and something bigger might be better. Let s be the smallest x such that $G_t(x) = K + G_t(S)$. Clearly $s \leq a$ because G_t cannot decrease by more than K to the right of a. That is, a is the largest possible value that s can attain. In short, $s \leq a \leq S$.

If we are going to order, we want to minimize G_t moving to the right, so the best we can do is order up to S. But the savings must exceed K to be worth it. Thus, if $x < s$, then $G_t(x) > K + G_t(S)$, so it is optimal to order up to S. If $s \leq x < S$, then, since G_t is quasi-K-convex, $G_t(x) \leq \max[G_t(s), K + G_t(S)] = K + G_t(S)$, so it is optimal not to order. Finally, if $x \geq S$, then, since G_t is non-K-decreasing on $[a, \infty)$ and $S \geq a$, it is optimal not to order: $G_t(x) \leq K + G_t(y)$ for any $y \geq x$.   □

Let V^* denote the set of continuous functions $f : \mathbf{R} \to \mathbf{R}$ such that, if $g(x) := cx + f(x)$ for $x \in \mathbf{R}$, then g is quasi-K-convex with changeover at 0, and let Δ^* denote the set of (s, S) policies.

Lemma 9.12   *If $f_{t+1} \in V^*$, then the following hold.*

(a) G_t is decreasing on $(-\infty, 0]$.

(b) (Attainment) There exists an (s, S) policy with $S \geq 0$ that is optimal in period t.

(c) (Preservation) $f_t \in V^*$.

Proof   (a) Decompose g_t into

$$g_t(x) = c\mu + \big[(1 - \alpha)cx + \mathcal{L}(x)\big] + \alpha\big[cx + f_{t+1}(x)\big],$$

which is the sum of a constant, a quasi-$(1-\alpha)K$-convex function with changeover at 0, and a quasi-αK-convex function with changeover at 0. Thus, by Lemma

9.5(d), g_t is quasi-K-convex with changeover at 0. Hence, by (9.2), (A2), and Exercise 9.4, G_t is quasi-K-convex with changeover at a for some $a \geq 0$. In particular, (a) holds.

Note that G_t is continuous even though g_t need not be. Part (b) then follows from Lemma 9.11.

(c) By Lemma 9.10, we need to show only that $cx + f_t(x)$ is decreasing for $x \leq 0$. Fix $x < y \leq 0$. As earlier, let $w_t(y) := L(y) + \alpha E f_{t+1}(y - D_t)$.

First consider the case in which $x < s$. In this case, since $S \geq 0 \geq y > x$, it follows that $C(S-x) = K + c(S-x) = K + c(S-y) + c(y-x) \geq C(S-y) + c(y-x)$. Consequently,

$$
\begin{aligned}
f_t(y) &\leq C(S - y) + w_t(S) && [S \text{ is feasible}] \\
&\leq C(S - x) - c(y - x) + w_t(S) && [\text{above}] \\
&= f_t(x) - c(y - x). && [x < s]
\end{aligned}
$$

That is, $cx + f_t(x)$ is decreasing in this case.

Finally, consider the case in which $x \geq s$. In this case, it is optimal not to order from both x and y. Therefore, by (9.4) and (9.5), $cx + f_t(x) = G_t(x)$ and $cy + f_t(y) = G_t(y)$. The result follows from (a).   □

Theorem 9.2   *If the ordering cost function is given by (9.1), (A1)–(A4) hold, and $v_T \in V^*$, then an (s, S) policy is optimal in each period t.*

Proof   By Lemma 9.12, Theorem 5.3 applies.   □

9.4   Generalized (s, S) Policies

Consider now a more significant generalization of Scarf's stochastic inventory model: The ordering cost function is now concave in general, instead of simply linear with a setup cost. To keep the exposition clear, we assume that the ordering cost function is piecewise linear with a setup cost. Any concave ordering cost function can be approximated by such a function, with a maximum error that decreases in the number of pieces used. Suppose there are M pieces in the ordering cost function. For instance, $M = 3$ in Figure 9.3. By extending each of the line segments as shown in Figure 9.3, it is possible to represent the ordering cost function c in the following form.

$$
C(z) = \begin{cases} 0 & \text{if } z = 0 \\ \min_i \left(K_i + c_i z \right) & \text{if } z > 0, \end{cases} \tag{9.6}
$$

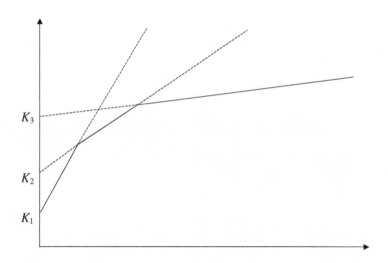

Figure 9.3   A Piecewise Linear Concave Ordering Cost Function

where $c_1 > c_2 > \cdots > c_M \geq 0$, and $0 \leq K_1 < K_2 < \cdots < K_M$. (Otherwise the original piecewise linear function would not be concave.)

It is convenient (and general) to think of there being M different suppliers (sources, different ways to manufacture the product, etc.) and that if $z > 0$ is ordered from supplier i, the cost is $K_i + c_i z$, where K_i and c_i can be interpreted as the setup cost and unit cost, respectively, if supplier i is used. The cheapest supplier will be used for each $z > 0$. This cost structure implies that we have a variety of options available: A low unit cost, high fixed-cost option, a high unit cost, low fixed-cost option, and perhaps lots of others in between. If there is no quantity $z > 0$ for which a supplier has the strictly lowest cost, such as when a supplier has both a higher setup cost and unit cost than another, then that supplier can be dropped from consideration.

We now make the following assumption about $\mathcal{L}$, the holding and shortage cost function of the ending inventory level.

(B1) $(c_1 - \alpha c_M)x + \mathcal{L}(x)$ is decreasing on $(-\infty, 0]$, and $(1 - \alpha)c_i x + \mathcal{L}(x)$ is non-$(1 - \alpha)K_i$-decreasing on $[0, \infty)$.

Exercises 9.9 and 9.10 explore some sufficient conditions for (B1) to hold. We assume henceforth in this section that (B1) and (A2)–(A4) hold.

A decision rule δ is called *generalized* (s, S) if there exist m and

$$s_m \leq s_{m-1} \leq \cdots \leq s_1 \leq S_1 \leq S_2 \leq \cdots \leq S_m$$

such that

$$\delta(x) = \begin{cases} S_m & \text{if } x < s_m \\ S_i & \text{if } s_{i+1} \leq x < s_i \text{ for } i = 1, 2, \ldots, m - 1 \\ x & \text{otherwise.} \end{cases}$$

Figure 9.4 illustrates the workings of such a policy for $m = 3$. If the initial level x of inventory before ordering is above s_1, then no order is placed. If that initial level x drops below s_1, then supplier 1, with the lowest setup cost and highest marginal cost, is used and the level of inventory after ordering is brought up to S_1. If x drops further, to below s_2, then we switch to supplier 2, with its higher fixed cost and lower unit cost, and bring the inventory level up to S_2, ordering a relatively large amount. If x drops below s_3, then we switch to the supplier with the lowest unit cost (and highest setup cost) and order an even larger amount, not only because x is lower but because the level after ordering is higher.

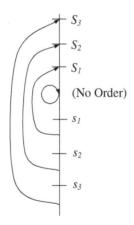

Figure 9.4   *Illustration of a Generalized (s, S) Policy*

In general, $m \leq M$, and equality may not occur, because some suppliers may never be used. It can be optimal to jump past some, including the first.

Given $f_{t+1}: \mathbf{R} \to \mathbf{R}$, define $G_{ti}: \mathbf{R} \to \mathbf{R}$ by

$$G_{ti}(y) := E g_{ti}(y - D_t) = \int_{\xi=0}^{\infty} g_{ti}(y - \xi)\phi(\xi)\, d\xi, \qquad (9.7)$$

where

$$g_{ti}(x) := c_i(x + \mu) + \mathcal{L}(x) + \alpha f_{t+1}(x),$$

so, by Exercise 9.7,

$$G_{ti}(y) = c_i y + L(y) + \alpha E f_{t+1}(y - D_t). \qquad (9.8)$$

Let

$$G_{ti}^*(x) := \min\left(G_{ti}(x), \inf_{y \geq x}\left[K_i + G_{ti}(y)\right]\right),$$

which represents the results of deciding how much to order, if any, when restricting consideration to supplier i. Thus, $-c_i x + G_{ti}^*(x)$ can be interpreted as the optimal return in period t if consideration is restricted to supplier i. The usual logic applies: If we are going to order from supplier i, we want to minimize G_{ti} moving to the right, but the savings must exceed K_i to be worth it.

The optimality equations can then be written as

$$f_t(x) = \min_{1 \leq i \leq m}\left\{-c_i x + G_{ti}^*(x)\right\}.$$

Lemma 9.13   *If G_{ti} is continuous and quasi-K_i-convex with changeover at a_i for each i ($\in \{1, 2, \ldots, M\}$), then there exist (s_i, S_i) for each i such that the following hold.*

(a) $s_i \leq a_i \leq S_i$ for each i.

(b) It is optimal in period t to follow an (s_i, S_i) policy if restricted to using supplier i (or ordering nothing).

(c) $a_1 \leq S_1 \leq S_2 \leq \cdots \leq S_M$.

(d) Let, for $i < j$,

$$s_{ij} := \frac{K_i - K_j + G_{ti}(S_i) - G_{tj}(S_j)}{c_i - c_j}$$

and

$$s_j^* := \min\left(s_j, \min_{1 \leq i < j} s_{ij}\right).$$

If $x \leq s_j^*$, then it is better (in period t) to order up to S_j rather than not order or to use any lower indexed supplier $i < j$. If $s_i^* \leq s_j^*$ for some $j > i$, then supplier i need never be used.

(e) There exists an optimal decision rule for period t that is a generalized (s, S) policy.

Proof   Parts (a) and (b) follow directly from Lemma 9.11.

(c) It follows from (9.8) that, for suppliers i and j,

$$G_{ti}(x) - G_{tj}(x) = (c_i - c_j)x.$$

Since $c_j < c_i$ for $j > i$, it therefore follows that $G_{t,i+1}'(x) \leq G_{ti}'(x)$ which, by Exercise 7.6, implies that $S_i \leq S_{i+1}$.

(d) By (b), it is optimal either to order nothing or to bring the inventory level after ordering up to S_i for some i. That is, if we are going to use (supplier) i, then we bring the level up to S_i. Fix j and consider arbitrary $i < j$. Starting period t at state x, the savings from using j compared to i, is

$$K_i - K_j + (c_j - c_i)x + G_{ti}(S_i) - G_{tj}(S_j).$$

Thus, s_{ij} is the initial inventory level at which we are indifferent between using i and j. Because $c_j < c_i$, it follows that $x \leq s_{ij}$ iff it is better to use j than i. Thus, by the definition of s_j^*, if $s < s_j^*$, it is better to use j than any lower indexed supplier and doing so is better than ordering nothing. Similarly, if $s \geq s_j^*$, then it is optimal to do something other than use j. Thus, if $s_i^* \leq s_j^*$, supplier i need never be used (in period t) and can be ignored when identifying the optimal policy for this period.

(e) After eliminating any suppliers that need not be used this period and renumbering, if necessary, we have $m \leq M$ active suppliers with $s_m^* < s_{m-1}^* < \cdots < s_1^* \leq S_1 < S_2 < \cdots < S_m$. If $x \geq s_1^*$, then not ordering dominates. If $s_{i+1}^* \leq x < s_i^*$, then ordering up to S_i dominates all lower indexed suppliers. Similarly, higher indexed suppliers are dominated by some lower numbered supplier, which must therefore be supplier i. Hence, it is optimal to order up to S_i from there.   □

Let V^* denote the set of continuous functions $f : \mathbf{R} \to \mathbf{R}$ such that $c_i x + f(x)$ is non-K_i-decreasing (in x) on $\mathbf{R}$ for each $i\,(= 1, 2, \ldots, M)$, and $c_M x + f(x)$ is decreasing on $(-\infty, 0]$. Let Δ^* denote the set of generalized (s, S) policies.

Lemma 9.14   *If $f_{t+1} \in V^*$, then the following hold.*

(a) g_{ti} is quasi-K_i-convex with changeover at 0 for each i.

(b) G_{ti} is decreasing on $(-\infty, 0]$ for each i.

(c) (Attainment) There exists a generalized (s, S) policy with $S_1 \geq 0$ that is optimal in period t.

(d) (Preservation) $f_t \in V^*$.

Proof   (a) For $x \leq 0$, decompose g_{ti} into

$$g_{ti}(x) = c_i\mu + \left[(c_1 - \alpha c_M)x + \mathcal{L}(x)\right] + (c_i - c_1)x + \alpha\left[c_M x + f_{t+1}(x)\right].$$

Each term is decreasing on $(-\infty, 0]$: the second term by (B1), the third because $c_i \leq c_1$, and the fourth because $f_{t+1} \in V^*$.

Similarly, for $x \geq 0$, decompose g_{ti} into

$$g_{ti}(x) = c_i\mu + \left[(1 - \alpha)c_i x + \mathcal{L}(x)\right] + \alpha\left[c_i x + f_{t+1}(x)\right].$$

By (B1), the second term is non-$(1-\alpha)K_i$-decreasing on $[0, \infty)$. Because $f_{t+1} \in V^*$ and by Lemma 9.5(c), the third term is non-αK_i-decreasing. Thus, g_{ti} is non-K_i-decreasing on $[0, \infty)$. That is, (a) holds.

(b) Hence, by (9.7) and Exercise 9.4, G_{ti} is quasi-K_i-convex with changeover at a_i for some $a_i \geq 0$ for each i. In particular, (b) holds.

(c) Note that G_{ti} is continuous even though g_{ti} need not be. Part (c) then follows from Lemma 9.13.

(d) (Exercise 9.13)   □

Theorem 9.3   If the ordering cost function is given by (9.6), (B1) and (A2)–(A4) hold, and $v_\mathbf{T} \in V^*$, then a generalized (s, S) policy is optimal in each period t.

Proof   By Lemma 9.14, Theorem 5.3 applies.   □

Exercises

9.1   A function $f : \mathbf{R} \to \mathbf{R}$ is *convex-concave* if f is either convex or concave or there exists a scalar a such that f is convex on $(-\infty, a]$ and concave on $[a, \infty)$. Prove that if f is convex-concave and ϕ is a PF_2 density, and

$$g(x) := \int_{\xi=-\infty}^{\infty} f(x - \xi)\phi(\xi)\,d\xi,$$

then g is also convex-concave. Assume as much differentiability as you wish. Hint: Apply Theorem 9.1.

9.2 Prove that if f is quasi-K-convex, then f is either (a) decreasing, (b) non-K-decreasing, or (c) nontrivially quasi-K-convex.

9.3 Prove Lemma 9.5.

9.4 Suppose that $X = \sum_{i=0}^{n} X_i$, where X_0 is a positive Pólya random variable and X_i is a positive, uniformly distributed random variable for each $i = 1, 2, \ldots, n$. Prove that if f is quasi-K-convex with changeover at a, then there exists $b \geq a$ such that $g(x) := Ef(x - X)$ is quasi-K-convex with changeover at b.

Hint: Let $g_0(x) := Ef(x - X_0)$, and, recursively, $g_i(x) := Eg_{i-1}(x - X_i)$ for $i = 1, 2, \ldots, n$, show that $g = g_n$, and apply Lemmas 9.6 and 9.7.

9.5 Consider the model of Section 9.3. Suppose that sufficiently many containers must be rented in each period to enclose the units in inventory at the end of the period. Each container has the capacity to enclose q units of inventory. Only containers needed must be rented. It is costless to rebalance containers each period, so at most one container will not be full. It costs $c_H(n)$ to rent n containers for one period. The function $c_H(n)$ is increasing but not necessarily convex or concave. The goods must be kept cool in the container, and it costs more for the energy when the container is almost empty than if full. In particular, the energy costs for a container that has x units in it are given by $c_E(x)$ for $0 \leq x \leq q$, where $c_E(0) - c_E(q) \leq (1 - \alpha)K$. Furthermore, the cost of having x units of shortage at the end of a period (ending inventory of $-x$), is given by

$$c_P(x) = \begin{cases} 0 & \text{if } x = 0, \\ c_{LS} + c_V x & \text{if } x > 0, \end{cases}$$

where $c_{LS} \geq 0$ and $c_V > (1 - \alpha)c$. Note that $c_P(x)$ incorporates a lump sum cost of c_{LS} and a variable cost of c_V per unit short.

Display $\mathcal{L}$ explicitly in this case and show that (A1) holds.

9.6 Prove Lemma 9.8.

9.7 Verify that (9.3) holds.

9.8 Suppose that (9.6) holds. Show that if $x \leq y \leq z$, then $C(z - x) \geq C(z - y) + c_M(y - x)$.

9.9   Suppose that

$$\mathcal{L}(x) = \begin{cases} -c_{\mathbf{P}}x & \text{for } x \le 0 \\ c_{\mathbf{H}}x & \text{otherwise.} \end{cases}$$

Prove that if $c_{\mathbf{P}} > c_1 - \alpha c_M$ and $c_{\mathbf{H}} + (1 - \alpha)c_M > 0$, then (B1) holds. Argue informally why (A3) will also hold.

9.10   Show that if (a) $\mathcal{L}$ is decreasing on $(-\infty, 0]$, differentiable on $(-\infty, 0)$, and $\mathcal{L}'(x) \le -(c_1 - \alpha c_M)$ for $x < 0$, and (b) $(1-\alpha)c_M x + \mathcal{L}(x)$ is non-$(1-\alpha)K_1$-decreasing on $[0, \infty)$, then (B1) holds.

9.11   Prove that if (B1) holds, then $(1-\alpha)c_i x + \mathcal{L}(x)$ is quasi-$(1-\alpha)K_i$-convex with changeover at 0 for each $i = 1, 2, \ldots, M$.

9.12   (Lippman, 1969)   Suppose that (9.6) holds. Show that, for each i, the function $c_i x + f_t(x)$ is non-K_i-decreasing in x.

9.13   Prove Lemma 9.14(d).

Hint: Modify the proof of Lemma 9.12 and apply Exercises 9.8 and 9.12.

References

Barlow, R., F. Proschan. 1965. *Mathematical Theory of Reliability*. John Wiley, New York.

Feller, W. 1968. *An Introduction to Probability Theory and Its Applications*. John Wiley, New York.

Karlin, S. 1968. *Total Positivity, Volume I*. Stanford University Press, Stanford, Calif.

Lippman, S. 1969. Optimal inventory policies with multiple set-up costs. *Management Science*. **16** 118–38.

Porteus, E. 1971. On the optimality of generalized (s, S) policies. *Management Science*. **17** 411–26.

Porteus, E. 1972. The optimality of generalized (s, S) policies under uniform demand densities. *Management Science*. **18** 644–46.

Schoenberg, I. 1951. On Pólya frequency functions I. The totally positive functions and their Laplace transforms. *Journal d'Analyse Mathématique*. **1** 331–74.

10
Empirical Bayesian Inventory Models

Consider the dynamic inventory model of Section 4.2. In particular, newly purchased units cost c each, all unmet demand is backlogged, and all leftover stock is available to be used in the following period. The big change is that the demand distribution is not known, so that not only must we manage the stock levels, we must simultaneously estimate the underlying probability distribution of demand. We take an empirical Bayesian approach.

For example, suppose that we have developed a new product and we are not sure what the demand for it will be each week, at the one location at which it will be sold. Each week, we must decide how many units to produce, at unit cost c, before any demands for the product are observed. (Production capacity is unlimited.) Unmet demands are backlogged and met in the following week. The products we have developed in the past turned out to be either *hits* or *bombs*, with about an equal number of each. The problem is that we don't know in advance what type our new product is. If the product is a hit, demand during a week will be for either 200 units, with probability 0.9, or 100 units, with probability 0.1. However, if the product is a bomb, then the probabilities are reversed. In the first week during which we sell the product, we will observe demand and learn about the type of the product. However, we will not know the type for sure, because both demand quantities can arise under both types of products.

With an empirical Bayesian approach, we start with a prior distribution on the underlying product type and update it using Bayes' rule (for example, DeGroot, 1970) each week after observing the demand that week. Suppose our prior probability that the product is a bomb is 0.5. Suppose further that demand in the first week is 100. Using Bayes' rule, we now calculate that our posterior probability that the product is a bomb is

$$\frac{0.9(0.5)}{0.9(0.5) + 0.1(0.5)} = \frac{0.45}{0.50} = 0.9.$$

Thus, we are now much more inclined to believe that the product is a bomb. However, if demand in the second week is 200, the new posterior probability (that the product is a bomb) is

$$\frac{0.1(0.9)}{0.1(0.9) + 0.9(0.1)} = \frac{0.09}{0.18} = 0.5,$$

and our beliefs are right back where we started. However, if 7 of the next 10 demands are 100, then the posterior probability (of a bomb) becomes 0.99985. That is, in general, as demands are observed over time, the type of the product will be revealed.

In this example, there are only two possible demand realizations and two types of products. In practice, there will usually be many, even possibly a continuum, of demand realizations. The same may be the case for types of products. Thus, this chapter focuses on the case in which there is a continuum of both demand realizations and product types. Hence, we will be working with probability densities of demand and prior (and posterior) densities on the type of product.

10.1   Model Formulation

To keep things from getting too complicated, assume that demands for the product in the various periods are i.i.d. positive random variables with a common unknown underlying demand distribution, which comes from a given (known) family of distributions. In particular, $\psi(\cdot|\omega)$ is the demand density, where ω is a single unknown parameter that specifies the product type, namely, which particular distribution from the given family is generating the demands. (In

general, there may be several unknown parameters, but we restrict consideration to estimating a single parameter, to keep the exposition as simple as possible.) For example, suppose the distribution comes from the family of *Weibull*
distributions with

$$\psi(\xi|\omega) = \omega k \xi^{k-1} e^{-\omega \xi^k}, \tag{10.1}$$

where k (> 0) is a known shape parameter and ω (> 0) is the unknown
positive scale parameter. (Because demand is positive, it goes without saying
that $\xi \geq 0$.) In this case, as shown in Exercise 10.4, the mean demand depends on ω but the coefficient of variation does not. Thus, this model can
be interpreted as one in which the unknown type of the product is the mean
demand. Given the type, the standard deviation of demand is a fixed multiple
of the mean, and the demand distribution is Weibull, which is similar in many
ways to the gamma distribution: Both reduce to the exponential distribution
when $k = 1$ (with rate ω), both are IFR for $k \geq 1$, and both are DFR for
$0 < k \leq 1$. They differ (Barlow and Proschan, 1965) in that, when they are
IFR and non-exponential $(k > 1)$, the failure rate of the gamma is bounded
above by the parameter ω, while the failure rate of the Weibull increases without bound, as does the normal distribution. This difference implies that the
Weibull (and the normal) have thinner tails than the gamma (in this case).

Before stocking the product and observing any sales, you, as the retailer, have a
prior density function g on the unknown parameter, which represents your beliefs about the underlying demand distribution. For instance, this new product
may fall into a category of products for which you are comfortable specifying
the family of distributions and merely seek to identify a single unknown parameter. (We keep the setting as simple as possible by assuming you are the
single decison maker who has an initial prior on ω. We then work together on
solving your problem.)

After unconditioning on this parameter, we get the *predictive demand density*

$$\phi(\xi) = \int_{\omega=-\infty}^{\infty} \psi(\xi|\omega) g(\omega) \, d\omega,$$

which, given your prior g on the product type, gives what you believe is the
density of demand in the next period. In the example of the previous section,
if your prior that the product is a bomb is 0.7, then the predictive probability
that demand will equal 100 next week is $0.9(0.7) + 0.1(0.3) = 0.66$.

Clearly, as observations of demands over successive periods accumulate, improved knowledge of the underlying parameter will be obtained. After sufficiently many observations, there will be little or no uncertainty about the originally unknown parameter, and inventory management would be applied as in Section 4.2. However, the question is how to manage the inventory as that evidence is accumulated.

There is a natural bullwhip effect in this model: A base stock policy will be optimal under the conditions assumed in this chapter. If a large demand is observed, then you are going to think that the underlying demand distribution is stochastically larger than what you thought before. So our new selection of the optimal base stock level will be larger than it was before. Hence, you will order enough to replenish the just observed large demand, plus the increase in the base stock level. However, if a small demand is observed, then your updated idea of the underlying demand distribution will be stochastically smaller, with a smaller base stock level than before. So you will order less than the small amount demanded, perhaps nothing. In particular, you will order more than the latest observed demand if it is large and less than demand if it is small, which is exactly the bullwhip effect. (See Lee, Padmanabhan, and Whang, 1997, for more on the bullwhip effect.)

There is nothing conceptually difficult about the dynamic analysis: We can augment the state space to include, in addition to the level of inventory at the beginning of a period, the vector of observed demands since the product was introduced. If there is only one period left in the problem, then Bayes' rule can be applied using the available observations, to determine the predictive density, and the quantity to stock can then be determined in the usual way. However, in earlier periods, our analysis must anticipate what the predictive densities will become as we make additional observations, and this approach is unsatisfactory from a practical perspective, as the computational burden becomes overwhelming.

Another approach is to augment the state space with a representation of the current prior distribution on the unknown parameter: After each observation of demand, Bayes' rule can be applied to obtain a posterior distribution on the parameter, which becomes the updated prior for the beginning of the next period. This approach can work well if the dimensionality of the representation of the prior is not too great. For instance, if there are only two different values of the unknown parameter, then one need keep track only of the probability that it equals one of those values. (The other probability is one minus the first and updating is straightforward, as illustrated in the previous section.) In most realistic situations, however, there will be at least several different values of the unknown parameter. The next section presents a framework in which there is a continuum of possible parameter values yet representation of the prior requires only a small number of parameters, which will be state variables in our analysis.

10.2   Conjugate Priors

The idea is to find conditions under which (a) the prior distribution on the unknown parameter has a specific form that can be characterized by a small number of parameters, (b) the posterior distribution on the parameter (after updating using Bayes' rule based on what is observed during the period) has the same distributional form as the prior (with the same set of parameters), and (c) updating these parameters can be done easily.

In this case, the state need include only the level of inventory and the current values of these parameters. The optimality equations will still have a simple form, and fruitful analyses can be carried out.

The trick is to find one family for the demand distributions and another for the prior on the unknown parameter such that (b) and (c) hold. When these conditions hold, the two families are said to be *conjugate*. It turns out that there are quite a few combinations of conjugate distributions. Raiffa and Schlaifer (1961) developed the concept and presented many of them. See also DeGroot (1970) for a useful exposition, including basic underlying material.

Weibull-Gamma

Assume for the remainder of this subsection that demand is Weibull as in (10.1) (with k known, ω unknown, and both strictly positive) and the prior on ω has a *gamma* distribution with shape parameter $a > 0$ and scale parameter $S > 0$: The prior density on the unknown parameter $\omega > 0$ is given by

$$g(\omega | a, S) = \frac{S^a \omega^{a-1} e^{-\omega S}}{\Gamma(a)},\tag{10.2}$$

where the gamma function $\Gamma(\cdot)$ is defined in Exercise 10.1, and Exercise 10.2 shows that it is a natural generalization to noninteger positive real numbers of the factorial function: $\Gamma(a) = (a-1)!$ for $a = 1, 2, \ldots$.

It is useful to recall that when a is an integer (and S remains a general scale parameter), the gamma distribution is an *Erlang* distribution, namely, the distribution of the sum of a independent random variables, each of which is exponentially distributed with rate S (and therefore mean $1/S$). The mean of the gamma distribution is a/S, and the variance is a/S^2, so the coefficient of variation is $\sqrt{1/a}$.

Letting D denote the random demand in a period, then, given ω, by Exercise 10.3, D^k is exponentially distributed with rate ω. In particular, by Exercise 10.5, the smaller the unknown rate is, the (stochastically) larger the demand is. Thus, when the prior distribution has a small mean, the demand is apt to be large.

Lemma 10.1   *(Azoury, 1985)   In the Weibull-Gamma case as given by (10.1) and (10.2), the following hold.*

(a) The predictive density is given, for $\xi \geq 0$, by

$$\phi(\xi|a, S) = \frac{ak S^a \xi^{k-1}}{[S + \xi^k]^{a+1}}. \tag{10.3}$$

(b) The predictive distribution is given, for $\xi \geq 0$, by

$$\Phi(\xi|a, S) = 1 - \left(\frac{S}{S + \xi^k}\right)^a. \tag{10.4}$$

(c) The posterior density (on the unknown parameter, after updating based on observing demand ξ in a period) is gamma with updated shape parameter equal to $a + 1$ and updated scale parameter, denoted by $S \circ \xi$, equal to

$$S \circ \xi = S + \xi^k.$$

Proof   (a) In this case,

$$\phi(\xi|a, S) = \int_{-\infty}^{\infty} \psi(\xi|\omega)g(\omega|a, S)\, d\omega$$

$$= \int_{0}^{\infty} \omega k \xi^{k-1} e^{-\omega \xi^k} \frac{S^a \omega^{a-1} e^{-\omega S}}{\Gamma(a)}\, d\omega$$

$$= \frac{k S^a \xi^{k-1}}{\Gamma(a)} \int_{0}^{\infty} \omega^a e^{-\omega(S+\xi^k)}\, d\omega$$

$$= \frac{a k S^a \xi^{k-1}}{[S + \xi^k]^{a+1}}.$$

The first two equalities are by definition. The third is the result of combining terms. The fourth comes from Exercise 10.2(b) and from

$$\int_{-\infty}^{\infty} g(\omega|\hat{a}, \hat{S})\, d\omega = 1,$$

which, using $\hat{a} = a + 1$, and $\hat{S} = S + \xi^k$, reveals that

$$\int_{0}^{\infty} \omega^a e^{-\omega(S+\xi^k)}\, d\omega = \frac{\Gamma(a+1)}{[S + \xi^k]^{a+1}},$$

Part (b) follows from direct integration of (10.3), using $u = S + \xi^k$ so that $du = k\xi^{k-1}\, d\xi$.

(c) In this case,

$$g(\omega|a, S, \xi) = \frac{\psi(\xi|\omega)g(\omega|a, S)}{\int_{\omega'=-\infty}^{\infty} \psi(\xi|\omega')g(\omega'|a, S)\, d\omega'}$$

$$= \frac{\psi(\xi|\omega)g(\omega|a, S)}{\phi(\xi|a, S)}$$

$$= \frac{[S + \xi^k]^{a+1} \omega^a e^{-\omega[S+\xi^k]}}{\Gamma(a+1)}$$

$$= \frac{[\hat{S}]^{\hat{a}} \omega^{\hat{a}} e^{-\omega \hat{S}}}{\Gamma(\hat{a})},$$

where $\hat{a} := a + 1$ and $\hat{S} := S + \xi^k$. The first equality uses Bayes' rule. The second uses the definition of the predictive density. The third comes from plugging in the specific formulas, including (10.3), and rearranging terms. Finally, this is exactly the gamma density, with parameters $\hat{a}$ and $\hat{S}$.

$\square$

Thus, the shape parameter increases by one after each observation and can be expressed in terms of the number of observations: At the beginning of period t, there have been $t-1$ observations of demand, so the updated shape parameter at the beginning of period t can be given (deterministically) by $a_t = a_1 + t - 1$, where a_1 is the initial shape parameter specified before any observations are made. In short, at the beginning of period t, the only other information needed to specify the prior distribution on the unknown parameter is S, the current scale parameter of that prior. Thus, the predictive demand density for period t can be written as

$$\phi_t(\xi|S) := \phi(\xi|a_t, S) = \frac{(a_1 + t - 1)kS^{a_1+t-1}\xi^{k-1}}{[S + \xi^k]^{a_1+t}}.$$

Because the coefficient of variation of the gamma prior is $\sqrt{1/a_t}$, the shape parameter completely determines the precision of the system's information on the unknown parameter ω. Thus, as the number of observations increases, the relative uncertainty about the unknown parameter ω decreases. In the limit, ω is known exactly: Demand is still stochastic, but the missing parameter is known precisely. (The specific value of that parameter is revealed by the sequence of observed demands.)

By Lemma 10.1(b), the scale parameter increases each period by the demand observation raised to the kth power. However, because the shape parameter is also increasing each period, whether or not a demand observation in this period leads to a stochastically larger demand distribution for next period is unclear. Exercises 10.5 and 10.11 shed some light on this issue.

Gamma-Gamma

Suppose that demand is gamma distributed with known shape parameter $k > 0$ and unknown scale parameter ω:

$$\psi(\xi|\omega) = \frac{\omega^k \xi^{k-1} e^{-\omega\xi}}{\Gamma(k)}. \tag{10.5}$$

As indicated in the previous subsection, the mean and coefficient of variation of this distribution are k/ω and $\sqrt{1/k}$, respectively. Thus, as in the Weibull-Gamma case, we are assuming that the mean of the distribution is unknown and that the standard deviation is a fixed multiple of that unknown mean.

Furthermore, suppose that the prior on ω has a gamma distribution with shape parameter a and scale parameter S, so that the prior density on the unknown parameter ω is given by (10.2) again. The following result is the analog of Lemma 10.1 for this case.

Lemma 10.2   *(Scarf, 1960)   In the Gamma-Gamma case as given by (10.5) and (10.2), the following hold.*

(a) The predictive density is given, for $\xi \geq 0$, by

$$\phi(\xi | a, S) = \frac{\Gamma(a+k)}{\Gamma(k)\Gamma(a)} \frac{S^a \xi^{k-1}}{(S+\xi)^{a+k}}.$$

(b) The posterior density (on the unknown parameter, after updating based on observing demand ξ in a period) is gamma with updated shape parameter equal to $a + k$ and updated scale parameter equal to

$$S \circ \xi = S + \xi.$$

That is, the shape parameter increases by k after each observation and the scale parameter increases by the demand observation. Thus, as in the previous subsection, the uncertainty about the unknown parameter ω decreases (to zero) as the number of observations increases. Similarly, the shape parameter is a known function of the number of observations ($a_t = a_1 + k(t - 1)$) and the predictive demand density for period t can be written as

$$\phi_t(\xi | S) = \frac{\Gamma(a_1 + kt)}{\Gamma(k)\Gamma(a_1 + k(t-1))} \frac{S^{a_1 + k(t-1)} \xi^{k-1}}{(S+\xi)^{a_1 + kt}}.$$

10.3   Scalable Problems

We say that a problem is a *single-parameter conjugate problem* if there is a single unknown parameter of the underlying distribution, the initial prior on that parameter is conjugate to that distribution, and the prior at the beginning of period t is fully specified by a single (dimensional) parameter S (in addition to the period index t). Both of the examples discussed in the previous section are single-parameter conjugate problems. We assume henceforth in this chapter that we are solving a single-parameter conjugate problem.

This section explores conditions in which the single parameter of the prior is a scale parameter, and it is possible, as will be seen in the next section, to convert the problem into an equivalent problem with no scale parameter. We start the exploration by assuming the single parameter S must be positive and considering the properties of the *normalized case* in which the parameter S equals one. The parameter S will be suppressed from the notation in this case. For instance, $\phi_t(\xi) = \phi_t(\xi|1)$ denotes the predictive demand density for period t when $S = 1$.

A problem is called *scalable using q and U* if $q : \mathbf{R}_+ \to \mathbf{R}_+$, $U : \mathbf{R}_+ \to \mathbf{R}_+$, $q(1) = 1$, $\int_{\xi=0}^{\infty} U(\xi)\phi_t(\xi)\, d\xi < \infty$ for all t,

$$\phi_t(\xi|S) = \frac{\phi_t\big(\xi/q(S)\big)}{q(S)}, \tag{10.6}$$

and

$$q(S \circ \xi) = q(S)U\big(\xi/q(S)\big). \tag{10.7}$$

The problem is called *scalable* if there exist functions q and U such that the problem is scalable using q and U. The function q can be interpreted as a scaling function and U can be interpreted as the updating function for the normalized case. Equation (10.6) shows how the predictive density of a scalable problem can be determined in terms of the normalized density. If demand is observed to be ξ, the updated scale parameter is given by (10.7). In particular, we normalize the demand observation ξ by dividing by $q(S)$, update that using U, the updating function for the normalized case, and then convert the result back into the unnormalized case, by multiplying by $q(S)$.

We shall see in the next section that there is tremendous value to having a scalable problem, because the problem then only needs to be analyzed for the normalized case of $S = 1$: This normalized case can be coherently formulated in that the recursion refers only to solutions of other normalized problems. The solution for all other cases can be easily derived from the solution to this case. Thus, solving a scalable finite-horizon problem only requires solving a nonstationary normalized problem with a known demand distribution.

Lemma 10.3   *(Azoury, 1985)   A Weibull-Gamma problem, as given by (10.1) and (10.2), is scalable using $q(S) = S^{1/k}$ and $U(x) = (1 + x^k)^{1/k}$.*

Lemma 10.4   *(Scarf, 1960)   A Gamma-Gamma problem, as given by (10.5) and (10.2), is scalable using $q(S) = S$ and $U(x) = 1 + x$.*

These are not the only two known cases of scalable problems. For instance, Azoury (1985) shows that a Uniform-Pareto problem is scalable. In particular, the underlying demand distribution is uniform over $[0, \omega]$ with ω unknown and the prior on ω is a Pareto distribution.

10.4   Dimensionality Reduction

This section presents the results of Scarf (1960) and Azoury (1985), who show that with scalable problems, it is possible to first solve a normalized problem in which the scale parameter S is set to one and then determine the solution to the original, unnormalized problem by scaling the results of the normalized problem in a relatively simple way. In particular, the normalized problem can be interpreted as solving a nonstationary problem with a known demand distribution.

First, let $f_t(x|S)$ denote the minimum expected cost over periods t through N starting with inventory level x and scale parameter S (for the prior) at the beginning of period t. The optimality equations become

$$f_t(x|S) = \min_{y \geq x} \big[G_t(y|S) - cx \big],$$

where

$$G_t(y|S) := cy + L_t(y|S) + \alpha \int_{\xi=0}^{\infty} f_{t+1}(y - \xi|S \circ \xi)\phi_t(\xi|S)\, d\xi,$$

and

$$L_t(y|S) := \int_{\xi=0}^{\infty} \mathcal{L}(y - \xi)\phi_t(\xi|S)\, d\xi.$$

Lemma 10.5   *(Azoury, 1985; Scarf, 1960)*   *(Exercise 10.14)*   If $\mathcal{L}$ and v_{T} *are convex, then a base stock policy is optimal in each period. The optimal base stock level, $S_t(S)$, is a function of the period t and the scale parameter S at the beginning of that period.*

As indicated earlier, the scale parameter S is suppressed when it equals one. For example, $f_t(x) = f_t(x|1)$ and $L_t(y) = L_t(y|1)$.

Lemma 10.6   (Azoury, 1985; Scarf, 1960)   *If a problem is scalable using q and U, and $\mathcal{L}$ is homogeneous of degree one: $\mathcal{L}(ax) = a\mathcal{L}(x)$ for all $a > 0$, then*

$$L_t(y|S) = q(S)L_t\big(y/q(S)\big).$$

Proof   Here,

$$
\begin{aligned}
L_t(y|S) &= \int_{\xi=0}^{\infty} \mathcal{L}(y - \xi)\phi_t(\xi|S)\, d\xi \\
&= \int_{\xi=0}^{\infty} \mathcal{L}(y - \xi)\frac{\phi_t\big(\xi/q(S)\big)}{q(S)}\, d\xi && \text{[by (10.6)]} \\
&= \int_{x=0}^{\infty} \mathcal{L}(y - xq(S))\phi_t(x)\, dx && [x = \xi/q(S)] \\
&= \int_{x=0}^{\infty} \mathcal{L}(zq(S) - xq(S))\phi_t(x)\, dx && [z = y/q(S)] \\
&= \int_{x=0}^{\infty} q(S)\mathcal{L}(z - x)\phi_t(x)\, dx && \text{[homogeneity]} \\
&= q(S)L_t(z) = q(S)L_t\big(y/q(S)\big)
\end{aligned}
$$

$\square$

Define the following functions recursively, for $1 \le t \le N$:

$$
F_t(x) = \min_{y \ge x}\left\{ c(y - x) + L_t(y) + \alpha \int_{\xi=0}^{\infty} U(\xi)F_{t+1}\left(\frac{y - \xi}{U(\xi)}\right)\phi_t(\xi)\, d\xi\right\}, \quad (10.8)
$$

where

$$F_{N+1}(x) := v_{\mathrm{T}}(x).$$

The following result shows that $F_t(x) = f_t(x)$ for all t and x. In particular, (10.8) therefore gives the optimality equations for the normalized problem (in which the scale factor equals one). First, let's interpret (10.8), which has the appearance of the optimality equations for a nonstationary single variable inventory problem with a known demand distribution, ϕ_t, for each t. The only difference is that the optimal value of continuing is scaled: If demand is observed to be ξ in period t, then the inventory level at the beginning of period $t+1$ is divided by $U(\xi)$ to scale it back into an equivalent problem with a scale parameter of $S = 1$. The value of arriving at that normalized state is then scaled back up by $U(\xi)$ to give the appropriate value to the problem being solved.

Theorem 10.1 (*Azoury, 1985*) (*Exercise 10.16*) *If the updating is scalable using* q *and* U, *and* $\mathcal{L}$ *and* v_T *are convex and homogeneous of degree 1, then*

(a) $f_t(x|S) = q(S)F_t(x/q(S))$ *for all* t. *In particular,* $f_t(x) = F_t(x)$.

(b) *The optimal base stock level for a period can be determined by scaling the optimal base stock level for the normalized problem for that period:*

$$S_t(S) = q(S)S_t(1).$$

Exercises

10.1 Given $r > -1$, the gamma function is defined as

$$\Gamma(r+1) := \int_{x=0}^{\infty} x^r e^{-x}\, dx,$$

which can be interpreted as $E(X^r)$, the rth moment of a random variable X that is exponentially distributed with a mean of one. Suppose the random variable Y is exponentially distributed with rate λ (mean $1/\lambda$). Show that

$$E(Y^r) = \frac{\Gamma(r+1)}{\lambda^r}.$$

10.2 (Continuation of Exercise 10.1) Show that

(a) $\Gamma(1) = 1$,

(b) if $r > 0$, then $\Gamma(r+1) = r\Gamma(r)$, and

(c) if $r \geq 2$ is an integer, then $\Gamma(r) = (r-1)! = (r-1)(r-2)\cdots(1)$.

10.3 Suppose D is Weibull with density given by (10.1). Show that D^k is exponentially distributed with rate ω.

Hint: Show that $P(D^k \geq x) = e^{-\omega x}$.

10.4 Suppose that D is Weibull with density given by (10.1). Let $\theta := 1/k$.

(a) Show that the mean of D equals $\omega^{-\theta}\Gamma(1+\theta)$.

(b) Show that the variance of D equals

$$\omega^{-2\theta}\Big[\Gamma(1+2\theta) - \Gamma^2(1+\theta)\Big].$$

(c) Show that the coefficient of variation of D equals

$$\sqrt{\frac{2\Gamma(2\theta)}{\theta\Gamma^2(\theta)} - 1}.$$

Hint: Use Exercises 10.1–10.3.

10.5   Suppose D_1 and D_2 are Weibull random variables. In particular, both have the same shape parameter k but D_1 has scale parameter ω_1 and D_2 has ω_2. Show that D_1 dominates D_2 under FSD (first-order stochastic dominance as in Appendix D) iff $\omega_1 \le \omega_2$.

Hint: Use Exercise 10.3.

10.6   Suppose that (10.1)–(10.3) hold and that $k = 1$: The underlying demand distribution is exponential with an unknown mean.

(a) Show that if $a > 1$, then the mean of the predictive demand distribution is finite and equals $S/(a-1)$.

(b) Show that if $a > 2$, then the variance of the predictive demand distribution is finite and equals $aS^2/[(a-1)^2(a-2)]$, and the coefficient of variation equals $\sqrt{a/(a-2)}$.

10.7   Consider the failure rate of the distribution given in Lemma 10.1(a)–(b). Show that there exists $\gamma \ge 0$ such that the failure rate is increasing on $[0,\gamma)$ and decreasing on $[\gamma,\infty)$. Specify γ explicitly.

10.8   (*Newsvendor-Gamma*)   (Braden and Freimer, 1991)   A distribution Ψ is a *newsvendor distribution with rate ω and shape function d* if $d\colon \mathbf{R}_+ \to \mathbf{R}_+$, d is strictly increasing on $\mathbf{R}_+$, and

$$\Psi(\xi|\omega) = 1 - e^{-\omega d(\xi)}. \tag{10.9}$$

For example, the Weibull of (10.1) is a newsvendor distribution with rate ω and shape function $d(\xi) = \xi^k$. Consider the Newsvendor-Gamma case in which the demand distribution is given by (10.9) with $d(\cdot)$ known, continuous derivative $d'(\cdot)$, ω unknown, and gamma prior on ω given by (10.2). Show that the following hold.

(a) The predictive density is given, for $\xi \geq 0$, by

$$\phi(\xi|a, S) = \frac{aS^a d'(\xi)}{[S + d(\xi)]^{a+1}}.$$

(b) The predictive distribution is given, for $\xi \geq 0$, by

$$\Phi(\xi|a, S) = 1 - \left(\frac{S}{S + d(\xi)}\right)^a.$$

(c) The posterior density (on the unknown parameter, after updating based on observing demand ξ in a period) is gamma with updated shape parameter equal to $a + 1$ and updated scale parameter equal to

$$S \circ \xi = S + d(\xi).$$

10.9 (Continuation of Exercise 10.8) (Braden and Freimer, 1991) Consider an inventory problem in which unmet demands are not backlogged or even observed. If y units are stocked and there is a stockout at the end of the period, then only the fact that demand exceeded y is known. (The exact demand during the period is not observed.) See Lariviere and Porteus (1999) for more.

Show that the posterior density (on the unknown ω), after updating based on observing a stockout, is gamma with updated shape parameter equal to a (left unchanged) and updated scale parameter equal to

$$S \circ \xi = S + d(y).$$

10.10 Show that (10.4) is a newsvendor distribution (as defined in Exercise 10.8) with rate a and shape function $d(\xi) := \ln(1 + \xi^k/S)$.

10.11 Consider the Weibull-Gamma model of Section 10.2. Let μ_t denote the mean of the gamma prior distribution on the unknown rate (of the underlying Weibull) at the beginning of period t. Show that $\mu_{t+1} \leq \mu_t$ iff $\xi_t^k \geq 1/\mu_t$.

10.12   Suppose, given $0 < \zeta < 1$, we seek x such that $\bar{\Phi}(x) = \zeta$. Let $z := \zeta^{1/a}$. Prove that if Φ is given by (10.4), then the solution we seek is given by

$$x = \left(\frac{S(1-z)}{z} \right)^{\theta}.$$

10.13   Prove Lemma 10.2.

10.14   Prove Lemma 10.5.

10.15   Suppose that $f : \mathbf{R} \to \mathbf{R}$ is convex, $U : \mathbf{R}_+ \to \mathbf{R}_+$ is strictly positive on $(0, \infty)$, and $g : \mathbf{R} \to \mathbf{R}$ is defined by

$$g(y) := \int_{\xi=0}^{\infty} U(\xi) f \left(\frac{y - \xi}{U(\xi)} \right) \phi(\xi) \, d\xi,$$

where ϕ is a density of a positive random variable. Show that g is convex.

10.16   Prove Theorem 10.1.

References

Azoury, K. 1985. Bayes solution to dynamic inventory models under unknown demand distribution. *Management Science.* **31** 1150–60.

Barlow, R., F. Proschan. 1965. *Mathematical Theory of Reliability.* John Wiley, New York.

Braden, D., M. Freimer. 1991. Informational dynamics of censored observations. *Management Science.* **37** 1390–404.

DeGroot, M. 1970. *Optimal Statistical Decisions.* McGraw-Hill, New York.

Lariviere, M., E. Porteus. 1999. Stalking information: Bayesian inventory management with unobserved lost sales. *Management Science.* **45** 346–63.

Lee, H., V. Padmanabhan, S. Whang. 1997. Information distortion in a supply chain: The bullwhip effect. *Management Science.* **43** 546–58.

Raiffa, H., R. Schlaifer. 1961. *Applied Statistical Decision Theory.* Graduate School of Business Administration, Harvard University.

Scarf, H. 1959. Bayes solution of the statistical inventory problem. *Annals of Mathematical Statistics.* **30** 490–508.

Scarf, H. 1960. Some remarks on Bayes solutions to the inventory problem. *Naval Research Logistics Quarterly.* **7** 591–96.

11

Infinite-Horizon Theory

This chapter establishes conditions under which the optimality equations and the optimality conditions continue to hold after letting the time horizon of the finite-horizon problem of Chapter 5 go to infinity. Much of the notation of that chapter is used here without comment. After formulating the stationary infinite-horizon problem in general notation, this chapter emphasizes the finite state and action case, to keep the exposition relatively simple. A short discussion of generalizations is given at the end.

11.1 Problem Formulation

We now seek to maximize the expected present value of all returns received, over an infinite-horizon, in a *stationary problem*, in which the returns, transition probabilities, and state and action spaces do not change over time. Many ways exist to define the infinite-horizon values. We use limits of finite-horizon values here. The terminal (salvage, leftover) value function $v_{\mathbf{T}}$ is applied at the end of each possible finite-horizon. We now let n denote a generic planning horizon, so the process will terminate at the end of period n in some state s_{n+1}, and $v_{\mathbf{T}}(s_{n+1})$ will be the assigned terminal value. Many authors assume that the terminal value functions are identically zero, which simplifies the exposition. However, that approach can be unduly restrictive when working with general formulations and when proving the optimality of structured decision rules. We assume that the discount factor is strictly less than one $(0 \leq \alpha < 1)$, which puts us in the realm of what are known as *discounted* problems. Exercise 11.1 touches on some issues that arise in undiscounted problems (when $\alpha = 1$).

This chapter uses the term "policy" in place of "strategy," to conform to common usage. In particular, a generic policy (for implementation over a possibly infinite horizon) is denoted by $\pi = (\pi_1, \pi_2, \ldots)$. Let $v_t^n(\pi, s)$ denote the expected present value, evaluated at the beginning of period t, of the returns received in periods t through n given that the process starts period t in state s and policy π is implemented. It is the value of the returns received, including any terminal value, over periods t through n when implementing policy π. Thus,

$$v_t^n(\pi, s) = E\left\{ \sum_{\tau=t}^{n} \alpha^{\tau-t} r(s_\tau, \pi_\tau(s_\tau)) + \alpha^{n-t+1} v_{\mathbf{T}}(s_{n+1}) \right\}, \qquad (11.1)$$

where, as before, π_τ is the decision rule prescribed by policy π for period τ. Let

$$v_{n+1}^n(\pi, s) := v_{\mathbf{T}}(s)$$

for every π and s: The return in period $n+1$ (through the end of period n) simply equals the terminal value function. Thus, we can write (11.1) recursively, as in (5.1), as

$$v_t^n(\pi, s) = r\big(s, \pi_t(s)\big) + \sum_{j \in \mathcal{S}} q_{sj}^{\pi_t(s)} v_{t+1}^n(\pi, j), \qquad (11.2)$$

for $1 \leq t \leq n$, all states s, and all admissible π.

As usual, when we want to talk about the vector of present values yielded by a given policy, we suppress s from the notation and write $v_t^n(\pi)$. Thus, as in (5.4), (11.2) can be written in operator notation as

$$v_t^n(\pi) = H(\pi_t) v_{t+1}^n(\pi). \qquad (11.3)$$

Here and henceforth, when $t = 1$, we suppress the subscript and any reference to period 1. Thus, we write $v^n(\pi)$ for $v_1^n(\pi)$, the expected return over an n period horizon under policy π.

Let

$$\bar{v}_t(\pi, s) := \limsup_{n \to \infty} v_t^n(\pi, s),$$

and

$$\underline{v}_t(\pi, s) := \lim_{n \to \infty} v_t^n(\pi, s),$$

when it exists. We say $v_t(\pi, s)$ is the infinite-horizon value of starting at state s in period t and implementing policy π. It is the limit of the finite-horizon values when such limits exist. Sometimes the limits do not exist in all cases, so the limit superior is used. Formally,

$$\bar{v}_t(\pi, s) := \lim_{N \to \infty} \sup_{n \geq N} v_t^n(\pi, s).$$

For example, if we had the sequence $\{0, 1, 0, 1, \ldots\}$, then the liminf is 0 and the limsup is 1. Liminfs and limsups exist, although they are not necessarily finite for all sequences of real numbers. If a regular limit doesn't exist, then the limsup takes the limit of the best possible convergent subsequence.

A policy π^* is *(infinite-horizon) optimal at state s for period t* if

$$v_t(\pi^*, s) \geq \bar{v}_t(\pi, s) \text{ for every } \pi \in \Pi.$$

The limit of the finite-horizon values for such a policy must exist. Such a policy must yield the maximal value starting from state s in period t and continuing forever. And that value must be at least as good as the best of all possible convergent subsequences of values. Thus, we're asking a lot of an optimal policy: We do so because we can get it. A policy π^* is *optimal for period t* if it is optimal at state s for period t for every state $s \in \mathcal{S}$. When $t = 1$, we speak of policies that are *(infinite-horizon) optimal at state s* and *(infinite-horizon) optimal*.

Let

$$f_t(s) := \sup_{\pi \in \Pi} \bar{v}_t(\pi, s),$$

which is called the *optimal (infinite-horizon) value of starting at state s in period t*. We call the resulting function f_t the *optimal (infinite-horizon) value function for period t*. Thus, π^* is infinite-horizon optimal if $v(\pi^*) = f$.

11.2   Mathematical Preparations

Let V, the set of admissible value functions introduced in Chapter 5, be en-
dowed with what is called the L^∞ metric ρ, which is defined as

$$\rho(u,v) := \sup_{s \in S} |u(s) - v(s)| \tag{11.4}$$

and gives the maximum absolute distance between the two functions/vectors
u and v. See Exercises 11.2 and 11.3, Kolmogorov and Fomin (1957), Varga
(1962), Royden (1968), and Young (1971) for more about metrics and related
concepts.

A metric of two vectors is a relative measure of how far apart the two vectors
are. Think freely of it as a distance function. The pair (ρ, V) is a *metric
space*. When ρ is clear, we also say that V itself is a metric space. Note that
$u, v \in V$ implies that $\rho(u,v) < \infty$.

Given $u, v \in V$, let $a := \inf_s[u(s) - v(s)]$ and $b := \sup_s[u(s) - v(s)]$,
the smallest and largest differences (not absolute) between u and v. Then
$\rho(u,v) = \max(b, -a)$. Let e denote the vector of ones (the function equal to
one everywhere: $e_s = e(s) = 1$ for all $s \in S$). If a and b are arbitrary real
numbers such that $ae \le u - v \le be$, then $\rho(u,v) \le \max(b, -a)$.

An operator H $(H : V \to V)$ is an α-*contraction* if $\alpha \ge 0$ and, for all
$u, v \in V$,

$$\rho(Hu, Hv) \le \alpha\rho(u,v).$$

An operator H is a *contraction* if H is an α-contraction for some $\alpha \in [0,1)$:
If you apply the operator to two different vectors, the resulting vectors are
closer together. For example, if $\alpha = .9$, then the maximum distance between
Hu and Hv is no more than 90% of the maximum distance between u and
v.

Recall that $H_\delta : V \to V$, which was defined in Chapter 5 as

$$H_\delta v := r_\delta + Q_\delta v,$$

is isotone, by Lemma 5.2.

Lemma 11.1

(a) If $ae \le u - v \le be$, then, for each $\delta \in \Delta$,

$$\alpha ae \le H_\delta u - H_\delta v \le \alpha be. \tag{11.5}$$

(b) The operator H_δ is an α-contraction for each $\delta \in \Delta$.

(c) (Denardo, 1967)   The optimal value operator A is an α-contraction.

Proof   (a) Here, $H_\delta u - H_\delta v = Q_\delta(u - v) \le Q_\delta be = \alpha be$, the first equality by definition, the inequality by $Q_\delta \ge 0$, and the last equality by $Q_\delta e = \alpha e$. Similarly, $H_\delta u - H_\delta v \ge \alpha ae$.

(b) Let $a := \inf_s[u(s) - v(s)]$ and $b := \sup_s[u(s) - v(s)]$, so that $ae \le u - v \le be$, and, in particular, $\rho(u, v) = \max(b, -a)$. By (a), (11.5) holds. Thus,

$$\rho(H_\delta u, H_\delta v) \le \max(\alpha b, -\alpha a) = \alpha \max(b, -a) = \alpha \rho(u, v).$$

(c) A proof is given for the case in which an optimizing decision rule attains the optimization for each v: For each $v \in V$, there exists $\delta \in \Delta$ such that $H_\delta v = Av$.

Given u, select a decision rule δ such that $Au = H_\delta u$. Thus,

$$
\begin{aligned}
Au &= H_\delta u \\
&\le H_\delta v + \alpha be && [\text{H_δ is isotone}] \\
&\le Av + \alpha be. && [\text{definition of } A]
\end{aligned}
$$

Similarly, $Au \ge Av + \alpha ae$. Thus, $\alpha ae \le Au - Av \le \alpha be$. $\square$

We now present and prove the Banach fixed-point theorem, also called the contraction-mapping theorem, which states that a contraction mapping has a unique fixed point that can be computed as the limit of a recursion. This theorem can be found in most textbooks on functional analysis, such as Kolmogorov and Fomin (1957). We do this to illustrate the flavor of the proofs used in the infinite-horizon theory.

A *Cauchy sequence* is a sequence of elements/points in V such that

$$\rho(v_n, v_m) \to 0 \text{ as } n, m \to \infty.$$

A *complete metric space* is a metric space (ρ, V) in which all Cauchy sequences converge. That is, given a Cauchy sequence of elements of V, there exists a $v \in V$ such that

$$\lim_{n \to \infty} \rho(v_n, v) = 0.$$

Theorem 11.1   *(Banach Fixed-Point Theorem)   Suppose that H is a contraction defined on a complete metric space. For $v \in V$, define $H^0 v := v$, and, for $n \geq 1$, $H^n v := H(H^{n-1} v)$. Then the following hold.*

(a) For each $v \in V$, there exists $v^* \in V$ such that

$$v^* = \lim_{n \to \infty} H^n v. \tag{11.6}$$

That is, the limit exists and is an element of V.

(b) Each such v^* is a fixed point of H: $v^* = H v^*$. In particular, the operator H has at least one fixed point.

(c) The operator H has a unique fixed point in V. Consequently, every v^* constructed in (a), being a fixed point of H by (b), is the same: $\lim_{n \to \infty} H^n v$ is independent of v.

(d) Letting v^* denote the unique fixed point of H,

$$\rho(v^*, H^n v) \leq \alpha^n \rho(v^*, v) \quad \text{for every } n = 1, 2, \dots .$$

Proof   (a) Fix $v \in V$. Let $v_0 := v$, and $v_n := H v_{n-1}$ for $n \geq 1$. Assume without loss of generality that $n \leq m$. Then

$$
\begin{aligned}
\rho(v_n, v_m) &= \rho(H v_{n-1}, H v_{m-1}) \\
&\leq \alpha \rho(v_{n-1}, v_{m-1}) && [H \text{ is a contraction}] \\
&\leq \cdots \leq \alpha^n \rho(v, v_{m-n}) && [\text{recursion}] \\
&\leq \alpha^n [\rho(v, v_1) + \rho(v_1, v_2) + \\
&\qquad \cdots + \rho(v_{m-n-1}, v_{m-n})] && [\text{triangle inequality}] \\
&\leq \alpha^n [\rho(v, v_1) + \alpha \rho(v, v_1) + \\
&\qquad \cdots + \alpha^{m-n-1} \rho(v, v_1)] && [\text{contractions}] \\
&\leq \frac{\alpha^n \rho(v, v_1)}{(1 - \alpha)} && [\text{geometric series}] \\
&\to 0 \text{ as } m, n \to \infty. && [0 \leq \alpha < 1]
\end{aligned}
$$

So $\{v_n\}$ forms a Cauchy sequence. Since (ρ, V) is complete, there exists a limit (function) v^* that is an element of V such that (11.6) holds.

(b) We now show that v^* is a fixed point of H. Fix $\epsilon > 0$. Select N such that $n \geq N$ implies that $\rho(v_{n-1}, v^*) \leq \epsilon/2$. Then $n \geq N$ implies that

$$
\begin{aligned}
\rho(v^*, H v^*) &\leq \rho(v^*, v_n) + \rho(v_n, H v^*) && [\text{triangle inequality}] \\
&\leq \frac{\epsilon}{2} + \rho(H v_{n-1}, H v^*) && [n + 1 \geq N] \\
&\leq \frac{\epsilon}{2} + \alpha \rho(v_{n-1}, v^*) && [\text{contraction}] \\
&\leq \frac{\epsilon}{2} + \alpha \epsilon/2 \leq \epsilon.
\end{aligned}
$$

Since ϵ is arbitrary, we must have $\rho(v^*, Hv^*) = 0$, and, therefore, $v^* = Hv^*$.

(c) Suppose v° is another fixed point of H. Then

$$\rho(v^*, v^\circ) = \rho(Hv^*, Hv^\circ) \leq \alpha \rho(v^*, v^\circ),$$

which, since $0 \leq \alpha < 1$, implies that $\rho(v^*, v^\circ) = 0$, and v^* is the unique fixed point of H.

(d) That $\rho(v^*, H^n v) \leq \alpha^n \rho(v^*, v)$ follows directly from $v^* = H^n v^*$ and n contraction operations.

$\square$

11.3   Finite State and Action Theory

We assume in this section, as we did in Section 5.2, that the state space S is a finite set $\{1, 2, \ldots, S\}$ and that the set of admissible actions A_s is a finite set for each state s. All decision rules are admissible. All policies are admissible and denoted generically by $\pi = (\pi_1, \pi_2, \ldots)$, where each π_t is a decision rule. $V = \mathbf{R}^S$, so all admissible value functions are S-vectors. The probability of making a transition from state s into state j when action a is made is denoted by p_{sj}^a. The immediate returns are all finite. General notation is not needed to address the finite state and action case. However, the proofs can be easily understood in this case and do not require many changes for more general cases.

Theorem 11.2   *(Shapley, 1953)*

(a) *The infinite-horizon values exist for every policy: $v_t(\pi)$ exists and is finite for every t and $\pi \in \Pi$, and*

(b) *they satisfy the recursion*

$$v_t(\pi, s) = r\big(s, \pi_t(s)\big) + \alpha \sum_j p_{sj}^{\pi_t(s)} v_{t+1}(\pi, j),$$

which, in matrix notation, is

$$v_t(\pi) = r(\pi_t) + \alpha P(\pi_t) v_{t+1}(\pi),$$

which, in operator notation, as in (5.4), is

$$v_t(\pi) = H(\pi_t) v_{t+1}(\pi).$$

Proof   A routine explicit proof can be found in Porteus (1975, 1982).   □

Stationarity

A *stationary policy* uses the same decision rule in each period. Following convention, $\delta^\infty := (\delta, \delta, \cdots)$ denotes the stationary policy that applies decision rule δ in each period.

Lemma 11.2   *(Denardo, 1967)   For every decision rule $\delta \in \Delta$, there exists $v_\delta \in V$ with the following properties.*

(a) $v_\delta = \lim_{n \to \infty} H_\delta^n v$ for any $v \in V$.

(b) v_δ is the unique fixed point of H_δ.

(c) If $\pi = \delta^\infty$, then $v_t(\pi) = v_\delta$ for all t.

Proof   It is known that if V is a finite dimensional vector space, then (ρ, V) is complete. Fix $\delta \in \Delta$. Since $\alpha < 1$, H_δ is a contraction by Lemma 11.1. Let v_δ denote the unique fixed point of H_δ, guaranteed to exist by Theorem 11.1. Parts (a) and (b) then follow from Theorem 11.1.

(c) Suppose that $\pi = \delta^\infty$. Then, by (11.3),

$$v_t^n(\pi) = H_\delta v_{t+1}^n(\pi) = \cdots = H_\delta^{n-t+1} v_{\mathbf{T}}.$$

By (a), because $v_{\mathbf{T}} \in V$, the limit as n approaches ∞ not only exists but equals v_δ.   □

Thus, in this case, because the state space, the sets of admissible actions, and the immediate returns are all stationary, $v_t(\pi)$ is also stationary when $\pi = \delta^\infty$ and equals v_δ, which can therefore be interpreted as the infinite-horizon value from the stationary policy δ^∞, which uses decision rule δ in every period.

Because of the form of H_δ, we can write $v_\delta = H_\delta v_\delta$ as

$$v_\delta = r_\delta + Q_\delta v_\delta, \tag{11.7}$$

which, written pointwise, becomes

$$v_\delta(s) = r(s, \delta(s)) + \sum_j q_{sj}^{\delta(s)} v_\delta(j).$$

Note that, given a stationary policy δ^∞, the expected discounted value from using that policy over n periods is given by

$$v^n(\delta^\infty) = H_\delta^n v_{\mathrm{T}},$$

which, by Lemma 11.2, converges to the infinite-horizon value for that policy. Indeed, we will get the same result *regardless* of the particular terminal value function we use to define the infinite-horizon values.

Neumann Series

Recall from Chapter 5 that P_δ denotes the S by S matrix of transition probabilities when decision rule δ is implemented, with ijth element

$$[P_\delta]_{ij} = p_{ij}^{\delta(i)},$$

$Q_\delta := \alpha P_\delta$ denotes the effective transition matrix, and r_δ denotes the vector of immediate returns, with ith element

$$[r_\delta]_i = r(i, \delta(i)).$$

With a stationary policy δ^∞, we have, by iterating on (11.7), that

$$v_\delta = r_\delta + Q_\delta v_\delta$$
$$= r_\delta + Q_\delta r_\delta + Q_\delta^2 r_\delta + \cdots$$
$$= (I + Q_\delta + Q_\delta^2 + \cdots) r_\delta.$$

The series in parentheses is called a *Neumann Series*.

Lemma 11.3   *(Exercise 11.8)*   If $\alpha < 1$, then $I - Q_\delta$ is invertible, and

$$I + Q_\delta + Q_\delta^2 + \cdots = (I - Q_\delta)^{-1}.$$

Lemma 11.3 becomes particularly plausible if you reorganize (11.7) as

$$v_\delta - Q_\delta v_\delta = r_\delta,$$

which can be rewritten as

$$(I - Q_\delta) v_\delta = r_\delta.$$

If $I - Q_\delta$ is invertible, we get

$$v_\delta = (I - Q_\delta)^{-1} r_\delta.$$

Theorem 11.3   *(Shapley, 1953; Blackwell, 1965)*

(a) The optimal value functions are stationary and satisfy:

$$f_t(s) = f(s) = \max_{a \in A_s} \{ r(s, a) + \alpha \sum_j p_{sj}^a f(j) \}, \qquad \text{(OE)}$$

which, in operator notation, reduces to the single optimality equation

$$f = Af, \qquad \text{(OE)}$$

which states that the optimal value function is a fixed point of the optimal value operator.

(b) The optimal value function is the unique fixed point of the optimal value operator A, and satisfies

$$f = \lim_{n \to \infty} A^n v \quad \text{for every } v \in V.$$

Proof   A routine, explicit proof of (a) can be found in Porteus (1982).

(b) By Lemma 11.1, A is a contraction, so Theorem 11.1 applies.   □

In this case, the optimal value function is the same regardless of the terminal value function you use to define the finite-horizon values. The optimality equation is a *functional equation* because the function f appears on both sides of the equation.

Theorem 11.4   *(Blackwell, 1965)*

(a) (Optimality Criterion)   If a decison rule δ satisfies

$$H_\delta f = Af,$$

then the stationary policy δ^∞ is optimal.

(b) In the finite state and action case, a stationary optimal policy exists.

Proof   By Theorem 11.1(a), we have

$$f = Af = H_\delta f = \cdots = H_\delta^n f,$$

which, by Lemma 11.2, converges to v_δ as n get large, which implies that δ^∞ is optimal. In the finite case, the suprema in Af are attained, so there exists a decision rule for which (a) applies.   □

Suppose you somehow are given the optimal infinite-horizon value function f, which exists. You need consider only the one period problem with f as the arrival value function: If you pick out the maximizing action for each state and assemble those actions into a decision rule, then the resulting stationary policy will be optimal.

Optimality of Structured Policies

We now see conditions under which a structured policy is optimal. Significantly, the terminal value function v_T need not be structured, because the infinite-horizon values do not depend on the terminal value function used to define them.

Theorem 11.5   *If*

(a) $V^* \subset V$ and (ρ, V^*) is complete;

(b) (Attainment)   If $v \in V^*$, then there exists $\delta^* \in \Delta^*$ such that $H_{\delta^*} v = Av$; and

(c) (Preservation) $A: V^* \to V^*$; then

(d) The optimal value function f is structured; and

(e) There exists an optimal structured stationary policy.

Proof   Pick arbitrary $v \in V^*$. Then, by (c), $A^n v \in V^*$ for every n. It is straightforward to show that $\{A^n v\}$ is a Cauchy sequence in V^*. Thus, since (ρ, V^*) is complete, $f = \lim_{n\to\infty} A^n v$ must be structured (an element of V^*). That proves (d). Select $\delta \in \Delta^*$ such that $H_\delta f = Af$. Such a selection is justified, since $f \in V^*$ and by (b). Then δ^∞ is optimal by the Optimality Criterion of Theorem 11.4(a).   □

11.4   Generalizations

Appropriate generalizations of Theorems 11.2 through 11.4 exist. The state and action spaces need not be finite. The single-stage value operators corresponding to a given decision rule need not be affine, so that certain risk sensitive problems and stochastic games can be encompassed. The problems need not be stationary, so that returns, transition probabilities, state and actions spaces, and so on all can depend on the period. The discount factor can depend not only on the period but also on the state and action. See Porteus (1975, 1982) for details.

Exercises

11.1   Consider the following finite state, denumerable action infinite-horizon *undiscounted* model. There are two states: $S = \{0, 1\}$, and the set of admissible actions is denumerable: $A_s = \{1, 2, \ldots\}$ for each $s \in S$, $p_{00}^a = 1$ for each a, $p_{10}^a = 1/a$, and the returns consist of $r(0, a) = 0$, and $r(1, a) = 1$ for each a. The terminal values are zero.

(a) Develop an explicit expression for $v_t^n(\pi, s)$ for $t = 1$.

(b) Show that the expected total return, over an infinite horizon, for an arbitrary stationary policy δ^∞ is finite.

Hint: Show, for $t = 1$, that

$$\lim_{n \to \infty} v_t^n(\delta^\infty, s)$$

is finite for each $s \in S$ and $\delta \in \Delta$.

(c) Construct a nonstationary policy π such that $v_t(\pi, 1) = \infty$ for every t.

Hint: Construct a sequence of positive real numbers $\{a_t\}$ such that

$$\lim_{n \to \infty} (1 - 1/a_1)(1 - 1/a_2) \cdots (1 - 1/a_n) \geq \frac{1}{2}.$$

Show that such a sequence exists. Then let $\delta_t(1) = a_t$ for every t.

(d) What can you conclude from (b) and (c)?

(e) Analyze the example assuming a discount factor $0 < \alpha < 1$. (In particular, if there exists an optimal stationary policy, provide one. If there does not exist an optimal stationary policy but there exists an optimal nonstationary policy, provide one. If there do not exist any optimal nonstationary policies, explain why.)

11.2   A *metric* on V is a real valued function $\rho(\cdot, \cdot)$ defined on $V \times V$ such that, for every $u, v \in V$,

(a) $\rho(u, v) \geq 0$.

(b) $\rho(u, v) = 0$ iff $u = v$.

(c) $\rho(u, v) = \rho(v, u)$. (symmetry)

(d) $\rho(u, v) \leq \rho(u, w) + \rho(w, v)$ for every $w \in V$. (triangle inequality)

Suppose that $V = \mathbf{R}^S$. Show that ρ, as defined by (11.4), satisfies (a)–(d).

11.3   A *norm* on V is a real valued function $\|\cdot\|$ defined on V such that

(a) $\|v\| \geq 0$ for all $v \in V$.

(b) $\|av\| = |a|\|v\|$ for all scalars $a \in \mathbf{R}$.

(c) $\|v\| = 0$ iff $v = 0$.

(d) $\|u + v\| \leq \|u\| + \|v\|$ for all $u, v \in V$.

A norm of a vector is a relative measure of how large that vector is. If we start with a given norm, the *induced metric* is defined as

$$\rho(u, v) := \|u - v\|.$$

Suppose that $V = \mathbf{R}^S$. Identify the norm that induces the L^∞ metric on V given by (11.4). (Specify its explicit definition and show that it satisfies (a)–(d).)

11.4   Suppose that $V = \mathbf{R}$ and that ρ is given by (11.4). Show that (ρ, V) is complete.

11.5   Given real numbers $a < b$, suppose that V is the set of convex functions defined on $[a, b]$ and that ρ is given by (11.4). Show that (ρ, V) is complete.

Hint: Use Exercise 11.4 to guarantee the existence of a real valued (finite) limit function. Then show that this limit function must be convex.

11.6   Prove Lemma 11.1(c) for the case in which an optimizing decision rule does not necessarily attain the optimization for each v, but an ϵ-optimal decision rule does exist: For each $v \in V$ and $\epsilon > 0$, there exists $\delta \in \Delta$ such that $Av \le H_\delta v + \epsilon e$.

11.7   Suppose that, for every $v \in V$, there exists $M > 0$ such that $\rho(v, H_\delta v) \le M$, for all δ. Prove that, for arbitrary t and π, $v_t^n(\pi)$ forms a Cauchy sequence in n, for $n = t, t+1, \ldots$.

Hint: Modify the proof of Theorem 11.1(a).

11.8   Let P be a stochastic matrix, let $0 < \alpha < 1$, and let $Q := \alpha P$. Show that the matrix $(I - Q)$ is invertible and that

$$(I - Q)^{-1} = I + Q + Q^2 + \cdots = \sum_{n=0}^{\infty} Q^n.$$

References

Blackwell, D. 1965. Discounted dynamic programming. *Annals of Mathematical Statistics*. **36** 226–35.

Denardo, E. 1967. Contraction mappings in the theory underlying dynamic programming, *SIAM Review*. **9** 165–77.

Kolmogorov, A., S. Fomin. 1957. *Elements of the Theory of Functions and Functional Analysis, Volumes I and II*. Graylock Press, Rochester, N.Y.

Porteus, E. 1975. On the optimality of structured policies in countable stage decision processes. *Management Science*. **22** 148–57.

Porteus, E. 1982. Conditions for characterizing the structure of optimal strategies in infinite horizon dynamic programs. *Journal of Optimization Theory and Applications*. **37** 419–32.

Royden, H. 1968. *Real Analysis*. Macmillan, New York.

Shapley, L. 1953. Stochastic games. *Proceedings of the National Academy of Sciences*. **39** 1095–100.

Varga, R. 1962. *Matrix Iterative Analysis*. Prentice-Hall, Englewood Cliffs, N.J.

Young, D. 1971. *Iterative Solution of Large Linear Systems*. Academic Press, New York.

12

Bounds and
Successive Approximations

Suppose we have a stationary finite state and action problem, and we simply keep solving longer-horizon finite-horizon problems. That is, we start with the terminal value function v_T and apply the optimal value operator repeatedly, getting $A^n v_\mathrm{T}$ for $n = 1, 2, \ldots$. We know that the optimal value function f is the unique fixed point of A and that

$$f = \lim_{n \to \infty} A^n v \quad \text{for every } v \in V.$$

Since $v_\mathrm{T} \in V$, that approach will converge to the optimal value function. But if we have $A^n v_\mathrm{T}$ for some n, how close are we? And how good is the stationary policy formed from the latest decision rule? For example, recalling the e-Rite-Way example from Chapter 3, the same decision rule was optimal when the horizon was $n = 3$ and $n = 4$. Is that decision rule optimal for the infinite-horizon problem?

A closely related question revolves around the infinite-horizon value from a given stationary policy: We know from Lemma 11.2 that

$$v_\delta = \lim_{n \to \infty} H_\delta^n v \quad \text{for every } v \in V.$$

How close is $H_\delta^n v$ to v_δ for a given n? Is there a better estimate of v_δ than simply $H_\delta^n v$?

In addition, we shall show that as we get better bounds on the optimal value function, we may be able to eliminate certain decisions from further consideration by identifying them as being nonoptimal in the infinite-horizon problem.

12.1 Preliminary Results

Lemma 12.1   If $ae \leq u - v \leq be$, then, for $n = 1, 2, \ldots$,

$$\alpha^n ae \leq H_\delta^n u - H_\delta^n v \leq \alpha^n be.$$

Proof   Lemma 11.1(a) gives the result for $n = 1$. Given $\alpha^{n-1}ae \leq H_\delta^{n-1}u - H_\delta^{n-1}v \leq \alpha^{n-1}be$, the inductive step follows from Lemma 11.1(a) by a suitable assignment of roles: $\alpha^{n-1}a$ plays the role of a, $H_\delta^{n-1}u$ plays the role of u, and so on.   □

Suppose we have a vector estimate v of v_δ and have computed $H_\delta v$. For instance, v might be the terminal value function. We want to know how close $H_\delta v$ is to v_δ. Our answer will be given in Lemma 12.3, which builds on the following result.

Lemma 12.2   If $ae \leq H_\delta v - v \leq be$, then

$$\frac{\alpha(1 - \alpha^n)ae}{1 - \alpha} \leq H_\delta^{n+1}v - H_\delta v \leq \frac{\alpha(1 - \alpha^n)be}{1 - \alpha}.$$

Proof   Assume inductively that, for all $i \leq n$,

$$\frac{\alpha(1 - \alpha^{i-1})ae}{1 - \alpha} \leq H_\delta^i v - H_\delta v \leq \frac{\alpha(1 - \alpha^{i-1})be}{1 - \alpha}.$$

Pick the case when $i = n$. Have $H_\delta^n v$ play the role of u and $H_\delta v$ play the role of v in Lemma 11.1(a) to get

$$\frac{\alpha^2(1 - \alpha^{n-1})ae}{1 - \alpha} \leq H_\delta^{n+1}v - H_\delta^2 v \leq \frac{\alpha^2(1 - \alpha^{n-1})be}{1 - \alpha}.$$

Thus,

$$H_\delta^{n+1}v \leq H_\delta^2 v + \frac{\alpha^2(1 - \alpha^{n-1})be}{1 - \alpha} \qquad \text{[rewrite the right side]}$$

$$\leq H_\delta v + \alpha be + \frac{(\alpha^2 - \alpha^{n+1})be}{1 - \alpha} \qquad \text{[inductive hypothesis for } i = 2]$$

$$= H_\delta v + \frac{\alpha(1-\alpha)e}{1-\alpha} + \frac{(\alpha^2 - \alpha^{n+1})be}{1-\alpha}$$

$$= H_\delta v + \frac{\alpha(1-\alpha^n)e}{1-\alpha}.$$

The other inequality follows similarly.   □

Lemma 12.3   *If* $ae \le H_\delta v - v \le be$, *then*

$$v + \frac{ae}{1-\alpha} \le v_\delta \le v + \frac{be}{1-\alpha} \qquad (12.1)$$

and

$$H_\delta v + \frac{\alpha ae}{1-\alpha} \le v_\delta \le H_\delta v + \frac{\alpha be}{1-\alpha}. \qquad (12.2)$$

Proof   We obtain (12.2) by taking the limit as $n \to \infty$ in Lemma 12.2 and using the fact that $\lim_{n\to\infty} H_\delta^n v = v_\delta$, by Lemma 11.2.

We prove only the right-hand side of (12.1), since the left-hand side follows similarly:

$$v_\delta \le H_\delta v + \frac{\alpha be}{1-\alpha} \qquad \text{[by (12.2)]}$$

$$\le v + be + \frac{\alpha be}{1-\alpha} \qquad \text{[by hypothesis]}$$

$$= v + \frac{be}{1-\alpha}.$$

So (12.2) is a tighter bound than (12.1).   □

Bounds on the Optimal Value Function

Recall the definition of the optimal value operator A:

$$Av := \sup_{\delta \in \Delta} H_\delta v.$$

That is, Av gives the optimal value function for the one-period problem in which v is the arrival value function (for the end of that period). We defined $A^n v$ as $A^n v := A(A^{n-1}v)$.

Lemma 12.4   *(Exercise 12.1)*   *If* $ae \le u - v \le be$, *then*

$$\alpha^n ae \le A^n u - A^n v \le \alpha^n be.$$

Furthermore, if $ae \le Av - v \le be$, *then*

$$\frac{\alpha(1 - \alpha^n)ae}{1 - \alpha} \le A^{n+1}v - Av \le \frac{\alpha(1 - \alpha^n)be}{1 - \alpha},$$

Theorem 12.1   *(Exercise 12.2)*   *If* $ae \le Av - v \le be$, *then*

$$v + \frac{ae}{1 - \alpha} \le f \le v + \frac{be}{1 - \alpha}, \tag{12.3}$$

and

$$Av + \frac{\alpha ae}{1 - \alpha} \le f \le Av + \frac{\alpha be}{1 - \alpha}. \tag{12.4}$$

The bounds in (12.3) were first given by MacQueen (1966) and those in (12.4) by Porteus (1971). A successive approximation step will typically start with a function v and compute Av. A useful way to apply Theorem 12.1 is to select $a = \min_i[Av - v]_i$ and $b = \max_i[Av - v]_i$. The required condition $ae \le Av - v \le be$ then holds. The bounds in (12.3) are easily interpreted. The quantity a can be thought of as the minimum amount that will be gained in each period (starting from v). The present value of these gains is $a + \alpha a + \alpha^2 a + \ldots = a/(1 - \alpha)$. Thus, the worst that can be obtained is the left-hand side of (12.3). The right-hand side is interpreted analogously. The bounds in (12.4) follow similarly, but use the fact that Av has already been obtained.

Although either (12.3) or (12.4) can be used to construct bounds, the bounds given by (12.4) are tighter. Formally, we construct

$$\underline{f} = Av + \frac{\alpha ae}{1 - \alpha} \quad \text{and} \quad \bar{f} = Av + \frac{\alpha be}{1 - \alpha} \tag{12.5}$$

and obtain, by (12.4), $\underline{f} \le f \le \bar{f}$.

12.2   Elimination of Nonoptimal Actions

Recall the definition of the local income function in Chapter 5:

$$h_i^k v := h(i, k, v) = r(i, k) + \sum_j q_{ij}^k v_j,$$

where q_{ij}^k is the discounted probability of moving into state j in one period, starting in state i and making decision k. Thus, $h_i^k v$ is the expected present value in a one-period problem starting in state i and making decision k, given arrival value function v.

Suppose, after a successive approximation step, that upper and lower bounds, as in (12.5), are computed. This section shows how to use these bounds to identify decisions as being nonoptimal before getting the optimal value function exactly. Once a decision is known to be nonoptimal for a certain state, its $h_i^k v$ value need not be computed at subsequent successive approximation steps, which can reduce the computation time.

Theorem 12.2   *(MacQueen, 1966)   Suppose $\underline{f} \leq f \leq \bar{f}$. If, at state i, there are decisions k and d such that $h_i^k \bar{f} < h_i^d \underline{f}$, then decision k is nonoptimal for state i.*

Proof   The idea is that if the best you can get using one decision is strictly worse than the worst you can possibly get with another, then the first cannot be optimal. Pick any decision rule that uses decision k in state i. Then

$$
\begin{aligned}
[v_\delta]_i &= h_i^k v_\delta & &[v_\delta = H_\delta v_\delta] \\
&\leq h_i^k \bar{f} & &[v_\delta \leq \bar{f} \text{ and isotonicity}] \\
&< h_i^d \underline{f} & &[\text{hypothesis}] \\
&\leq h_i^d f & &[\underline{f} \leq f \text{ and isotonicity}] \\
&\leq \max_a h_i^a f & &[= [Af]_i] \\
&= f_i. & &[\text{Optimality Equation}]
\end{aligned}
$$

□

Theorem 12.3   *(Porteus, 1971, 1975)   (Exercise 12.3)   Given $v \in V$, let $a := \min_i [Av - v]_i$ and $b := \max_i [Av - v]_i$.*

(a) (Basic Optimality Test)   If

$$
h_i^k v < [Av]_i - \frac{\alpha(b - a)}{1 - \alpha},
$$

then k is nonoptimal at i.

(b) (Deferred Optimality Test)   If there exists a decision d such that

$$
h_i^k (Av) < h_i^d (Av) - \frac{\alpha^2 (b - a)}{1 - \alpha},
$$

then k is nonoptimal for i.

The basic optimality test is based on (12.3) and requires computation of Av before it can be applied. That is, after computing $h_i^k v$ for all i and k (to get Av), you must identify $h_i^k v$ for each decision k that you wish to test. If there are not too many states and actions, it is reasonable to store all such values and check them against the test quantity. However, if there are many states and actions, there may not be enough fast memory available to store everything needed. In this case, use of the basic test requires either regenerating the values (which takes time) or retrieving them from slower storage (which also takes time).

The deferred optimality test is designed for such an environment. Once one iteration is complete, Av, a, and b have all been computed. At the next iteration, Av will take the place of v and $A(Av)$ will be computed. That requires computing $h_i^k(Av)$ for each i and k. The deferred test can therefore be applied right when that quantity is computed. (The action d is the best action found so far during this iteration.) While this test is not as sharp as the basic one, it allows the $h_i^k(Av)$ quantities to be thrown out after seeing if it generates the best action so far during this iteration or can be eliminated as nonoptimal. Further details can be found in Porteus (1975).

Numerical Example: e-Rite-Way

We illustrate the bounds we obtain at each iteration of solving longer finite-horizon problems and illustrate the basic optimality test. Our initial guess, for the one-period problem, was $v = 0$. The first six columns of the table below come from Chapter 3.

One-Period Problem

i	v_i	$h_i^0 v$	$h_i^1 v$	$h_i^2 v$	$[Av - v]_i$	T_i	$\underline{f}_i$	$\bar{f}_i$
1	0	0.08	-0.01	-0.08	0.08	-142.48	8.00	150.56
2	0	1.52	1.39	0.97	1.52	-141.04	9.44	152.00

Column seven gives the test quantity for that state from Theorem 12.3(a), namely,

$$T_i := [Av]_i - \frac{\alpha(b - a)}{1 - \alpha}.$$

In particular, $h_i^k v$ must be less than this test quantity for k to be identified as nonoptimal at state i. To compute these test quantities, Theorem 12.3 says to select a as the smallest difference between Av and v, namely, $a = 0.08$, and b as the largest difference, namely, $b = 1.52$. Thus, since $\alpha = .99$, we have $\alpha/(1-\alpha) = 99$, and $\alpha(b-a)/(1-\alpha) = 142.56$. None of the decisions is even close to being identified as nonoptimal at this point.

Columns eight and nine give the lower and upper bounds on the optimal value function given by (12.5):

$$\underline{f} = \begin{pmatrix} 0.08 + 99(.08) = 8.00 \\ 1.52 + 99(.08) = 9.44 \end{pmatrix},$$

and

$$\bar{f} = \begin{pmatrix} 0.08 + 99(1.52) = 150.56 \\ 1.52 + 99(1.52) = 152.00 \end{pmatrix}.$$

No decisions are identified as being nonoptimal for the two- and three- period problems. The results for the four-, five-, and six-period problems are given below.

Four-Period Problem

i	v_i	$h_i^0 v$	$h_i^1 v$	$h_i^2 v$	$[Av - v]_i$	T_i	$\underline{f}_i$	$\bar{f}_i$
1	0.3529	0.4462	0.4575	0.5056	0.1527	0.3079	15.623	15.821
2	2.0402	2.1899	2.1949	2.1462	0.1547	1.9972	17.312	17.510

Five-Period Problem

i	v_i	$h_i^0 v$	$h_i^1 v$	$h_i^2 v$	$[Av - v]_i$	T_i	$\underline{f}_i$	$\bar{f}_i$
1	0.5056	**0.5974**	**0.6088**	0.6570	0.1515	0.6313	15.651	15.677
2	2.1949	2.3415	2.3466	**2.2983**	0.1517	2.3209	17.341	17.366

Six-Period Problem

i	v_i	$h_i^0 v$	$h_i^1 v$	$h_i^2 v$	$[Av - v]_i$	T_i	$\underline{f}_i$	$\bar{f}_i$
1	0.6570	**0.7474**	**0.7587**	0.8070	0.1500	0.8037	15.655	15.658
2	2.3466	**2.4915**	2.4967	**2.4484**	0.1500	2.4933	17.344	17.348

When a decision can be identified as nonoptimal, then its $h_i^k v$ value is displayed in boldface. For example, the decisions $k = 0$ and $k = 1$ are identified as nonoptimal for inactive customers $(i = 1)$, and the decision $k = 2$ is identified as nonoptimal in the five-period problem. The policy that was optimal in the three-period problem is confirmed to be optimal for the infinite-horizon problem after solving the six-period problem.

The bounds on the optimal value function keep getting tighter at each iteration. Exercise 12.4 shows that this will always be the case.

12.3   Additional Topics

Best Estimates

If you had to estimate f, what would you use? One plausible approach is to take an average of the upper and lower bounds on f. Using the bounds from (12.4) and (12.5), we get

$$f_{est} := Av + \frac{\alpha(a + b)e}{2(1 - \alpha)}.$$

Rewriting (12.4), we get

$$-\frac{\alpha(b - a)e}{2(1 - \alpha)} \le f - f_{est} \le \frac{\alpha(b - a)e}{2(1 - \alpha)}.$$

That is,

$$\rho(f, f_{est}) \le \frac{\alpha(b - a)}{2(1 - \alpha)}.$$

Using the Best Policy Found

Suppose you stop with a "good" decision rule and want to get a bound on how far away from optimal the value of the corresponding stationary policy is. The following result is useful in this regard.

Lemma 12.5   *(Exercise 12.7)*   *Suppose $H_\delta v = Av$ and $ae \le Av - v \le be$.*
Then
$$\rho(v_\delta, f) \le \frac{\alpha(b-a)}{1-\alpha}.$$

Unequal Row Sums

In semi-Markov decision chains and other examples, Q_δ has unequal row sums. Let α continue to denote the maximum row sum of Q_δ. Let β denote the minimum row sum of Q_δ. Porteus (1971) develops bounds for this case. They derive from the following results, whose proofs are straightforward and therefore omitted.

Lemma 12.6   *(Exercise 12.8)*   *Suppose that $ae \le u - v \le be$.*
(a) *If $a \ge 0$, then $\beta ae \le H_\delta u - H_\delta v \le \alpha be$.*
(b) *If $a \le 0 \le b$, then $\alpha ae \le H_\delta u - H_\delta v \le \alpha be$.*
(c) *If $b < 0$, then $\alpha ae \le H_\delta u - H_\delta v \le \beta be$.*

If $a \le 0 \le b$, then Theorem 12.1 continues to hold in its stated form. However, if $a > 0$, for example, then the bounds take a slightly different form.

Theorem 12.4   *(Exercise 12.9)*   *If $ae \le u - v \le be$, and $a \ge 0$, then*
$$\beta^n ae \le A^n u - A^n v \le \alpha^n be.$$

If $ae \le Av - v \le be$, and $a \ge 0$, then
$$\frac{\beta(1-\beta^n)ae}{1-\beta} \le A^{n+1}v - Av \le \frac{\alpha(1-\alpha^n)be}{1-\alpha},$$
$$v + \frac{ae}{1-\beta} \le f \le v + \frac{be}{1-\alpha},$$
and
$$Av + \frac{\beta ae}{1-\beta} \le f \le Av + \frac{\alpha be}{1-\alpha}.$$

If $b < 0$, then an analogous result (Exercise 12.10) holds.

Exercises

12.1   Prove Lemma 12.4.

12.2   Prove Theorem 12.1.

12.3   Prove Theorem 12.3.

12.4   Suppose that generic successive approximations are used: $f^n = A^n v$ for $n \geq 1$ and some initial $v \in V$. For convenience, let $f^0 := v$. For $n \geq 1$, let $a_n := \min_i[f_i^n - f_i^{n-1}]$, $b_n := \max_i[f_i^n - f_i^{n-1}]$, and $\underline{f}^n := f^n + \alpha a_n e / (1 - \alpha)$, and $\bar{f}^n := f^n + \alpha b_n e / (1 - \alpha)$. Prove that

$$\underline{f}^1 \leq \underline{f}^2 \leq \cdots \leq f \leq \cdots \bar{f}^2 \leq \bar{f}^1 .$$

12.5   Consider the following form of successive approximations: $f^0 = v$ for some $v \in V$. For $n \geq 1$, a real number c_n is identified and $f^n = Af^{n-1} + c_n e$. That is, a constant is added to each value before beginning the next iteration. In other words, a simple form of extrapolation is carried out at each iteration. For $n \geq 1$, let $a_n := \min_i[Af^{n-1} - f^{n-1}]_i$, $b_n := \max_i[Af^{n-1} - f^{n-1}]_i$, and $\underline{f}^n := Af^{n-1} + \alpha a_n e / (1 - \alpha)$, and $\bar{f}^n := Af^{n-1} + \alpha b_n e / (1 - \alpha)$. Prove that in the equal row sum case $(Q_\delta e = \alpha e)$ these bounds are independent of the sequence $\{c_1, c_2, \ldots\}$.

12.6   (Continuation of Exercise 12.5)   At each step $(n \geq 1)$ of the algorithm, a decision rule δ_n is found such that

$$Af^{n-1} = H_{\delta_n} f^{n-1} .$$

Prove that the sequence $\{\delta_1, \delta_2, \ldots\}$ is independent of the sequence $\{c_1, c_2, \ldots\}$.

12.7   Prove Lemma 12.5.

12.8   Prove Lemma 12.6.

12.9   Prove Theorem 12.4.

12.10   State and then prove the analogous result to Theorem 12.4 for the case in which $b < 0$.

12.11   Write a computer program (in whatever language you prefer) that will apply successive approximations to (approximately) solve infinite-horizon finite state and action Markov decision chains. Use it to analyze the generalization of e-Rite-Way presented below. Display the immediate returns and transition probabilities for each state/decision combination, an optimal policy (for the infinite-horizon problem), the best estimate you have of the corresponding optimal value function, and bounds on that optimal value function. Hand in a copy of your computer program and a listing of the output you used to obtain your estimates.

In managing e-Rite-Way, as presented in Chapter 3, you have developed an information system that allows you to implement a more sophisticated contingency plan. In particular, you believe that customer buying habits depend on how long it has been since their last purchase, rather than simply whether the customer bought something last month or not. You will now categorize the state of a customer by the number i of months since the last time this customer made a purchase of any kind, for $i = 0, 1, \ldots, 12$. State $s = 0$ represents customers who bought something during the last month. State $s = 11$ represents customers who bought something 11 months ago, but not more recently. State $s = 12$ is an aggregate that represents all customers who have not bought anything for more than a year. That is, once customers move into state 12, they will remain there until they purchase something. The economic parameters remain the same as in Chapter 3. For example, it still costs $0.50 to send a gift, and the expected value of a contribution from purchases made over a month given that a purchase is made is $8 if no promotion is offered to that customer. Any promotion offered is still valid for only one month, the month immediately following the offer. The one-month discount factor remains 0.99. However, the probabilities now differ. The effective (discounted) probability, expressed as a multiple of 0.001, of a customer making a purchase during the month is given below as a function of the state of that customer and the decision made by e-Rite-Way $(a = 0, 1, 2)$.

For example, there is no chance that a customer who hasn't bought anything in the last 12 months will purchase anything if s/he is sent nothing $(a = 0)$. However, the discounted probability increases to 0.015 if s/he is sent a gift and a minor promotion, and to 0.020 if s/he is offered a major promotion. Similarly, the discounted probability that a customer who last made a purchase five months ago will make a purchase next month is 0.025, 0.050, and 0.100 if s/he is sent nothing, a minor promotion, and a major promotion, respectively.

a	\multicolumn{13}{c}{i}
	0	1	2	3	4	5	6	7	8	9	10	11	12
0	50	45	40	35	30	25	20	15	10	7	4	2	0
1	110	92	80	69	59	50	42	35	29	24	20	17	15
2	220	180	160	140	120	100	80	70	60	50	40	30	20

References

MacQueen, J. 1966. A modified dynamic programming method for Markovian decision problems. *Journal of Mathematical Analysis and Applications.* **14** 38–43.

Porteus, E. 1971. Some bounds for discounted sequential decision processes. *Management Science.* **18** 7–11.

Porteus, E. 1975. Bounds and transformations for discounted finite Markov decision chains. *Operations Research.* **23** 761–84.

13

Computational
Markov Decision Processes

This chapter looks a little deeper at the issues of computing the optimal (stationary) policy and the accompanying optimal value function in stationary infinite-horizon Markov decision processes. We first examine what is called *policy iteration* and the use of linear programming. The bulk of the chapter examines what is called *value iteration*, namely, computing $A^n v$ for successively larger values of n starting with a given value function v. We know from Chapter 11 that value iteration converges geometrically to the optimal value function at a rate equal to the discount factor: $\rho(f, A^n v) \leq \alpha^n \rho(f, v)$. We shall see that the convergence occurs at a rate that is faster than that. After presenting what that rate is, we show how to get bounds on it. Doing so may be useful for determining what problems may be solved quickly. We then present some possible transformations that can be used to attempt to improve the convergence rate.

13.1 Policy Iteration

Howard (1960) popularized the concept of policy iteration, which generates a sequence of stationary policies whose infinite-horizon values strictly increase at each iteration. If there are only a finite number of policies, as in the case of a finite number of states and actions, then the algorithm will find the optimal policy in a finite number of steps.

Policy Iteration consists of the following steps:

[1] Select arbitrary $v \in V$ such that $v = v_\delta$ for some $\delta \in \Delta$.

[2] Select $\delta \in \Delta$ such that $H_\delta v = Av$.

[3] If $Av = v$, then stop. (Otherwise, continue to step [4].)

[4] Determine $v_\delta = H_\delta v_\delta$, replace v by v_δ and go to step [2].

For convenience, let u_1 denote the initial function and δ_1 the initial decision rule selected in step [1]. Let iteration n measure the number of times that step [2] is carried out. Let δ_n denote the candidate decision rule (forming the candidate stationary policy $(\delta_n, \delta_n, \ldots)$) entering iteration n, and let u_n denote the corresponding infinite-horizon value (from that stationary policy). Thus, at iteration n, step [2] computes Au_n. If, at step [3], the process stops, then $u_n = v_{\delta_n}$ is a fixed point of A, which must therefore equal the optimal value function, and the candidate stationary policy $(\delta_n, \delta_n, \ldots)$ is optimal. If the process does not stop at step [3], then the decision rule found in step [2] becomes δ_{n+1}, the candidate decision rule at iteration $n+1$. Let N denote the iteration at which the process stops. (Recall from the Preface that $v > u$ among functions means that $v(x) \geq u(x)$ for all x, and there exists y such that $v(y) > u(y)$.)

Lemma 13.1

(a) $Au_n \geq u_n$ for all $n = 1, 2, \ldots, N$.

(b) For $n = 1, 2, \ldots, N-1$, $u_{n+1} \geq Au_n > u_n$.

Proof (a) At each iteration n, there is a decision rule δ_n such that $u_n = v_{\delta_n} = H_{\delta_n} u_n$. Hence,

$$Au_n \geq H_{\delta_n} u_n = u_n.$$

(b) Thus, by (a), the only way for step [4] to be exercised is for $Au_n > u_n$. The decision rule selected in step [2] is denoted by δ_{n+1}, and we shall compute $u_{n+1} = v_{\delta_{n+1}}$. By (a), we have

$$H_{\delta_{n+1}} u_n = Au_n > u_n.$$

Iterating on this inequality yields

$$u_n < H_{\delta_{n+1}} u_n \leq H_{\delta_{n+1}}^2 u_n \leq \cdots \leq v_{\delta_{n+1}} = u_{n+1}. \qquad \square$$

By (b), $u_{n+1} > u_n$ for all n, so policy iteration must stop in a finite number of iterations if there is only a finite number of distinct decision rules. See Puterman (1994) for much more on policy iteration.

Example: e-Rite-Way

Starting with the decision rule $\delta = (0,0)$, corresponding to doing nothing for any customer, the infinite-horizon value is (approximately) $(9.7561, 11.5122)$. At the first iteration, step [2] yields the optimal decision rule $(2,1)$ and the corresponding infinite-horizon value, $(15.6552, 17.3448)$. The process then stops at iteration 2.

13.2   Use of Linear Programming

Assume henceforth in this section that our problem has a finite number of state and action combinations. We will see that the optimal value vector can be obtained in this case by using linear programming. (Manne, 1960, and D'Epenoux, 1960, introduced the use of linear programming in this context.) Recall that e is the vector of ones, so that, for example, $e^{\mathsf{T}}v = \sum_{s=1}^{S} v(s)$.

Consider the following primal problem, denoted by (P): Find $v \in V$ to

$$\min e^{\mathsf{T}}v$$

subject to

$$H_{\delta}v \le v \quad \text{for every } \delta \in \Delta.$$

Lemma 13.2

(a) The optimal value function f is feasible for (P).

(b) If v is feasible for (P), then $v \ge f$.

(c) The optimal value function f is the unique optimal solution to (P).

Proof

(a) By definition of the optimal value operator A, we have $H_{\delta}f \le Af$ for all $\delta \in \Delta$. The result follows since $Af = f$, by Theorem 11.3.

(b) If $H_\delta v \leq v$ for all δ, then $Av \leq v$. Iterating leads to $v \geq Av \geq A^2 v \geq \cdots \geq f$.

(c) By (a) and (b), f is optimal for (P). Suppose that v^* is optimal for (P) and $v^* \neq f$. By (b), it follows that $v^* > f$, and, therefore, $e^\mathsf{T} v^* > e^\mathsf{T} f$. However, by (a), that means we have a feasible solution, f, that does strictly better than v^*, which is a contradiction.   □

The primal becomes the following linear program (LP): Find $v_1, v_2, \ldots, v_S$ to

$$\min \sum_{s=1}^{S} v_s \tag{13.1}$$

subject to

$$r(s, a) + \sum_j q_{sj}^a v_j \leq v_s \quad \text{for every } s \in \mathcal{S} \text{ and } a \in A(s). \tag{13.2}$$

This LP has S decision variables, and a constraint for every feasible state/action combination. LPs with many constraints are more difficult to solve numerically than ones with fewer constraints. Thus, it makes sense to formulate and solve the dual LP, which will have only one constraint for each state. (It will have one decision variable for every feasible state/action combination.) Exercise 13.1 shows that this dual LP can be written as follows. Find x_s^a for all s and a to

$$\max \sum_{s,a} r(s, a) x_s^a \tag{13.3}$$

subject to

$$\sum_{a \in A(s)} x_s^a - \sum_{i \in \mathcal{S}} \sum_{a \in A(i)q} q_{is}^a x_i^a = 1 \quad \text{for every } s \in \mathcal{S}, \tag{13.4}$$

and $x_s^a \geq 0$ for every s and a. At the optimal solution of the primal, the binding constraints correspond to the optimal actions for that state. These binding constraints correspond to the strictly positive dual variables. That is, the strictly positive decision variables in the optimal solution to the dual indicate the optimal actions in the Markov decision process. Furthermore, the shadow prices in the optimal solution to the dual give the optimal values of the decision variables in the primal, namely, the optimal value function.

Example: e-Rite-Way

The nonzero variables in the optimal solution to the dual are $x_1^2 = 166.67$ and $x_2^1 = 33.33$, which confirm that the optimal policy is $(2,1)$. The shadow prices are 15.6552 and 17.3448, which confirm the values of the optimal value function.

13.3   Preparations for Further Analysis

We now turn our attention to value iteration, which was studied by Bellman (1957) as the classical technique of successive approximations. For many purposes, it is appropriate to limit consideration to policy iteration or linear programming. However, if the number of states is extremely large, then the computational burden can become huge, even with high-speed computers. Furthermore, if there is structure in the problem so that determining the optimal decision rule at an iteration is far simpler than having to numerically evaluate the value from every feasible action for every state, then value iteration can offer substantial benefits over policy iteration and/or linear programming. It can even be possible to solve problems numerically for infinite-state problems using value iteration. It is therefore appropriate to explore value iteration in more depth, with initial emphasis on the finite state and action case.

We first need some preliminary concepts from matrix theory. Suppose P is an arbitrary N by N real matrix. Recall that it has N eigenvalues, say $\alpha_1, \alpha_2, \cdots, \alpha_N$, not necessarily all real, each of which has corresponding left and right eigenvectors. Consider the absolute values of these eigenvalues, $|\alpha_1|, |\alpha_2|, \cdots, |\alpha_N|$. Assume, without loss of generality, that $|\alpha_1| \geq |\alpha_2| \geq \cdots \geq |\alpha_N|$. The *spectral radius* $\rho(P)$ is defined to be the largest of these absolute values:

$$\rho(P) := \max_i |\alpha_i| = |\alpha_1|.$$

Similarly, the *(spectral) subradius* $\rho^*(P)$ is the second largest: $\rho^*(P) = |\alpha_2|$.

Lemma 13.3   *(Theorem 3.4, Young, 1971)   Any norm of a matrix is an upper bound on the spectral radius of that matrix:*

$$\rho(P) \leq \|P\|.$$

Unless indicated otherwise, we shall use the L^∞ norm henceforth: If v is a vector and P is a matrix, then

$$\|v\| = \max_i |v_i| \text{ and } \|P\| = \max_i \left\{ \sum_j |P_{ij}| \right\}.$$

That is, the (L^∞) norm of a vector is its maximum absolute component, and the norm of a matrix equals its maximum absolute row sum. See Exercise 11.3 and, for example, Young (1971) for more.

Lemma 13.4 *If P is a positive matrix $(P \geq 0)$ with equal row sums $(Pe = \alpha e$ for some $\alpha \geq 0)$, then the spectral radius of P equals its row sum: $\rho(P) = \alpha$.*

Proof Since $P \geq 0$ and $Pe = \alpha e$, α is an eigenvalue of P and e is a corresponding right eigenvector. Since α is only one of N eigenvalues and is a positive real, the spectral radius of a stochastic matrix must be at least α. Because the absolute row sums of a positive matrix are its (simple) row sums, the (L^∞) norm of P equals α, which, by Lemma 13.3, is an upper bound on the spectral radius of that matrix. Thus, α is both an upper and lower bound on the spectral radius. □

Note that P can be expressed as the product of a positive scalar (which, for now, need not be less than one) and a *stochastic matrix*: $P = \alpha Q$, where $Q \geq 0$ and $Qe = e$. A *stationary vector* π, also called the *steady-state probability vector*, satisfies

$$\pi Q = \pi.$$

Multiplying through by α yields $\pi P = \alpha \pi$, so that π is a left eigenvector of P associated with α.

There is a great deal more that can be said about nonnegative matrices. In preparation, a matrix is *irreducible* if it cannot be permuted, by relabeling the states, into the form

$$\begin{pmatrix} P_1 & 0 \\ P_2 & P_3 \end{pmatrix},$$

where each P_i is a nonzero matrix. A matrix is *aperiodic* if $P^n \gg 0$ for some integer n. We are now ready to state the famous Perron-Frobenius Theorem. See Varga (1962) and/or Young (1971) for the original citations, and Çinlar (1975) for, in addition, a nice, probabilistically oriented proof.

Theorem 13.1   *(Perron-Frobenius Theorem)   If P is an irreducible, positive matrix, then its spectral radius $\rho(P)$ is an eigenvalue of P. There exist strictly positive right and left corresponding eigenvectors. If P is aperiodic, then the (spectral) subradius of P is strictly less than the radius of P:*

$$\rho^*(P) < \rho(P).$$

Theorem 13.2   *(Çinlar, 1975)   Suppose that P is irreducible, aperiodic, and stochastic. Let S denote the matrix of stationary vectors: Each row of S is π. Then*

$$\lim_{n \to \infty} P_{ij}^n = \pi_j$$

independent of i, and convergence to S is geometric at the rate of the subradius: For every $\beta > \rho^*(P)$, there exists $M > 0$ such that

$$\|P^n - S\| \leq \beta^n M \quad \text{for every } n.$$

13.4   Convergence Rates for Value Iteration

Given v, we know that value iteration converges geometrically at the rate of the discount factor: There exists M such that

$$\rho(f, A^n v) \leq \alpha^n M.$$

Given an arbitrary decision rule δ, the effective transition matrix $Q_\delta = \alpha P_\delta$ satisfies Lemma 13.4. We now prepare for a result given by Morton and Wecker (1977) that, after making one small adjustment, value iteration converges at a rate that is faster than the spectral radius of every effective transition matrix: Convergence is geometric at the rate of the *subradius* of the optimal effective transition matrix.

Relative Value Iteration

Suppose we designate a particular state, say state 0, and, given v, after computing Av, we subtract $[Av](0)$ from the value at every state. Let v^n denote the resulting vector after n iterations. We then have, pointwise,

$$v^n(s) = \max_{a \in A(s)} \{r(s, a) + \alpha \sum_j p_{sj}^a v^{n-1}(j)\} - v^n(0),$$

where v^0 was given. The resulting algorithm is called *relative value iteration*, and we shall see that it essentially converges in the same way that (regular) value iteration does. Incidentally, relative value iteration was first used in undiscounted problems, because the expected present value of infinite-horizon values in such cases may be infinite.

Lemma 13.5   *(Exercise 13.2)   Relative value iteration and (regular) value iteration both yield the same decision rules and bounds on the optimal value function at each iteration.*

If relative value iteration converges, we can get the optimal value function easily: If $v^n = v^{n-1}$, then, suppressing $n-1$ so that $v = v^{n-1}$, we have

$$Av - be = v$$

for some $b \in \mathbf{R}$. (Indeed, $b = [Av](0)$.) Let $u := v + be/(1-\alpha)$. Then

$$Au = A(v + be/(1-\alpha))$$
$$= Av + \frac{\alpha be}{1-\alpha}$$
$$= v + be + \frac{\alpha be}{1-\alpha}$$
$$= v + \frac{be}{1-\alpha}$$
$$= u.$$

So $u = f$, the optimal value function. We capitalize the unadjusted value at the designated state and add it to v.

Theorem 13.3   *(Morton and Wecker, 1977)   If every P_δ is irreducible and aperiodic, and the optimal decision rule is unique, then relative value iteration converges to the optimal relative value function at the rate of the subradius of the optimal effective transition matrix: Let P denote the optimal transition matrix, so $\alpha \rho^*(P)$ is the subradius of the optimal effective transition matrix. Then, for every $\beta > \alpha \rho^*(P)$, there exists $M \in \mathbf{R}$ such that*

$$\rho(v^n, \hat{f}) \leq \beta^n M \quad \text{for every } n,$$

where $\hat{f}$ is the optimal relative value function: $\hat{f}(s) = f(s) - f(0)$.

Example: e-Rite-Way

Let 1 be the designated state. Thus, we need only to examine the relative value at state 2. We have: $v^0 = 0$, $v^1 = 1.44$, $v^2 = 1.672$, $v^3 = 1.6874$, and $v^4 = 1.6894$. We saw in Chapter 12 that the optimal decision rule δ is $(2, 1)$. Thus, $f = v_\delta$, and v_δ can be computed by solving the system of linear equations $v_\delta = r_\delta + Q_\delta v_\delta$. Solving that system numerically reveals that the optimal values are 15.65517 and 17.34482, respectively. Thus the optimal relative value is $17.34482 - 15.65517 = 1.68965$, so relative value iteration has converged very quickly in this case.

The effective transition matrix of the optimal decision rule is

$$Q_\delta = \begin{pmatrix} 0.85 & 0.14 \\ 0.72 & 0.27 \end{pmatrix}.$$

The radius is 0.99. By Theorem A.8, the trace of a matrix, which equals 1.12 in this case, equals the sum of the eigenvalues. Therefore, the subradius equals $1.12 - 0.99 = 0.13$. No wonder convergence is so fast.

13.5   Bounds on the Subradius

Assume that P is irreducible and aperiodic. As in Theorem 13.2, let S denote the matrix of stationary vectors. Then, by that theorem, $\lim_{n \to \infty} \|P^n - S\| = 0$. In Isaacson and Luecke (1978) terminology, P is *strongly ergodic*.

Lemma 13.6   (Isaacson and Luecke, 1978)   If P is irreducible and aperiodic, then
$$\rho^*(P) = \rho(P - S).$$

Thus, while the radius of a matrix measures how different it is from the zero matrix, Lemma 13.6 says that the subradius measures how different it is from its stationary matrix.

The *delta coefficient* of a stochastic matrix is defined as follows:

$$\delta(P) := \sup_{i,s} \frac{\sum_j |p_{ij} - p_{sj}|}{2}.$$

To compute the delta coefficient of a matrix, take any two rows of P, find the absolute value of the difference between the elements in each column, and add them up. Repeat that process over all possible pairs of rows. Pick the largest resulting value, and divide it by two. That is the delta coefficient.

Lemma 13.7   *(Isaacson and Luecke, 1978)   If P is irreducible and aperiodic, then*

$$\rho^*(P) \le [\delta(P^n)]^{1/n} \quad \text{for every } n.$$

Lemma 13.7 gives us "easily" computable upper bounds on the subradius.

Example: e-Rite-Way

In this case, continuing study of the effective transition matrix, $Q = Q_\delta$, of the optimal policy,

$$\delta(Q) = \frac{0.13 + 0.13}{2} = 0.13,$$

which equals the subradius of Q. Also

$$Q^2 = \begin{pmatrix} 0.8233 & 0.1568 \\ 0.8064 & 0.1737 \end{pmatrix},$$

so

$$\delta(Q^2) = \frac{0.0169 + 0.0169}{2} = 0.0169.$$

Thus, $\sqrt{\delta(Q^2)} = 0.13$, which is also a tight upper bound in this example.

13.6   Transformations

We now examine the possibility of transforming a given problem into one that may be easier to solve. Three different examples are given. More can be found in Porteus (1975).

Column Reduction

For each state, find the smallest probability of moving into that state from all other states. Subtract that from all probabilities of moving into that state. Repeat for all states. The following result, which is specialized to the case of finding the infinite-horizon value of a fixed stationary policy, shows that this transformation yields an equivalent problem.

Lemma 13.8   *(Porteus, 1975)   Suppose that $P \geq 0$ and $Pe = \alpha e$, where $0 \leq \alpha < 1$. Let v be the infinite-horizon value: $v = r + Pv$. Let p_j denote the minimum value in column j: $p_j := \min_i P_{ij}$, and subtract p_j from each entry in column j of P to create $\tilde{P}$:*

$$\tilde{P}_{ij} = P_{ij} - p_j.$$

Let $\tilde{v}$ denote the corresponding infinite-horizon value: $\tilde{v} = r + \tilde{P}\tilde{v}$. Then v can be computed pointwise via $v_i = \tilde{v}_i + K/(1 - \alpha)$, where $K := \sum_j p_j \tilde{v}_j$.

Once you have found the infinite-horizon value for this problem, it is easy to compute the original infinite-horizon value. If the minimal probabilities in a column are nonzero, then this approach can yield much better bounds when you are using successive approximations. This approach works when you are optimizing, too. See Porteus (1975) for details.

Example: e-Rite-Way

Suppose we seek the infinite-horizon value from the decision rule $(2, 1)$. We start with

$$P = \begin{pmatrix} 0.85 & 0.14 \\ 0.72 & 0.27 \end{pmatrix}.$$

We end up with

$$\tilde{P} = \begin{pmatrix} 0.13 & 0.00 \\ 0.00 & 0.13 \end{pmatrix}.$$

The new effective transition matrix has a discount factor of 0.13. Now explicit computable bounds are available.

In this case,

$$(I - \tilde{P})^{-1} = \begin{pmatrix} 1/0.87 & 0 \\ 0 & 1/0.87 \end{pmatrix} \text{ and } r = \begin{pmatrix} -0.08 \\ 1.39 \end{pmatrix},$$

so the infinite-horizon value for the modified problem is

$$\tilde{v} = (I - \tilde{P})^{-1}r = \begin{pmatrix} -0.08/0.87 \\ 1.39/0.87 \end{pmatrix} \cong \begin{pmatrix} -0.091954 \\ 1.597701 \end{pmatrix}.$$

Thus, by Lemma 13.8, to compute the original infinite-horizon value, we compute $K = 0.72(-0.091954) + 0.14(1.597701) = 0.157471$, and, since $K/(1 - \alpha) = 15.7471$, we have

$$v = \begin{pmatrix} -0.091954 \\ 1.597701 \end{pmatrix} + \begin{pmatrix} 15.7471 \\ 15.7471 \end{pmatrix} = \begin{pmatrix} 15.65517 \\ 17.34483 \end{pmatrix}.$$

Diagonal Reduction

For this transformation, we find the smallest diagonal element in the matrix, say p, subtract it from each diagonal value, and divide the resulting matrix through by $1 - p$. We also divide the immediate return vector through by the same quantity. The resulting matrix still has equal row sums, which are smaller than α.

Lemma 13.9   (*Porteus, 1975*)   *Suppose that* $P \geq 0$ *and* $Pe = \alpha e$, *where* $0 \leq \alpha < 1$. *Let* v *be the infinite-horizon value:* $v = r + Pv$. *Let* p *denote the minimum value in the diagonal of* P: $p := \min_i P_{ii}$. *Let* $\tilde{r}_i := r_i/(1 - p)$ *and*

$$\tilde{P}_{ij} := \begin{cases} P_{ij}/(1 - p) & \text{if } j \neq i \\ (P_{ii} - p)/(1 - p) & \text{if } j = i. \end{cases}$$

Let $\tilde{v}$ *denote the infinite-horizon value for the transformed problem:* $\tilde{v} = r + \tilde{P}\tilde{v}$. *Then* $v = \tilde{v}$.

Example: e-Rite-Way

We continue to seek the infinite-horizon value from the decision rule $(2, 1)$. If we start with the output of the column reduction, we have

$$P = \begin{pmatrix} 0.13 & 0.00 \\ 0.00 & 0.13 \end{pmatrix}.$$

The smallest diagonal element is 0.13, so we have the following transformed problem:

$$\tilde{r} = \begin{pmatrix} -0.08/0.87 \\ 1.39/0.87 \end{pmatrix} = \begin{pmatrix} -0.091954 \\ 1.597701 \end{pmatrix} \text{ and } \tilde{P} = \begin{pmatrix} 0 & 0 \\ 0 & 0 \end{pmatrix}.$$

As the effective transition matrix is null, the new immediate return vector is the infinite-horizon value, which is confirmed by the results of the previous example.

Gauss-Seidel Iteration

Suppose we seek the infinite-horizon value from a fixed policy, which we suppress from the notation in the remainder of this section, for convenience. Using (regular) value interation, given v^{n-1}, we compute $Hv^{n-1} = r + Qv^{n-1}$, which can be expressed pointwise as

$$r(i) + \sum_j q_{ij} v^{n-1}(j).$$

When computing the infinite-horizon value from a fixed policy, Gauss-Seidel has you use the latest values as soon as you compute them:

$$v^n(i) = \frac{r(i) + \sum_{j<i} q_{ij} v^n(j) + \sum_{j>i} q_{ij} v^{n-1}(j)}{1 - q_{ii}}.$$

Gauss-Seidel is what you get if you reserve storage space for only one vector v, so whenever you compute the value for a state, it replaces the old value.

To analyze this method, decompose Q into $L + D + U$, where L is lower triangular, D is diagonal, and U is upper triangular.

Then we have

$$v^n = (I - D)^{-1}(r + Lv^n + Uv^{n-1}),$$

which can be rewritten as

$$(I - D)v^n - Lv^n = r + Uv^{n-1},$$

which becomes

$$v^n = (I - D - L)^{-1}(r + Uv^{n-1}),$$

which means that we have transformed the problem into an equivalent one with an effective immediate return vector of $\tilde{r} = (I - D - L)^{-1}r$ and an effective transition matrix of

$$\tilde{P} = (I - D - L)^{-1}U.$$

In general, the new effective transition matrix has a smaller maximum row sum, but it no longer has equal row sums. Thus, bounds from Chapter 12 may be superior, but convergence is no longer guaranteed at the rate of the subradius, and it is possible that convergence is slower with Gauss-Seidel than with relative value iteration. The reason for this is, essentially, that relative value iteration normalizes its values by subtracting a multiple of e, which is a right eigenvector corresponding to the dominant eigenvalue (spectral radius) of every transition matrix. In the Gauss-Seidel case, even when seeking only the infinite-horizon value from a fixed decision rule, we usually do not know either the dominant eigenvalue or a corresponding right eigenvector.

Gauss-Seidel can also be used with optimization. However, the difficulty of modifying it to converge at the rate of a subradius is compounded, as even if we know the dominant eigenvalue and a corresponding right eigenvector for a given effective transition matrix, those objects typically depend on the decision rule, making it difficult to normalize in the same way at each iteration. Nevertheless, see Porteus (1980) for some different modifications to Gauss-Seidel that can yield improved performance over relative value iteration.

Example: e-Rite-Way

For example, in e-Rite-Way with the policy $(2, 1)$, we have

$$Q = L + D + U = \begin{pmatrix} 0 & 0 \\ 0.72 & 0 \end{pmatrix} + \begin{pmatrix} 0.85 & 0 \\ 0 & 0.27 \end{pmatrix} + \begin{pmatrix} 0 & 0.14 \\ 0 & 0 \end{pmatrix}.$$

Here we have

$$(I - D - L) = \begin{pmatrix} 0.15 & 0 \\ -0.72 & 0.73 \end{pmatrix} \text{ and } (I - D - L)^{-1} = \begin{pmatrix} 6.66667 & 0 \\ 6.5753425 & 1.369863 \end{pmatrix},$$

so the effective transition matrix is

$$\tilde{P} = (I - D - L)^{-1}U = \begin{pmatrix} 6.6667 & 0 \\ 6.57534 & 1.36986 \end{pmatrix} \begin{pmatrix} 0 & 0.14 \\ 0 & 0 \end{pmatrix} = \begin{pmatrix} 0 & 0.93333 \\ 0 & 0.92055 \end{pmatrix}.$$

Thus, as pointed out above, the new effective transition matrix no longer has equal row sums. However, the maximum row sum is now 0.93333, which is smaller than the 0.99 of the original effective transition matrix.

Exercises

13.1 Show that the linear programming dual of (13.1) and (13.2) is given by (13.3) and (13.4).

13.2 Prove Lemma 13.5.

Hint: Apply Exercises 12.5 and 12.6.

13.3 Consider the following effective transition matrix:

$$P = \begin{pmatrix} 0.4 & 0.5 & 0 \\ 0 & 0.3 & 0.6 \\ 0.2 & 0.1 & 0.6 \end{pmatrix}.$$

(a) Compute the delta coefficient of P.

(b) Compute the delta coefficient of P^2 and its square root.

13.4 The *Hajnal measure* of a stochastic matrix is

$$h(P) := \sup_{i,s} \sum_j (p_{ij} - p_{sj})^+,$$

where $x^+ := \max(x, 0)$ for $x \in \mathbf{R}$. Prove that the delta coefficient and Hajnal measure of a stochastic matrix are identical.

13.5 Prove Lemma 13.8.

13.6 Prove Lemma 13.9.

13.7 (a) Show how to compute the row sums of the effective transition matrix (for a single decision rule) when using Gauss-Seidel with the work of a single value iteration (with approximately the same number of multiplications and additions required by a single value iteration).

(b) Demonstrate your method presented in (a) on the matrix in Exercise 13.2.

(c) Show how to compute the effective transition matrix of Gauss-Seidel with the work of N single value iterations, where N is the number of rows.

(d) Demonstrate your method presented in (c) on the matrix in Exercise 13.2.

References

Bellman, R. 1957. *Dynamic Programming*. Princeton University Press, Princeton, N.J.

Çinlar, E. 1975. *Introduction to Stochastic Processes*. Prentice-Hall, Englewood Cliffs, N.J.

D'Epenoux, F. 1960, Sur un problème de production et de stockage dans l'aléatoire, *Revue Française Autom. Inf. Recherche Op.* **14** 3–16. English translation: 1963. A probabilistic production and inventory problem. *Management Science.* **10** 98–108.

Howard, R. 1960. *Dynamic Programming and Markov Processes*. MIT Technology Press, Boston, Mass.

Isaacson, D., G. Luecke. 1978. Strongly ergodic Markov chains and rates of convergence using spectral conditions. *Stochastic Processes and Their Applications.* **7** 113–21.

Manne, A. 1960. Linear programming and sequential decisions. *Management Science.* **6** 259–67.

Morton, T., W. Wecker. 1977. Discounting, ergodicity, and convergence for Markov decision processes. *Management Science.* **23** 890–900.

Porteus, E. 1975. Bounds and transformations for discounted finite Markov decision chains. *Operations Research.* **23** 761–84.

Porteus, E. 1980. Improved iterative computation of the expected discounted return in Markov and semi-Markov chains. *Zeitschrift für Operations Research.* **24** 155–70.

Puterman, M. 1994. *Markov Decision Processes: Discrete Stochastic Dynamic Programming*. John Wiley and Sons, New York.

Varga, R. 1962. *Matrix Iterative Analysis*. Prentice-Hall, Englewood Cliffs, N.J.

Young, D. 1971. *Iterative Solution of Large Linear Systems*. Academic Press, New York.

14

A Continuous Time Model

So far in this book, all the dynamic problems have been discrete-time models. In this chapter, we examine a continuous time model. In such a model, one can formulate the decision-making process continuously over time. In many applications, transitions in the state of the system occur at distinct points in time, rather than continuously. For example, demands for a product often arise at specific points in time such as with the arrival of distinct customers in the system. In such cases, the distribution of the time it takes before a transition occurs is a critical factor.

For instance, suppose that exactly 100 units of a product are demanded exactly every seven days, and the supplier has a two-day replenishment lead time. (The interarrival times for demands are deterministic.) Then it is clearly optimal to order the 100 units just the right amount of time in advance of the demand, without holding the units all week, say.

However, suppose that the time between transitions is exponentially distributed. Then, because of the memoryless property of the exponential distribution, given any amount of time that has elapsed without a transition, the system looks exactly the way it did when the last state transition took place: The time until the next transition is still exponentially distributed with the same mean. Thus, it is reasonable to consider making a new decision only when a *change* in the state of the system has occurred. For instance, don't order any new replenishment until a new demand occurs. The resulting formulation is an *embedded Markov decision process*, in which a period represents the (random) time it takes for a state transition to occur. To illustrate the ideas of such models, we focus on a particular model, studied by Ha (1997).

14.1   A Two-Product Production/Inventory Model

We seek to manage an integrated manufacturing and sales organization. There are two products that are produced at a single production facility, one unit of one product at a time, and are sold directly to consumers, perhaps through the Internet. The time to produce a unit of product i is exponentially distributed with rate μ_i. Producing to stock (inventory) is allowed, but all units of product i in inventory accumulate cost at a positive (holding cost) rate of h_i per unit time. There is no cost to switching from producing one product to the other, and, because of the memoryless property of the exponential distribution, any accumulated time spent producing the other product is lost, because the time to complete the product remains exponential with the same parameter.

The demand process for product i is a Poisson process with intensity λ_i, so the time between demands for that product is exponentially distributed with rate λ_i (mean $1/\lambda_i$). Arriving demands are met immediately from inventory, if possible. If no inventory is available, then the demand is backlogged and accumulates cost at a positive (shortage/backlogging/delay cost) rate of p_i per unit time. Figure 14.1 diagrams the model.

Costs are discounted at continuous rate $\beta > 0$, so that, for example, the present value of receiving one dollar t time units from now is $e^{-\beta t}$. Hence, the one period discount factor would be $\alpha = e^{-\beta}$. We seek to minimize the expected present value of all costs incurred while the system is managed over an infinite horizon.

This is the dynamic problem of what to make next, if anything, in a setting with no economies of scale. Intuitively, when the stock level is low, something should be produced, and when the stock level is high, production should cease. We are interested in whether there is a simple form for the optimal policy.

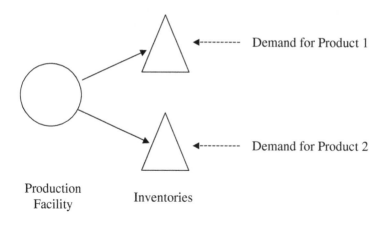

Figure 14.1   Diagram of the Two-Product Model

14.2   Formulation and Initial Analysis

The state of the system is denoted by (x_1, x_2), the inventory levels of each product. Backlogs are represented by negative inventory, as usual. The decisions are to produce nothing $(k = 0)$, to produce product 1 $(k = 1)$, or to produce product 2 $(k = 2)$.

Define the holding and shortage cost *rate* function as follows:

$$\mathcal{L}_i(x_i) := \begin{cases} h_i x_i & \text{if } x_i \geq 0 \\ -p_i x_i & \text{otherwise.} \end{cases}$$

Lemma 14.1   *(Exercise 14.1)   If costs are incurred at a rate of r per unit time over the time interval $[0, T]$ and T is exponentially distributed with rate λ, then the expected present value of the costs incurred over time $[0, T]$ equals*

$$E \int_{\xi=0}^{T} e^{-\beta \xi} r \, d\xi = \int_{t=0}^{\infty} \left(\int_{\xi=0}^{t} e^{-\beta \xi} r \, d\xi \right) \lambda e^{-\lambda t} \, dt = r/(\beta + \lambda).$$

Lemma 14.2   *If T_i is a sequence of independent, exponentially distributed random variables, with rates λ_i, respectively, then*

(a) $T := \min_i T_i$ is exponentially distributed with rate $\lambda := \sum_i \lambda_i$, and

(b) $P(T = T_i) = P(T = T_i | T = t) = \lambda_i / \lambda$ for every $t \geq 0$.

(c) If, in addition, (a lump sum) cost c_i is incurred at time T if $T = T_i$ (that is, the first of the possible events to occur is event i), then the expected present value (evaluated at time 0) of the costs to be incurred at time T is

$$Ee^{-\beta T}c = \frac{\sum \lambda_i c_i}{\beta + \sum_i \lambda_i}.$$

Proof   (a) The event that $\{T \geq t\}$ is equivalent to $\{T_i \geq t\}$ for every i. The probability of that is

$$e^{-\lambda_1 t}e^{-\lambda_2 t} \cdots e^{-\lambda_n t} = e^{-\lambda t}.$$

Exercise 14.2 proves parts (b) and (c).   □

Thus, for example, if we start at state (x_1, x_2), and decide to produce item 1, then the time until the first state transition is exponentially distributed with rate

$$\nu := \mu_1 + \lambda_1 + \lambda_2, \tag{14.1}$$

and, given that a transition has taken place, it is due to (a) production of a unit of product 1 with probability μ_1/ν, (b) demand for a unit of product 1 with probability λ_1/ν, and (c) demand for product 2 with probability λ_2/ν.

Thus, since $\mathcal{L}_i(x_i)$ denotes the holding and shortage cost rate for product i, we can set $r = \mathcal{L}_1(x_1) + \mathcal{L}_2(x_2)$ as the cost rate and get, by Lemma 14.1, that the expected holding and shortage costs incurred until the first transition occurs is

$$\frac{1}{\beta + \nu} \sum_{i=1}^{2} \mathcal{L}_i(x_i).$$

The original (infinite-horizon) optimality equation is therefore as follows:

$$f(x_1, x_2) = \min_{k=0,1,2} g_k(x_1, x_2),$$

where, using Lemma 14.2(c), the expressions corresponding to producing nothing, producing product 1, and producing product 2, are, respectively,

$$g_0(x_1, x_2) = \left(\frac{1}{\beta + \lambda_1 + \lambda_2} \right) \left(\sum_i \mathcal{L}_i(x_i) + \lambda_1 f(x_1 - 1, x_2) \right.$$
$$\left. + \lambda_2 f(x_1, x_2 - 1) \right),$$

$$g_1(x_1, x_2) = \left(\frac{1}{\beta + \mu_1 + \lambda_1 + \lambda_2} \right) \left(\sum_i \mathcal{L}_i(x_i) + \mu_1 f(x_1 + 1, x_2) \right.$$
$$\left. + \lambda_1 f(x_1 - 1, x_2) + \lambda_2 f(x_1, x_2 - 1) \right),$$

and

$$g_2(x_1, x_2) = \left(\frac{1}{\beta + \mu_2 + \lambda_1 + \lambda_2} \right) \left(\sum_i \mathcal{L}_i(x_i) + \mu_2 f(x_1, x_2 + 1) \right.$$
$$\left. + \lambda_1 f(x_1 - 1, x_2) + \lambda_2 f(x_1, x_2 - 1) \right).$$

The first key to this formulation is that times are all exponentially distributed. Regardless of what the first event is (a demand for a product or production of a unit), the times until the next transition remain exponentially distributed. For example, suppose that the time to produce a unit was not exponentially distributed: Suppose this time is deterministic and we initiate production on product 2. If the first event is a demand for product 1, which triggers consideration of a new decision, the remaining time until completion of the unit currently in production is no longer exponentially distributed. In this case, there is a deterministic amount of time left. In particular, the state of the system must include the time that the current unit has been in production. (It would be silly to switch over to begin production on product 1 if there was only a small amount of work left to do on the product—of type 2—in production, and that product might have to start production anew if it wasn't completed once started.) This sort of augmentation of the state space will be required for each time that was not exponentially distributed. (Because of the memoryless property of the exponential distribution, augmenting the state space with the current accumulated time of each random variable adds no relevant information to our formulation of the problem, and, therefore, need not be done.)

The second key to this formulation is that there is an infinite horizon. Our conceptual approach to solving an infinite-horizon problem is to solve a sequence

of finite-horizon problems with successively longer time horizons. In particular, the time horizon is represented by a given number of *periods*. In this
formulation, a period represents a state transition, and the expected time until
a transition occurs depends on the action. That is, a finite-horizon problem
with n transitions remaining corresponds, unnaturally, to a problem with a
random remaining time horizon, which, even worse, depends on the decisions
made during that time. For example, because higher costs tend to accumulate
during periods in which the transition takes a long time, there can be an inappropriate incentive in such a finite-horizon problem to pick actions that lead to
short periods.

A more reasonable formulation of a finite-horizon problem would have a set time
horizon, say τ, and the goal would be to minimize the relevant costs incurred
over $[0, \tau]$, regardless of how many transitions occurred during that time. That
is, this formulation would essentially be an infinite-horizon problem (in the sense
of no limit on the number of decisions) with an added state variable, the time
remaining in the horizon. In short, the infinite-horizon problem with no time
limit as an appended state variable is much easier to formulate and solve. Once
a transition is made, a new infinite-horizon problem is faced, with no limit on
the number of transitions or time.

Lippman's Transformation

In general, this sort of problem can be detected by the fact that the effective
transition matrix has unequal row sums. For any state in which the action
$k = 0$ is selected, the row sum is $(\lambda_1 + \lambda_2)/(\beta + \lambda_1 + \lambda_2)$, which we interpret
as the effective discount factor. When action $k = 1$ is selected, the effective
discount factor is $(\mu_1 + \lambda_1 + \lambda_2)/(\beta + \mu_1 + \lambda_1 + \lambda_2)$. The effective discount
factor for $k = 2$ is similar. All three effective discount factors can differ. Each
can be interpreted as the discount factor for a period equal to the expected
time to make a transition under this action.

From a conceptual point of view, this problem is not serious: The optimal policy
will be found for the infinite-horizon problem, even if inappropriate decision
rules are found for short-horizon problems. The more serious problem is that
it has proven difficult to characterize the form of optimal policies using this
representation.

Lippman (1975) presented an equivalent way to represent the problem that makes the resulting optimality equation easier to analyze. His approach can be interpreted as transforming the problem into an equivalent one with equal row sums. It is quite easy to understand and interpret.

Assume, without loss of generality, that the products are numbered so that $\mu_1 \geq \mu_2$. Thus the transition time with the highest rate, and lowest expected value, corresponds to producing item 1 $(k = 1)$, and the rate is $\beta + \nu$, where ν is defined in (14.1). The effective discount factor is highest when this decision is selected. For $k = 0$, corresponding to producing nothing, an *artificial transition*, with rate μ_1 is introduced, with the actual "transition" being made to the same state (x_1, x_2). This addition changes the form but not the substance of the formulation. The new effective discount factor for this decision is the same as for the decision $k = 1$. Similarly, for $k = 2$, corresponding to producing item 2, an artificial transition, with rate $\mu_1 - \mu_2$ is introduced, with the actual "transition" being no change in the state, as above. Importantly, the mean transition time is now probabilistically the same for every action. In particular, the effective discount factor for every state is the same, namely $\nu/(\beta + \nu)$. The distortion effect has been eliminated. For example, in a problem formulated with a finite number of transitions remaining, the time for that number of transitions to take place would be a random variable, but it wouldn't depend on any decisions made during that time.

Rescaling Time

Before stating the optimality equations, we rescale time to simplify the formulation further. For example, suppose the initial time unit is a year and that the present value of one dollar received one year from now is \$0.90. Thus, $\beta = \beta_1$ must satisfy $e^{-\beta_1} = 0.9$. If we rescale time, so that a time unit is now a day, then we must select a new $\beta = \beta_2$ that satisfies $e^{-365\beta_2} = 0.9$. That is, $\beta_2 = \beta_1/365$. In particular, the discount rate β and all transition rates scale proportionally in the time unit. (The cost and revenue rates must also be adjusted accordingly.) This approach yields the following simplifying result.

Lemma 14.3   *(Exercise 14.3)   Time can be scaled so that*

$$\beta + \mu_1 + \lambda_1 + \lambda_2 \quad (= \beta + \nu) = 1.$$

Using this scaling of time, the effective discount factor is simply ν, which is strictly less than 1, for every state, regardless of the decision. Thus, the terms in the optimality equations can be expressed as follows.

$$f(x_1, x_2) = \min_{k=0,1,2} G_k(x_1, x_2),$$

where

$$G_0(x_1, x_2) = \sum_i \mathcal{L}_i(x_i) + \mu_1 f(x_1, x_2) + \lambda_1 f(x_1 - 1, x_2) + \lambda_2 f(x_1, x_2 - 1),$$

$$G_1(x_1, x_2) = \sum_i \mathcal{L}_i(x_i) + \mu_1 f(x_1 + 1, x_2) + \lambda_1 f(x_1 - 1, x_2)$$
$$+ \lambda_2 f(x_1, x_2 - 1),$$

and

$$G_2(x_1, x_2) = \sum_i \mathcal{L}_i(x_i) + (\mu_1 - \mu_2) f(x_1, x_2) + \mu_2 f(x_1, x_2 + 1)$$
$$+ \lambda_1 f(x_1 - 1, x_2) + \lambda_2 f(x_1, x_2 - 1).$$

Final Form of Optimality Equations

Finally, by defining $G_0(x_1, x_2)$ as the base comparison quantity and pulling it out of the minimization, we can rewrite the optimality equations as

$$f(x_1, x_2) = \sum_i \mathcal{L}_i(x_i) + \mu_1 f(x_1, x_2) + \lambda_1 f(x_1 - 1, x_2) + \lambda_2 f(x_1, x_2 - 1)$$
$$+ \min[0, \mu_1 \Delta_1 f(x_1, x_2), \mu_2 \Delta_2 f(x_1, x_2)],$$

where
$$\Delta_1 v(x_1, x_2) := v(x_1 + 1, x_2) - v(x_1, x_2), \text{ and}$$
$$\Delta_2 v(x_1, x_2) := v(x_1, x_2 + 1) - v(x_1, x_2).$$

That is, Δ_1 computes the first difference in the first component of the function and Δ_2 the first difference in the second component.

14.3   Results

We now use the optimality criterion to characterize the optimal policy. Starting in state (x_1, x_2), it is optimal to produce product one if the second term in the minimization is smallest, namely,

$$\Delta_1 f(x_1, x_2) \leq 0, \text{ and } \mu_1 \Delta_1 f(x_1, x_2) \leq \mu_2 \Delta_2 f(x_1, x_2).$$

Similarly, it is optimal to produce product two if

$$\Delta_2 f(x_1, x_2) \leq 0 \text{ and } \mu_1 \Delta_1 f(x_1, x_2) \geq \mu_2 \Delta_2 f(x_1, x_2).$$

Finally, it is optimal to produce nothing if

$$\Delta_1 f(x_1, x_2) \geq 0 \text{ and } \Delta_2 f(x_1, x_2) \geq 0.$$

Theorem 14.1   *(Exercise 14.6)   Suppose that $p_2 \mu_2 > p_1 \mu_1$. If $x_2 < 0$, then it is optimal to produce product two, regardless of the stock level of product one.*

Theorem 14.1 is closely connected to the famous $c\mu$ rule for scheduling customers of different types in a potentially congested service system. In that setting, let c_i denote the waiting cost rate and μ_i the service rate (defined to be the inverse of the mean service time) for customers of type i. The $c\mu$ rule is a static priority rule (being independent of the state of the system) that gives priorities to the customer classes in descending order of their $c\mu$ values. Cox and Smith (1961) show that the $c\mu$ rule is optimal under an average cost formulation among the class of all static priority rules for an $M/G/1$ queue. In the model here, p_i plays the role of c_i.

Note that negative inventory in the model here corresponds to backlogged orders: $-x_2$ represents the number of orders for product 2 that are backlogged, each accumulating cost at the rate p_2. If all production in this system were done to order, then stock levels would always be negative, we could multiply the state space through by minus one, and the state of the system would be the number of customers of each type (orders for product one and two, respectively) in the system. That is, we would have a standard queueing model. Theorem 14.1 says that whenever there are type two customers in the system, then they should be given priority. However, a standard queueing system does not allow for a negative number of customers, which represents inventory of the product. Thus, this model can be viewed as a generalization of a queueing priority model that allows for inventories, which can be viewed as customer services that are carried out in advance and incur a holding cost until they are needed.

Assume henceforth that $\mu_1 = \mu_2$: The products have equal production rates. (The form of the optimal policy has not been established for the general case yet.) Let

$$S(x_1) := \min\{x_2 | \Delta_1 f(x_1, x_2) \geq 0, \Delta_2 f(x_1, x_2) \geq 0\},$$

which, given x_1, the inventory level of product one, is the smallest inventory level of product two such that it is optimal not to produce, starting at (x_1, x_2). Similarly, let

$$C(x_1) := \min\{x_2 | \Delta_2 f(x_1, x_2) \geq \Delta_1 f(x_1, x_2)\},$$

which, given x_1, is the smallest inventory level of product two such that it is better to produce product 1 than product 2, starting at (x_1, x_2).

Theorem 14.2   (Ha, 1997)   Suppose that $\mu_1 = \mu_2$. Then $S(x_1)$ is a decreasing function, and $C(x_1)$ is an increasing function, of x_1. Starting at (x_1, x_2), it is optimal to act as follows: If $x_2 \geq S(x_1)$, then stop production. If not, then produce product 1 if $x_2 \geq C(x_1)$ and produce product 2 otherwise.

Ha's (1997) proof identifies the structured value functions as those that are supermodular and satisfy a diagonal dominance condition on the matrix of second differences that is analogous to Corollary A.1. That is, if these were functions of two continuous real variables rather than integer variables, this condition would imply that the functions were convex.

It is interesting to observe how differently this system works from a decentralized inventory sytem in which there are separate managers of the inventories of each product. Suppose the managers follow base stock policies in that system. Usually when a unit is demanded, an order to replenish it is placed on the central production system. When there is a surge in demand, many orders are placed on the system. Stock levels are low, and the lead time until a new order will be received is high. Thus, each inventory manager may anticipate the need to have a larger base stock level, so they order additional units. After a long period of slow demand, so that inventory levels are near the base stock levels, the managers will recognize that the order lead times are now low and may

select smaller base stock levels, deferring placing new orders until the inventory
level drops below the new base stock level. This is an example of the bullwhip
effect discussed by Lee, Padmanabhan, and Whang (1997). In particular, it
generates a rush-and-wait atmosphere in the production facility. In addition,
the inventory policies say nothing about what unit should be produced next in
the production facility. It should be clear that a first-come-first-served priority
rule is not optimal. By contrast, the model in this chapter shows that if product
2 is stocked out, then it should be produced next. If product 2 is not stocked
out, but product 1 is, then product 1 should be produced next. Otherwise, as
illustrated in Figure 14.2, the decision depends on the relative scarcity of one
versus the other. If one of the products is overstocked, then a smaller number
of the other product is needed to stop production.

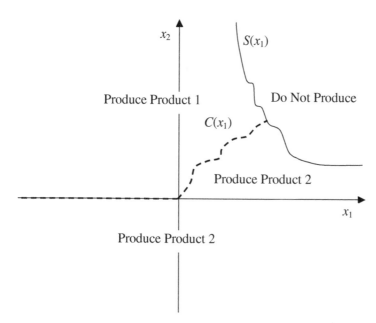

Figure 14.2   *Illustration of the Optimal Policy*

Once it is ensured that there is no excess stock of either product, the optimal
policy cannot be described simply by a base stock level for each product such
that a product is no longer produced once its inventory level reaches its base
stock level. For example, suppose, as in Figure 14.3, that it is optimal to
produce product 1 if the state is $(0, 2)$, to produce product 2 if the state is

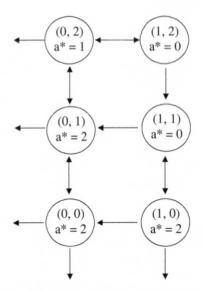

Figure 14.3   Multiple Production Stopping States

$(0,0)$, $(0,1)$, and $(1,0)$, and to produce nothing if the state is $(1,1)$, or
$(1,2)$. The arrows show the only possible transitions out of the states shown
under the optimal policy. For example, the only transitions out of state $(1,1)$
are to either $(0,1)$, corresponding to a demand for product 1 arising, or to
$(1,0)$, corresponding to a demand for product 2 arising. Then, starting at
$(0,0)$, production is initiated on a unit of product 2. If that unit is completed
before a demand occurs, the system moves to state $(0,1)$, where another unit
of product 2 is begun. If that unit is also finished before a demand arises, then
the state becomes $(0,2)$, where a unit of product 1 is begun. If that unit is
completed before a demand arises, the state becomes $(1,2)$, where production
is stopped. So $(1,2)$ is one realizable production stopping state. Now, if a
demand for product 2 arises, the state becomes $(1,1)$, and it is still optimal
to produce nothing. If another demand for product 2 arises, then the state
becomes $(1,0)$, where a unit of product 2 is begun. If that unit is completed
before a demand arises, then the state becomes $(1,1)$, where production is
stopped. That is, state $(1,1)$ is another realizable production stopping state.
We cannot say that the optimal base stock levels are $S_1 = 1$ and $S_2 = 2$,
because it is optimal to produce nothing when in state $(1,1)$. We cannot say
that the optimal base stock levels are $S_1 = S_2 = 1$, because it is optimal to
begin production of a unit of product 2 when in state $(0,1)$.

Exercises

14.1   Prove Lemma 14.1.

14.2   Prove Lemma 14.2(b) and (c).

14.3   Prove Lemma 14.3.

14.4   Let V^* denote the set of functions v of two integer variables such that if $x_2 < 0$, then $\Delta_2 v(x_1, x_2) < 0$ and $\mu_2 \Delta_2 v(x_1, x_2) \leq \mu_1 \Delta_1 v(x_1, x_2)$. Show that (ρ, V^*) is a complete metric space, where ρ is the L^∞ metric: $\rho(u, v) = \sup_x |u(x) - v(x)|$.

14.5   Define V^* as in Exercise 14.4. Given $v \in V^*$, prove that if $x_2 < 0$, then $\Delta_2[Av](x_1, x_2) < 0$ holds, where A is the usual optimal value operator and $\Delta_2[Av](x_1, x_2) = [Av](x_1, x_2 + 1) - [Av](x_1, x_2)$.

14.6   Prove Theorem 14.1.

Hint: Apply Exercises 14.4 and 14.5.

References

Cox, D., W. Smith. 1961. *Queues*. John Wiley and Sons, New York.

Ha, A. 1997. Optimal dynamic scheduling policy for a make-to-stock production system. *Operations Research*. **45** 42–53.

Lee, H., V. Padmanabhan, S. Whang. 1997. Information distortion in a supply chain: The bullwhip effect. *Management Science*. **43** 546–58.

Lippman, S. 1975. Applying a new device in the optimization of exponential queueing systems. *Operations Research*. **23** 687–710.

Convexity

This appendix assumes the reader has some familiarity with convex sets and functions. Readers not familiar with examples and basic properties of convex sets and functions can find them in many references, such as Heyman and Sobel (1984:521–4) and Zangwill (1969:25–30). This appendix also assumes that we have an optimization problem to solve: We seek to maximize or minimize an objective function by specifying numerical values to each of the decision variables subject to satisfying all the constraints. The important role that convex and concave functions play in such problems is reviewed: Theorem A.1(b) says that if we face an unconstrained minimization [maximization] problem, and the objective function is a convex [concave] function of the (continuous) decision variables, then setting the partial derivatives of the objective function with respect to the decision variables equal to zero and solving leads to an optimal solution. Convexity [concavity] of the functions defining the constraints also plays an important role in determining how manageable the optimization problem is. This appendix emphasizes basic results and the role of the Hessian, and ends with some extensions of the convexity concept. Advanced readers will find Rockafellar (1970) indispensable.

A.1   Basic Definitions and Results

We assume in this appendix that the set X is a subset of $\mathbf{R}^n$ unless specified otherwise. The set X is *convex* if it contains all line segments connecting points in the set. That is, X is convex if $x \in X$, $y \in X$, and $0 \le \theta \le 1$ imply that $\theta x + (1 - \theta)y \in X$.

Equivalently, X is *convex* if all *convex combinations* of points in X are in X. That is, suppose we start with m points in X, namely, $x^1, x^2, \cdots, x^m$, and m nonnegative weights $\theta^1, \theta^2, \cdots, \theta^m$ that sum to one: $\sum_j \theta^j = 1$. If X is convex, then the point represented by the convex combination

$$w = \theta^1 x^1 + \theta^2 x^2 + \cdots + \theta^m x^m$$

must be a member of the set.

A real valued function f defined on a convex set X is *convex* if $x \in X$, $y \in X$, and $0 \le \theta \le 1$ imply that $f(\theta x + (1 - \theta)y) \le \theta f(x) + (1 - \theta)f(y)$. For example, as in Figure A.1(a) below, a convex function of a single variable lies on or below the line connecting any two of its values. Note that the function depicted in Figure A.1(b) is not convex because the function does not completely lie below one such line. The function f is *strictly convex* if $0 < \theta < 1$ implies that $f(\theta x + (1 - \theta)y) < \theta f(x) + (1 - \theta)f(y)$. A function f defined on a convex set is *[strictly] concave* if $-f$ is [strictly] convex.

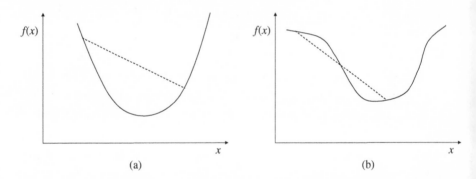

$$\text{(a)} \qquad\qquad\qquad\qquad \text{(b)}$$

Figure A.1   Examples of Functions That Are
(a) Convex and (b) Nonconvex, Respectively

Fundamental Role of Convexity in Optimization

Assume in this appendix, unless indicated otherwise, that the objective function f is twice continuously (partially) differentiable on its domain X. Recall from the conventions (following the preface) that $\nabla f(x)$ denotes the gradient of f

evaluated at the point x, the vector of partial derivatives of f. We can then state an equivalent definition of convexity and follow with strong motivation for studying convexity in optimization problems.

Theorem A.1   *Suppose X is a convex set.*

(a) (Zangwill, 1969:28)   A function f is convex on X iff

$$f(y) \geq f(x) + \nabla f(x)^{\mathrm{T}}(y - x)$$

for all $x, y \in X$.

(b) (Zangwill, 1969:31)   If f is convex on X, $\nabla f(x) = 0$, and $x \in X$, then x minimizes f over X.

Proof   The proof of (b) is simple and insightful. Let y be an arbitrary point in X. Then, by (a),

$$f(y) \geq f(x) + \nabla f(x)^{\mathrm{T}}(y - x) = f(x),$$

because $\nabla f(x) = 0$ is given. Thus, x is a minimizer of f over X.   □

In the single variable case $(n = 1)$, one can pick an arbitary point x and draw a straight line through the value $f(x)$. Part (a) says, in part, that if the slope of this line is $f'(x)$, the derivative of f at x, then the function will lie above this line. Part (b) is what makes optimization researchers so interested in determining whether or not their objective functions are convex [concave] or not: If we have a convex [concave] objective function and a feasible point at which the first-order conditions hold (the gradient of the objective function vanishes), then we know we have found a minimizer [maximizer].

Assuring Convexity

Thus, we are frequently interested in ensuring that certain functions that arise in our analysis of models are convex. Sometimes, there are simple basic results that are useful in this regard, such as the following.

Theorem A.2   *(Zangwill, 1969:32–33)   Positive linear combinations of convex functions are convex.*

However, frequently more powerful results are needed. The following two results are extremely useful in applications and are cited numerous times elsewhere in this book. Their importance justifies including their proofs.

Theorem A.3   *(Convexity Preservation under Maximization)   (Heyman and Sobel, 1984:525)   If Y is a nonempty set and $g(\cdot, y)$ is a convex function on a convex set X for each $y \in Y$, then*

$$f(x) := \sup_{y \in Y} g(x, y)$$

is a convex function on X.

Proof   Let x and $\bar{x}$ be arbitrary elements of X, let $0 \le \theta \le 1$, and let $\bar{\theta} := 1 - \theta$. Then,

$$
\begin{aligned}
f(\theta x + \bar{\theta}\bar{x}) &= \sup_{y \in Y} g(\theta x + \bar{\theta}\bar{x}, y) & \text{[definition]} \\
&\le \sup_{y \in Y} [\theta g(x, y) + \bar{\theta} g(\bar{x}, y)] & \text{[convexity of } g(\cdot, y)] \\
&\le \sup_{y \in Y} \theta g(x, y) + \sup_{y \in Y} \bar{\theta} g(\bar{x}, y) & \text{[separate maximizations]} \\
&= \theta f(x) + \bar{\theta} f(\bar{x}). & \text{[definition of } f]
\end{aligned}
$$

□

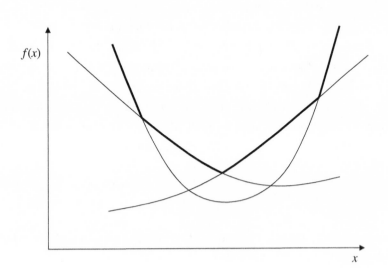

Figure A.2   Preservation of Convexity Under Maximization

Figure A.2 illustrates the basic idea of Theorem A.3: The (pointwise) maximum of three different convex functions, denoted by the thick line, is clearly convex as well. The minimum in that example is clearly *not* convex. However, if there is a continuum of convex functions and they satisfy the following joint convexity property, then the minimum will be convex.

Theorem A.4   *(Convexity Preservation under Minimization)*   *(Heyman and Sobel, 1984:525)   If X is a convex set, $Y(x)$ is a nonempty set for every $x \in X$, the set $C := \{(x, y) | x \in X, y \in Y(x)\}$ is a convex set, $g(x, y)$ is a convex function on C ,*

$$f(x) := \inf_{y \in Y(x)} g(x, y),$$

and $f(x) > -\infty$ for every $x \in X$, then f is a convex function on X .

Proof   Let x and $\bar{x}$ be arbitrary elements of X . Let $0 \le \theta \le 1$, and let $\bar{\theta} := 1 - \theta$. Select arbitrary $\delta > 0$. By the definition of f , there must exist $y \in Y(x)$ and $\bar{y} \in Y(\bar{x})$ such that $g(x, y) \le f(x) + \delta$ and $g(\bar{x}, \bar{y}) \le f(\bar{x}) + \delta$. Then,

$$\begin{aligned}
\theta f(x) + \bar{\theta} f(\bar{x}) &\ge \theta g(x, y) + \bar{\theta} g(\bar{x}, \bar{y}) - \delta &&\text{[properties of } y \text{ and } \bar{y}] \\
&\ge g(\theta x + \bar{\theta}\bar{x}, \theta y + \bar{\theta}\bar{y}) - \delta &&\text{[convexity of } g(\cdot, \cdot) \text{ on } C] \\
&\ge f(\theta x + \bar{\theta}\bar{x}) - \delta. &&[(\theta x + \bar{\theta}\bar{x}, \theta y + \bar{\theta}\bar{y}) \in C]
\end{aligned}$$

Because δ is arbitrary, the inequality must hold for $\delta = 0$. (Otherwise, a contradiction can be reached.)   □

Figure A.3 illustrates the idea of the theorem for the two-dimensional case in which all (x, y) points are feasible and a minimizing $y(x)$ exists for each x . The solid lines are *iso-cost* lines that give the locus of points in (x, y) space at which the objective function $g(x, y)$ has the same value. You can think of the figure as indicating contour lines on a map, in this case of a depression in the ground. One way to seek the bottom of the depression is to alter both x and y in the search. Another, which corresponds to this theorem, is, for each x , to find the lowest elevation (cost) possible by varying y . The optimal such y is $y(x)$. The question is whether $f(x) = g(x, y(x))$, the induced minimal elevation, is convex, a well-behaved function of x . If so, then, for example, if a point x^* can be found such that f only increases when x is changed from x^* , then x^* is optimal in the sense that $(x^*, y(x^*))$ minimizes $g(x, y)$. We now return to why $f(x)$ is indeed convex in this setting. Picking two arbitrary (feasible) points x and $\bar{x}$, the figure plots $(x, y(x))$ and $(\bar{x}, y(\bar{x}))$, which correspond to $f(x)$ and $f(\bar{x})$, respectively. Note that because $y(x)$ minimizes $g(x, y)$ over (feasible) y , a vertical line drawn (parallel to the y axis) through that

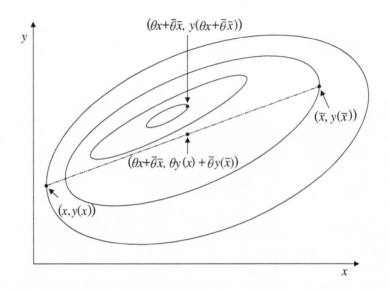

Figure A.3   Preservation of Convexity Under Minimization

point cannot intersect a lower iso-cost line. (Otherwise a point other than $y(x)$ would yield a lower cost.) Because all (x, y) points are feasible, the convex combination of the two feasible points $(x, y(x))$ and $(\bar{x}, y(\bar{x}))$, namely, $(\theta x + \bar{\theta}\bar{x}, \theta y(x) + \bar{\theta}y(\bar{x}))$, is also feasible. Because $g(x, y)$ is jointly convex in (x, y), its value at that convex combination, namely, $g(\theta x + \bar{\theta}\bar{x}, \theta y(x) + \bar{\theta}y(\bar{x}))$, is no bigger than the convex combination of the values of $f(x)$ and $f(\bar{x})$. The value of $f(\theta x + \bar{\theta}\bar{x})$ comes from minimizing $g(\theta x + \bar{\theta}\bar{x}, y)$ over y and is therefore even smaller. That is, $g(\theta x + \bar{\theta}\bar{x}, \theta y(x) + \bar{\theta}y(\bar{x}))$ corresponds to a feasible, but not necessarily optimal value of y. In short, $f(\theta x + \bar{\theta}\bar{x}) \leq \theta f(x) + \bar{\theta}f(\bar{x})$.

Counterexample

One might conjecture that if a function is convex in each variable separately, and there is a unique solution to the first-order conditions, then that solution is a local minimum. This conjecture is false, as seen by the following counterexample.

Suppose $f(x) = c^{\mathsf{T}}x + x^{\mathsf{T}}Ax$, $c^{\mathsf{T}} = (-4, 12)$, and

$$A = \begin{pmatrix} 2 & -3 \\ -3 & 4 \end{pmatrix}.$$

That is,

$$f(x) = -4x_1 + 2x_1^2 - 6x_1x_2 + 12x_2 + 4x_2^2,$$

which is strictly convex in each coordinate direction. The first-order conditions are

$$c + 2Ax = 0.$$

That is,

$$-4 + 4x_1 - 6x_2 = 0$$

$$12 - 6x_1 + 8x_2 = 0.$$

The first can be solved for x_1 in terms of x_2 :

$$x_1^*(x_2) = 3x_2/2 + 1,$$

which minimizes f in the x_1 direction for each x_2. If we plug that expression back into the second equation, we get $x_2 = 6$, which yields $x_1^*(x_2) = 10$, so the unique solution to the first-order conditions is $x^* = (10, 6)$. But if we plug $x_1^*(x_2)$ into the objective function, we get the *induced* objective function, as a function of x_2 alone as

$$f(x_1^*(x_2), x_2) = -2 + 6x_2 - x_2^2/2,$$

which is clearly unbounded below. We can always reduce the objective function by increasing x_2. The induced function is *concave* rather than convex. Its first-order conditions lead to a maximum along the given trajectory. The problem is that the original function is not *jointly* convex. We explore direct conditions that ensure (joint) convexity in the next section.

Connection to Team Theory

Suppose x_1 is selected by player 1 and x_2 by player 2, and each wants to minimize the same (organization wide) objective function. (This is an example of a team theory problem.) The point $(10, 6)$ is a *Nash equilibrium* in that neither player would choose to alter her decision, given the decision of the other player. However, it would be a terrible solution for the organization as a whole, as far better solutions are possible. Luckily, the point identified is unstable: If one player deviates a little bit from it, a *tatonnement* process (of alternating optimal responses by each player to the latest proposed decision of the other) never returns to it. If the objective function is jointly convex, then any Nash equilibrium yields a global optimum and a tatonnement process terminates at a global optimum. When analyzing best-response strategies for players of a general game, in which each player has separate objective functions, similar issues arise.

A.2   Role of the Hessian

There are other ways to ensure that a function is convex, and we pursue some of them in this section. We examine some optimization issues in more depth along the way. Readers not familiar with the definitions of *local maximum* and *local minimum* can find them in many references, such as Avriel (1976:9–10).

The *Hessian matrix* of a (twice differentiable) function f, evaluated at the point x, is the symmetric matrix of second partial derivatives, each evaluated at the point x. The diagonal of the Hessian gives the second derivatives with respect to each of the decision variables, and the off-diagonal elements are the cross-partial derivatives.

A *strict local minimum* is a local minimum whose objective function value is strictly lower than all other points in a specified neighborhood. The definition of a *strict local maximum* is analogous.

An $n \times n$ (square) matrix A is *positive definite* if $x^{\mathrm{T}}Ax > 0$ for every nonzero $x \in \mathbf{R}^n$. It is *positive semidefinite* if $x^{\mathrm{T}}Ax \geq 0$ for every x.

Theorem A.5

(a) (Avriel, 1976:11)   If the gradient (of the objective function) vanishes at an interior point and the Hessian is positive definite at that point, then that point is a local minimum.

(b) (Avriel, 1976:11)   If the gradient vanishes at an interior point and the Hessian is positive semidefinite in a neighborhood of that point, then that point is a local minimum.

(c) (Avriel, 1976:11)   If an interior point is a local minimum, then the gradient must vanish at that point and the Hessian must be positive semidefinite at that point.

(d) (Avriel, 1976:13)   If the gradient vanishes at an interior point and the Hessian is positive definite in a neighborhood of that point, then that point is a strict local minimum.

Connection Between Convexity and Hessians

Theorem A.6

(a) *(Zangwill, 1969:30)   A function is convex iff its Hessian is positive semidefinite at every point of its domain.*

(b) *(Bernstein and Toupin, 1962:67–72)   If a function's Hessian is positive definite at every point of its domain, then it is strictly convex.*

For example, by (a), a function of a single variable is convex iff its second derivative is positive. The converse of (b) is false: A (twice continuously differentiable) strictly convex function need not have a positive definite Hessian everywhere (Exercise A.14).

We aim for a direct approach to determining whether a given function is convex or not, using this result.

Connection Between Positive Definiteness and Eigenvalues

Assume in this appendix, unless indicated otherwise, that all matrices are real and that A is n by n. A real or complex number λ is an *eigenvalue* of A and a nonzero real or complex n-vector v is a *right eigenvector* corresponding to λ if $Av = \lambda v$. A nonzero real or complex n-vector v is a *left eigenvector* corresponding to λ if $v^{\mathsf{T}}A = \lambda v^{\mathsf{T}}$ (that is, $A^{\mathsf{T}}v = \lambda v$).

Theorem A.7   *(Young, 1971:14)   The number λ is an eigenvalue of A iff λ is a root of the characteristic equation*

$$\det(A - \lambda I) = 0,$$

where $\det(\cdot)$ is the determinant and I is the identity matrix.

The characteristic equation is a polynomial of degree n. Hence, there are n eigenvalues, some possibly repeated.

Theorem A.8   *(Young, 1971:14)   The eigenvalues $\lambda_1, \lambda_2, \cdots, \lambda_n$ satisfy*

$$\prod_{i=1}^{n} \lambda_i = \det(A) \text{ and } \sum_{i=1}^{n} \lambda_i = \text{trace}(A),$$

where trace($\cdot$) *is the sum of diagonal elements of the matrix, which must be square.*

The eigenvalues of two by two matrices can be found using this result. For example, consider the matrix

$$A = \begin{pmatrix} 2 & -3 \\ -3 & 4.5 \end{pmatrix}.$$

Its determinant is 0, and its trace is 6.5. Hence, its eigenvalues are 6.5 and 0.

Theorem A.9

(a) *(Ostrowski, 1960)   The eigenvalues of a matrix are continuous functions of its elements.*

(b) *(Young, 1971:16)   All eigenvalues of a symmetric matrix are real.*

(c) *(Young, 1971:21)   A symmetric matrix is positive semidefinite [definite] iff all its eigenvalues are [strictly] positive.*

(d) *(Young, 1971:21)   A symmetric matrix is positive semidefinite [definite] iff the determinant of every principal minor (submatrix formed by striking out arbitrary rows and their corresponding columns) is [strictly] positive.*

Thus, for a symmetric matrix to be positive definite, all its diagonal elements must be strictly positive, and the determinant of the entire matrix must be strictly positive. For two by two matrices, these conditions are both necessary and sufficient for positive definiteness. Is the example matrix above positive definite?

Theorem A.10   *(Gerschgorin Bounds on Eigenvalues)   (Varga, 1962:16) Let δ_i denote the sum of the absolute values of the off-diagonal elements in row i. That is, $\delta_i := \sum_{j \neq i} |a_{ij}|$. All eigenvalues of A lie in the union of the following sets:*

$$\{\lambda \,|\, |\lambda - a_{ii}| \leq \delta_i\} \text{ for } 1 \leq i \leq n.$$

A matrix is *diagonally dominant* if the absolute value of each diagonal element exceeds the sum of the absolute values of the off-diagonal elements in its row:

$$|a_{ii}| \geq \sum_{j \neq i} |a_{ij}| \text{ for all } i.$$

Strict diagonal dominance calls for a strict inequality for each i.

Corollary A.1   *If a symmetric matrix has positive diagonal elements and is
[strictly] diagonally dominant, then it is positive semidefinite [definite].*

The following is an example of a strictly diagonally dominant matrix:

$$A = \begin{pmatrix} 5 & -1 & -2 \\ -1 & 4 & 1 \\ -2 & 1 & 4 \end{pmatrix}.$$

The following is an example of a positive definite matrix that is not diagonally
dominant:

$$A = \begin{pmatrix} 2 & -3 \\ -3 & 5 \end{pmatrix}.$$

Testing Convexity by Analyzing the Hessian Directly

One way to determine if a (twice continuously differentiable) function of several
variables is convex is to consider its Hessian directly. The diagonal elements
must be positive. Nothing more is required if there are no cross-product terms.
(We simply have the sum of n convex functions of single variables.) If there are
off-diagonal entries, check for diagonal dominance. If you don't have diagonal
dominance but you have only two variables, simply check whether the determinant is positive. If there are three variables, it might be reasonable to compute
the determinants of all principal minors to ensure that they are positive.

Analyzing the Hessian Indirectly

If the Hessian of a function can be expressed in terms of other matrices, one
of the following theorems may be useful in guaranteeing that the function is
convex.

Theorem A.11

*(a) (Heyman and Sobel, 1984:537)   Any matrix of the form $A^{\mathsf{T}}A$ is positive
semidefinite.*

*(b) (Heyman and Sobel, 1984:537)   If A is positive definite, then A is
nonsingular and A^{-1} is positive definite.*

*(c) (Heyman and Sobel, 1984:537)   If A is $n \times n$ and positive definite and
B is $n \times m$ with rank m, and $m \leq n$, then $B^{\mathsf{T}}AB$ is positive definite.*

A.3 Generalizations of Convexity

Theorem A.1(b) provided great incentive to show that an objective function was convex, and much of this appendix was aimed at providing useful tools in this regard. However, there are several generalizations of Theorem A.1(b) that expand the class of functions among which the result holds. We touch on the topic here and refer the reader to Avriel (1976) for more.

A function f is *quasi-convex* on X if X is a convex set and if x and y in X and $0 \leq \theta \leq 1$ imply that $f(\theta x + (1 - \theta)y) \leq \max[f(x), f(y)]$. A function f is *strictly quasi-convex* on X if x and y in X, $x \neq y$, and $0 < \theta < 1$ imply that $f(\theta x + (1 - \theta)y) < \max[f(x), f(y)]$. This latter definition follows Diewert, Avriel, and Zang (1981), which differs from Ponstein (1967) and Avriel (1976) but has the attractive feature that strictly quasi-convex functions are quasi-convex.

Theorem A.12

(a) *(Avriel, 1976:146)*   If f is quasi-convex on a convex set and x is a strict local minimum, then x is a strict global minimum.

(b) *(Diewert, Avriel, and Zang, 1981)*   If f is strictly quasi-convex on a convex set and x is a local minimum, then x is the unique global minimum.

(c) *(Quasi-convexity Preservation under Maximization)*   If Y is a nonempty set and $g(\cdot, y)$ is a quasi-convex function on a convex set X for each $y \in Y$, then $f(x) := \sup_{y \in Y} g(x, y)$ is a quasi-convex function on X.

(d) *(Quasi-convexity Preservation under Minimization)*   If $Y(x)$ is a nonempty set for every $x \in X$, the set $C := \{(x, y) | x \in X, y \in Y(x)\}$ is a convex set, and $g(x, y)$ is a quasi-convex function on C, then $f(x) := \inf_{y \in Y(x)} g(x, y)$ is a quasi-convex function on any convex subset of $\{x \in X | f(x) > -\infty\}$.

A strictly quasi-convex function possesses the strong property that it cannot be flat at its minimum and therefore must have a unique global minimum. For example, not all convex functions are strictly quasi-convex. Nevertheless, a strictly quasi-convex function can have points of inflection, so that points at which the gradient vanishes are not necessarily even local minima. Yet another class of functions is called for: A (differentiable) function f is *pseudo-convex* if $\nabla f(x)^{\mathrm{T}}(y - x) \geq 0$ implies that

$$f(x) \leq f(y).$$

Theorem A.13 (*Avriel, 1976:146*) *If* f *is pseudo-convex on an open convex set, then any point at which the gradient vanishes is a global minimum.*

Exercises

A.1 Consider the conjecture created by replacing "convex function" by "strictly convex function" in Theorem A.4.

(a) Prove that the conjecture is valid if the minimization over y is always attained.

(b) Provide a counterexample to the conjecture if the minimization over y is not necessarily always attained.

A.2 Consider the optimal value function f of a linear program:

$$f(b) := \min_{\substack{Ax=b \\ x \geq 0}} c^T x,$$

where x is the n-vector of decision variables, c is a given n-vector and A is a given $m \times n$ matrix, as a function of the right-hand side m-vector b. Let B denote a convex subset of $\mathbf{R}^m$ such that $f(b)$ is finite for each $b \in B$. Prove that f is a convex function on B.

A.3 Suppose that $g(x, y)$ is a (jointly) convex function, twice continuously partially differentiable, defined on $\mathbf{R}^2$. For convenience, we use subscripts to denote partial differentiation. For example,

$$g_2(x, y) = \frac{\partial g(x, y)}{\partial y}.$$

Suppose, for every x, there exists $y(x)$ such that $g_2(x, y(x)) = 0$. That is, a minimizer $y(x)$ of $g(x, \cdot)$ exists for each $x \in \mathbf{R}$. Assume that $g_{22}(x, y(x)) > 0$ for all x. Use Theorem A.4 and the implicit function theorem, stated below, to prove that

$$g_{11}(x, y(x)) g_{22}(x, y(x)) - g_{12}^2(x, y(x)) \geq 0.$$

(Do *not* use Theorem A.6. What you are doing here sheds some insight on that result.)

Theorem A.14   *(Implicit Function)   If $f(x, y)$ and $f_2(x, y)$ are continuous in a neighborhood $N_{(a,b)}$ of the point (a, b) in $\mathbf{R}^2$, $f(a, b) = 0$, and
$f_2(a, b) \neq 0$, then there exist neighborhoods N_a of a and N_b of b and a
function $\phi(x)$ defined on N_a such that*

(a) *for all $x \in N_a$, $\phi(x) \in N_b$, $(x, \phi(x)) \in N_{(a,b)}$, and $f(x, \phi(x)) = 0$,*

(b) *$\phi(a) = b$,*

(c) *$\phi(x)$ is continuous in N_a, and*

(d) *if $f_1(x, y)$ exists and is continuous in $N_{(a,b)}$, then $\phi'(x)$ exists, is continuous in N_a, and*

$$\phi'(x) = -\frac{f_1(x, \phi(x))}{f_2(x, \phi(x))}.$$

A.4   (Zheng, 1992)   For strictly positive real numbers $x > 0$ and real
numbers $y \in \mathbf{R}$, define

$$f(x, y) := \frac{a + \int_{t=y}^{x+y} c(t)\, dt}{x},$$

where a is a strictly positive real number, $c(\cdot)$ is a nonnegative, continuously
differentiable, and convex function that is minimized at a unique strictly positive
finite point t_0.

(a) Fix $x > 0$. Show that y minimizes $f(x, \cdot)$ if and only if y satisfies

$$c(y) = c(x + y).$$

(b) Let $y(x)$ denote a minimizer of $f(x, \cdot)$ for each given $x > 0$. Assume
that $y(x)$ exists, is continuously differentiable and is strictly positive for each
such x. Prove that

$$c'(y(x)) \leq 0 \leq c'(x + y(x)).$$

(c) (Continuation) Use the implicit function theorem to prove that

$$-1 \leq y'(x) \leq 0.$$

(d) (Continuation) Define

$$g(x) := c(y(x)).$$

Prove that g is convex on the positive orthant. You may assume that g is
twice differentiable.

A.5 (Mendelson, 1985) Consider the following two-variable nonlinear maximization problem. The objective function is

$$f(x, y) = kx - vg(x/y) - cy;$$

the decision variables, x and y, must be strictly positive; and k, v, and c are strictly positive constants such that $k > c$. Furthermore, g is a continuously twice differentiable, strictly increasing, and convex function defined for $x < y$. Assume that $g(x/y) = \infty$ for $x \geq y$. Find an explicit solution (each variable expressed as an explicit function of the parameters of the problem) to the first-order optimality conditions: (Set the partial derivatives equal to zero and solve.) Is this solution an optimal solution to the stated maximization problem? Why or why not? If not, what is the optimal solution?

A.6 Suppose that X is a convex subset of $\mathbf{R}$. Prove that a real valued function f of a single real variable is convex on X iff $f(x + y) - f(x)$ is increasing in x (on X) for every (fixed) $y > 0$.

A.7 (Barlow and Proschan, 1965) Let Φ denote the distribution function and ϕ the density function for a positive continuous random variable T. That is, $\Phi(x) = P(T \leq x)$ for $x \geq 0$. Letting $\bar{\Phi}(x) := 1 - \Phi(x)$ as usual, define $g(x) := \ln[\bar{\Phi}(x)]$ and

$$r(x, y) := \frac{\Phi(x + y) - \Phi(x)}{\bar{\Phi}(x)}.$$

Let $X := \{x | \Phi(x) < 1, x \geq 0\}$. Prove that (a) for every fixed $y > 0$, the function $r(\cdot, y)$ is increasing on X iff (b) g is concave on X.

Hint: Express r in terms of g and use Exercise A.6.

A.8 (Karush, 1958) Suppose that $f : \mathbf{R} \to \mathbf{R}$ and that f is convex on $\mathbf{R}$. That is, $f(x)$ is a real valued convex function of a single real variable x. For $y \leq z$, define $g(y, z)$ as follows:

$$g(y, z) := \min_{x \in [y, z]} f(x).$$

(a) Show that g can be expressed as

$$g(y, z) = F(y) + G(z),$$

where F is convex increasing, and G is convex decreasing, on $\mathbf{R}$.

(b) Suppose that S is a minimizer of f over $\mathbf{R}$. Show that g can be expressed as

$$g(y,z) = \begin{cases} f(y) & \text{if } S \le y, \\ f(S) & \text{if } y \le S \le z, \\ f(z) & \text{if } z \le S. \end{cases}$$

A.9 Suppose $f : \mathbf{R} \to \mathbf{R}$. The *right derivative* of f is defined at x as

$$f'_+(x) = \lim_{h \downarrow 0} \frac{f(x+h) - f(x)}{h}.$$

If f'_+ exists for all $x \in \mathbf{R}$, then f is *right differentiable*. Prove that f is convex on $\mathbf{R}$ iff f is right differentiable on $\mathbf{R}$ and f'_+ is increasing on $\mathbf{R}$.

Hint: You may use without proof (Bazaraa and Shetty, 1979:83) that a convex function on $\mathbf{R}$ is right differentiable on $\mathbf{R}$. You may also use the fact that, for $y \ge x$,

$$f(y) = f(x) + \int_{t=x}^{y} f'_+(t)\, dt.$$

Hint: Use Exercise A.6.

A.10 Let X denote the set of integers: $X = \{0, \pm 1, \pm 2, \ldots\}$, and let f denote a real valued function defined on X. f is said to be *convex on* X if

$$f(\theta x + (1-\theta)y) \le \theta f(x) + (1-\theta)f(y)$$

whenever $x, y \in X$, $0 \le \theta \le 1$, and $\theta x + (1-\theta)y \in X$.

(a) Prove that f is convex on X if and only if $\Delta f(x) := f(x+1) - f(x)$ is increasing in x: $\Delta f(x+1) \ge \Delta f(x)$ for all $x \in X$.

(b) Prove that f is convex on X if and only if $f(x+i) - f(x)$ is increasing in x (on X) for every strictly positive integer i.

A.11 Let X denote the set of integers. Suppose that T is a finite set and that $g(x,t)$ is a real valued function defined for $x \in X$ and $t \in T$. Use Exercise A.10 to prove that $f(x) := \min_{t \in T} g(x,t)$ is convex on X if $g(x+1,t) - g(x,\tau)$ is increasing in x for every $t, \tau \in T$.

A.12 (Li, Porteus, and Zhang, 2001) Let X denote the set of integers. Suppose that c is a given, not necessarily positive, real number. Show that if f is convex on X, then so is the function $g(x) := \min[f(x+1) + c, f(x)]$.

Hint: Use Exercises A.10 and A.11.

A.13 Consider the matrix

$$A = \begin{pmatrix} 1 & 2 \\ 2 & 4 \end{pmatrix}.$$

Is A positive definite? Explain.

A.14 Give an example of a twice continuously differentiable strictly convex function defined on all of $\mathbf{R}^n$ whose Hessian is not positive definite everywhere. Your example should be a mathematical expression. Show that it has the required properties.

A.15 (Zangwill, 1969) Let X denote a convex set and f a real valued function defined on X. Prove that f is quasi-convex on X if and only if the set

$$Y(a) := \{x | f(x) \le a\}$$

is convex for every real number a.

A.16 Prove Theorem A.12(c).

A.17 Prove Theorem A.12(d).

References

Avriel, M. 1976. *Nonlinear Programming: Analysis and Methods.* Prentice-Hall, Englewood Cliffs, N.J.

Barlow, R., F. Proschan. 1965. *Mathematical Theory of Reliability.* Wiley, New York.

Bazaraa, M., C. Shetty. 1979. *Nonlinear Programming.* Wiley, New York.

Bernstein, B., R. Toupin. 1962. Some properties of the Hessian matrix of a strictly convex function. *Journal für die reine und angewandte Mathematik* **210** 67–72.

Diewert, W., M. Avriel, I. Zang. 1981. Nine kinds of quasiconcavity and concavity. *Journal of Economic Theory.* **25** 397–420.

Heyman, D., M. Sobel. 1984. *Stochastic Models in Operations Research, Volume II.* McGraw-Hill, New York.

Karush, W. 1958. A theorem in convex programming. *Naval Research Logistics Quarterly.* **5** 245–60.

Li, L., E. Porteus, H.-T. Zhang. 2001. Optimal operating policies for multiplant stochastic manufacturing systems in a changing environment. *Management Science.* **47** 1539–51.

Mendelson, H. 1985. Pricing computer services: queueing effects. *Communications of the ACM.* **28** 312–21.

Ostrowski, A. 1960. *Solution of Equations and Systems of Equations.* Academic Press, New York.

Ponstein, J. 1967. Seven kinds of convexity. *SIAM Review.* **9** 115–19.

Rockafellar, T. 1970. *Convex Analysis.* Princeton University Press, Princeton, N.J.

Varga, R. 1962. *Matrix Iterative Analysis.* Prentice-Hall, Englewood Cliffs, N.J.

Young, D. 1971. *Iterative Solution of Large Linear Systems.* Academic Press, New York.

Zangwill, W. 1969. *Nonlinear Programming: A Unified Approach.* Prentice-Hall, Englewood Cliffs, N.J.

Zheng, Y.-S. 1992. On properties of stochastic inventory systems. *Management Science.* **38** 87–103.

Duality

Suppose we have a constrained optimization problem, called the primal problem, that we'd like to solve. Duality theory can be very helpful in this regard, sometimes even revealing an explicit, closed form, optimal solution. It also sheds insight into the workings of markets and decentralization schemes. We begin with some basic optimization concepts, follow with a section on what is called the Everett result, and end with duality theory.

B.1   Basic Concepts

The *primal* (*P*) is the problem of maximizing an *objective function* f over the set of points that satisfy some given *constraints*, which consist of the *explicit constraints* $g(x) \leq b$ and the *implicit constraints* $x \in X$:

$$\max_{x \in X} f(x) \text{ subject to } g(x) \leq b, \qquad (P)$$

where X is a subset of $\mathbf{R}^n$, x is the n-vector of *decision variables*, $f \colon X \to \mathbf{R}$, $g \colon X \to \mathbf{R}^m$, b is a given m-vector, and n and m are strictly positive integers.

The explicit constraints can be written in pointwise form as

$$g_i(x) \leq b_i \text{ for } i = 1, 2, \ldots, m.$$

Example B.1   There are two decision variables $(n = 2)$ that are required implictly to be positive: $X = \{x = (x_1, x_2)|x_1 \geq 0, x_2 \geq 0\}$. There is one explicit constraint $(m = 1)$: $g(x) = g(x_1, x_2) = x_1 - x_2$, and $b = b_1 = 1$. The objective function is

$$f(x) = f(x_1, x_2) = -x_1^2 + 10x_1 + 4x_2 - 2x_2^2.$$

A solution x is *explicitly [implicitly] feasible* if it satisfies the explicit [implicit] constraints. A *feasible solution* is explicitly and implicitly feasible. An *optimal solution*, say x^*, is a feasible solution that yields at least as large an objective function value as every other feasible solution: $x^* \in X$, $g(x^*) \leq b$, and $f(x^*) \geq f(x)$ for all $x \in X$ such that $g(x) \leq b$. For convenience, f and g are assumed to be partially differentiable.

Interpretation of the Primal

The owner of a firm seeks to determine the level at which to operate each of the firm's n activities. Each activity is managed by a separate manager, and x_j denotes the level of activity j. The vector x is the *schedule* of activity levels. The owner's objective is to maximize her resulting return, $f(x)$ over schedules that satisfy the two kinds of constraints, explicit and implicit.

The owner has m scarce resources available for use. In particular, she has an amount b_i of resource i available, and $g_i(x)$ denotes the amount of resource i used to implement schedule x. The explicit constraints insist that only the resources available can be used.

The implicit constraints represent any other limitations on the schedule x, such as that the solutions be integers. These are represented by the requirement that x be an element of X. If there are no implicit constraints, then we set $X = \mathbf{R}^n$.

The owner of the firm wants to design an objective function that will induce her managers to select an optimal schedule. The objective function that we examine in this regard is called the *Lagrangian*, and it deals differently with the explicit and implicit constraints: Prices are established for the resources identified by the explicit constraints and a form of decentralized market is established. The implicit constraints are dealt with internally, directly.

Definition of the Lagrangian

The *Lagrangian* for (P) is defined as

$$L(x, \lambda) := f(x) - \lambda^{\mathrm{T}}[g(x) - b],$$

where $\lambda \geq 0$ is an m-vector of *Lagrange multipliers*. The Lagrangian can be written as

$$L(x, \lambda) = f(x) - \sum_{i=1}^{m} \lambda_i[g_i(x) - b_i].$$

Interpretation of the Lagrangian

The *Lagrange multipliers*, also called *dual variables* in Section B.3, are unit prices for each of the scarce resources. The Lagrangian is the (decentralized) net return from schedule x, corresponding to the given prices. The owner of the firm sets these prices and directs her managers to concentrate on maximizing the net return, rather than on coordinating their use of resources so that their resulting schedule is feasible. If the managers use exactly what is available of a resource $(g_i(x) = b_i,)$ then they (collectively) get charged nothing. If the managers use more than what is available, then they get charged at the set unit price for each excess unit used. If the managers use less, they get paid a bonus for each unit left unused. The idea is that the owner will specify a vector λ (of positive Lagrange multipliers), and the managers will respond with a schedule $x(\lambda)$ that maximizes the Lagrangian. We shall see that if the owner can find $\lambda \geq 0$ such that $x(\lambda)$ is feasible and uses exactly the amount available of resource i for each i such that $\lambda_i > 0$, then $x(\lambda)$ is optimal for the original, constrained, primal problem (P).

Only one form of the primal and Lagrangian needs to be presented because minimization problems can be represented as equivalent maximization problems, and equality constraints can be represented by two inequalities. For example, Exercise B.7 shows that if the explicit constraints are given by $g(x) = b$, then the Lagrangian has the same form, but the Lagrange multipliers are unconstrained in sign. Intuitively, when forming the Lagrangian, you want to penalize the objective function if the constraints are not satisfied. (With equality constraints, it is not clear in advance whether a violation will be higher or lower than the required amount, so the sign of the corresponding Lagrange multiplier must be allowed to be either negative or positive.)

It is possible to assume, without loss of generality, by redefining the constraint functions, that $b = 0$. However, separating the resource level vector b from the definition of g facilitates the statement and interpretation of Theorem B.1. It is also possible to exclude the $\lambda^\intercal b$ term from the definition of the Lagrangian, but including it leads to simpler forms of the results, such as Theorem B.2.

The Separable Case

Problem (P) is *separable* if f has the form

$$f(x) = \sum_{j=1}^{n} f_j(x_j),$$

g has the form

$$g_i(x) = \sum_{j=1}^{n} g_{ij}(x_j) \text{ for every } i,$$

and X is the *Cartesian Product*

$$X = X_1 \times X_2 \times \cdots \times X_n.$$

In this case, the total return consists of the sum of the returns from the different activities, resource usage is similarly separable, and the implicit constraints are separable in the sense that if $x_j \in X_j$ for every j, then the resulting schedule will be implicitly feasible.

In separable problems, the Lagrangian is also separable:

$$L(x, \lambda) = \sum_{j=1}^{n} L_j(x_j, \lambda) + \lambda^\intercal b,$$

where

$$L_j(x_j, \lambda) := f_j(x_j) - \sum_i \lambda_i g_{ij}(x_j)$$

is the *decentralized Lagrangian* for manager j. In particular, if each $x_j(\lambda)$ maximizes $L_j(x_j, \lambda)$ over X_j, then the vector $x(\lambda) = (x_1(\lambda), x_2(\lambda), \ldots, x_n(\lambda))$

will maximize the Lagrangian over X. Note that the $\lambda^\mathsf{T} b$ term in the Lagrangian need not (and therefore is not) incorporated into the decentralized Lagrangian terms, because it has no influence on what decision variables maximize the Lagrangian, for a given λ.

Example B.1 (continued)   This problem is separable and has only a single Lagrange multiplier $\lambda = \lambda_1$. The decentralized Lagrangians are given as follows:

$$L_j(x_j, \lambda) = \begin{cases} -x_1^2 + 10x_1 - \lambda x_1 & \text{if } j = 1 \\ -2x_2^2 + 4x_2 + \lambda x_2 & \text{if } j = 2. \end{cases}$$

The Optimal Response Function

Consider the following modification of the primal:

$$\max_{x \in X} f(x) \text{ subject to } g(x) \le \beta, \tag{P_β}$$

where β is an m-vector. We have simply parameterized the vector of resources available, and called it β to clarify that it may differ from the original level of resources available. The primal (P) is therefore (P_b). Let $F(\beta)$ denote the optimal value for (P_β). It is called the *optimal response function* and the *perturbation function*. That is,

$$F(\beta) := \sup_{x \in X} \{ f(x) | g(x) \le \beta \}.$$

The optimal value for (P) is, of course, $F(b)$.

B.2   The Everett Result

Theorem B.1   (*The Everett Result*)   (*Everett, 1963*)   If, given $\lambda \ge 0$, $x(\lambda)$ maximizes $L(x, \lambda)$ over $x \in X$, then $x(\lambda)$ is optimal for (P_β) for every $\beta \in \mathbf{R}^m$ that satisfies

$$\beta \ge g(x(\lambda)) \text{ and } \lambda^\mathsf{T}[g(x(\lambda)) - \beta] = 0. \tag{B.1}$$

Proof Suppose β satisfies the conditions. Note that $x(\lambda)$ is feasible for (P_β) . Let x denote an arbitrary feasible solution to (P_β) . Since $x(\lambda)$ maximizes $L(x, \lambda)$, we have

$$L(x(\lambda), \lambda) \geq L(x, \lambda).$$

That is, rewriting, we have

$$
\begin{aligned}
f(x(\lambda)) &\geq f(x) + \lambda^{\mathbf{T}}[g(x(\lambda)) - g(x)] \\
&= f(x) + \lambda^{\mathbf{T}}[g(x(\lambda)) - \beta] + \lambda^{\mathbf{T}}[\beta - g(x)] \qquad \text{[add and subtract } \lambda^{\mathbf{T}}\beta.\text{]} \\
&\geq f(x). \qquad\qquad\qquad\qquad\qquad\qquad\qquad\qquad\qquad \text{[(B.1) and } \lambda \geq 0\text{]}
\end{aligned}
$$

Thus, $x(\lambda)$ is optimal for (P_β) .   □

Example B.1 (continued)   Since each decentralized Lagrangian is concave, the maximizer of the Lagrangian can be found by examining the first-order conditions. For example, $\nabla_1 L_1(x_1, \lambda) = -2x_1 + 10 - \lambda$, so $x_1 = 5 - \lambda/2$ is a maximizer, if it is feasible (positive). That is, $x_1(\lambda) = \max(0, 5 - \lambda/2)$ is the maximizer. Similarly, $x_2(\lambda) = \max(0, 1 + \lambda/4)$ is the other maximizer. For example, $x_1(2) = 4$ and $x_2(2) = 3/2$, which use $4 - 3/2 = 5/2$ units of resource, so $(4, 1.5)$ is optimal if there are 2.5 units of resource available, rather than 1. Thus, if $\lambda \leq 10$, then $x_1(\lambda) = 5 - \lambda/2$ and $x_2(\lambda) = 1 + \lambda/4$. In this case, the amount of the resource used, as a function of λ is

$$g(x_1(\lambda), x_2(\lambda)) = (5 - \lambda/2) - (1 + \lambda/4) = 4 - 3\lambda/4.$$

Setting that quantity equal to 1 leads to $\lambda = 4$, so that $x_1(4) = 3$, and $x_2(4) = 2$, is optimal for the original problem.

Indeed, the optimal solution can be obtained for every positive level β of resources available. In particular, $(5, 1)$ is optimal for all $\beta \geq 4$, and $(7/3, 7/3)$ is optimal for $\beta = 0$.

Example B.2   *(Knapsack Problem)*   Here, the problem is

$$\max 3x_1 + 20x_2 + 35x_3 + 18x_4 \text{ over } x_i \in \{0, 1\} \text{ for every } i$$

subject to

$$x_1 + 5x_2 + 7x_3 + 3x_4 \leq 13.$$

Knapsack problems are discussed in more generality in Section 2.7. The purpose of including this problem here is to illustrate that the Everett result can facilitate finding the optimal solution for some values of β , but not all values.

The decentralized Lagrangians are given as follows:

$$L_j(x_j, \lambda) = \begin{cases} (3 - \lambda)x_1 & \text{if } j = 1 \\ 5(4 - \lambda)x_2 & \text{if } j = 2 \\ 7(5 - \lambda)x_3 & \text{if } j = 3 \\ 3(6 - \lambda)x_4 & \text{if } j = 4. \end{cases}$$

Optimizing the decentralized Lagrangians is immediate. For example, $x_1(\lambda)$ is 0 if $\lambda > 3$, 1 if $\lambda < 3$, and can be selected to be either 0 or 1 if $\lambda = 3$. It can be shown that the five distinct Lagrangian maximizers are found using only four different Lagrange multipliers, 6, 5, 4, and 3. The resource usages of those five solutions are 0, 3, 10, 15, and 16, respectively. Thus, five different primal problems can be solved with this approach. For example, if $\lambda = 4$, one of the Lagrangian maximizers is $(0, 0, 1, 1)$, which yields the optimal value (53) when there are only 10 units of the resource available.

Incidentally, these solutions are the same as the ones that can be found using *marginal analysis:* Find the object that yields the highest *bang-per-buck* ratio, and select it. "Bang" is the objective function coefficient, the value of the object. "Buck" is the constraint coefficient, the volume required by the object. Record the number of bucks spent. Go to the next highest ratio, and repeat. This approach is predicated on having a knapsack problem.

Interpretation

Any time you set prices for the resources defined by the explicit constraints, and maximize the resulting Lagrangian, you obtain an optimal solution to a particular primal problem: Take the vector of levels of resources that are used by a Lagrangian maximizing solution and call it β. Now form a new primal that seeks to maximize the return subject to not using more of the resources than β. The Lagrangian maximizing solution is optimal for that new primal.

In fact, you may have found the optimal solution to a multitude of primal problems. For example, if any of the prices is zero, then you can set the right-hand side for the corresponding resource to be any value larger than the amount used: If $\lambda_i = 0$, then you can set β_i to be any value such that $\beta_i \geq g(x(\lambda))$, and the Lagrangian maximizing solution is optimal for all such primals.

If the owner can set prices on the resources such that the managers, in their attempt to maximize the Lagrangian, want to implement a solution that uses exactly what is available of the resources with a strictly positive price and less than what is available of the resources with a zero price, then she has found an optimal solution to the original problem.

In addition, suppose you have a separable problem that is linear in some variable, say x_j, so that $L_j(x_j, \lambda) = c_j x_j - \sum_i \lambda_i a_{ij} x_j$, where c_j and all a_{ij} values are scalars, not all of which are zero. If the price vector for which you have a Lagrangian maximizer has the property that the marginal value of changing x_j under the current price vector is zero; that is, $c_j - \sum_i \lambda_i a_{ij} = 0$, then every feasible value of x_j in X_j leads to an optimal solution to a different primal problem. For example, if X_j is a set of integers, then plugging in a series of feasible integers for x_j leads to a series of primals for which you have the optimal solution.

The Everett result can be useful for planning purposes to specify a number of optimal solutions and corresponding returns for different resource levels: You maximize the Lagrangian for a number of different price vectors. Each gives an optimal solution for a specific level of resources. Displaying the results shows how sensitive the optimal return is to the availability of resources and sheds insight on the way in which resources should be optimally used. In practice, resource levels can often be changed, and this approach is useful for addressing what changes might fruitfully be made.

Note that use of the Everett result (Lagrangian approach) does not obtain optimal solutions for every possible primal problem (found by varying β) and is therefore not a panacea. However, any other optimal solution is dominated by a convex combination of solutions found with this approach. In particular, this approach avoids the possibility of finding an optimal solution for a postulated problem that could be dramatically improved by slightly increasing the availability of one of the resources.

Geometric Interpretation

Figure B.1, which is based on Example B.2, provides useful intuition about how the Lagrangian approach works. Maximizing the Lagrangian is equivalent to minimizing its negative, which is equivalent to minimizing $\lambda g(x) - f(x)$ in the single constraint case. If, as in Figure B.1, every solution $x \in X$ is plotted as

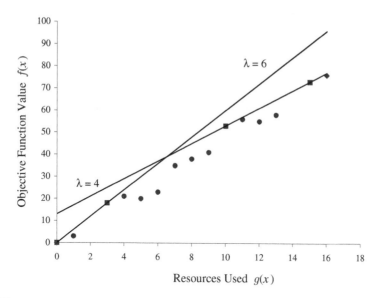

Figure B.1   Knapsack Problem Approached with Lagrangians

the point $(g(x), f(x))$, in two dimensions, then, for fixed λ, $\lambda g(x)$ plots along a straight line. (In this example, two such solutions, $(1, 0, 1, 0)$ and $(0, 1, 0, 1)$, have identical plots.) Minimizing the difference $\lambda g(x) - f(x)$ is equivalent to minimizing $\lambda g(x) - f(x) + a$ for any real number a. Thus, we are free to select a so that it is clear what point (or points) maximize the Lagrangian. If we select a so that $a + \lambda g(x)$ exceeds $f(x)$ everywhere and equals $f(x)$ at one or more points, then these points maximize the Lagrangian for this choice of λ: Every difference is positive, so any that equals zero is smaller than all others and is therefore optimal. Visually, you start with an arbitrary a such that $a + \lambda g(x)$ dominates $f(x)$. You then decrease a until $a + \lambda g(x)$ first touches one of the feasible points. In general, we obtain the minimal dominating hyperplane.

The result of this process is shown for two different values of λ, in Figure B.1. When $\lambda = 6$, the (resulting) line goes through two points, $(0, 0)$ and $(3, 18)$, so both of these points correspond to maximizers of the Lagrangian for that price. (The corresponding values of the decision variables are the feasible solutions, namely $(0, 0, 0, 0)$ and $(0, 0, 0, 1)$, that were found to generate those points before they were plotted. This geometric representation is useful to develop intuition but not as a method for finding the actual solutions.) These two points correspond to optimal solutions to two different primal problems, one with $\beta = 0$ and the other with $\beta = 3$. Two more solutions to primal problems are found when $\lambda = 4$: $(10, 53)$ and $(15, 73)$. There is only one more point, $(16, 76)$, that can be found with the Lagrangian approach to this problem, and it is found when $\lambda \leq 3$. Importantly, the optimal solution to the primal problem of interest, when $\beta = 13$, cannot be found by the Lagrangian approach. That optimal solution is $(1, 1, 1, 0)$, which plots as $(13, 58)$.

B.3   Duality

The *dual function* for (P) is defined as

$$L^*(\lambda) := \sup_{x \in X} L(x, \lambda).$$

Given the dual variables (prices) that have been set on resource usage, the dual function gives the maximum net return over all schedules that satisfy the implicit constraints.

Weak Duality

Theorem B.2   *(Weak Duality)   (Zangwill, 1969:48)   If $\lambda \geq 0$ and x is feasible for (P), then*
$$L^*(\lambda) \geq f(x).$$

Proof   Here,

$$\begin{aligned}
L^*(\lambda) &\geq L(x, \lambda) && \text{[defn. of } L^* \text{ and } x \in X] \\
&= f(x) - \lambda^{\mathsf{T}}[g(x) - b] && \text{[defn. of } L] \\
&\geq f(x). && [-\lambda \leq 0 \text{ and } g(x) - b \leq 0]
\end{aligned}$$

□

For *any* set of positive prices that the owner sets on the resources, the resulting maximum net return is an upper bound on the optimal return.

Example B.1 (continued)   Building on previous work, and letting $x(\lambda)$ denote a Lagrangian maximizer, we see that, for $\lambda \leq 10$,

$$L^*(\lambda) = L(x_1(\lambda), x_2(\lambda), \lambda)$$
$$= 27 - 3\lambda + 3\lambda^2/8,$$

which is an explicit upper bound on the value of the primal.

Definition of the Dual Problem

The *dual (problem)* (D) to (P) is

$$\min L^*(\lambda) \text{ over } \lambda \geq 0. \hspace{2cm} (D)$$

Interpretations

The owner seeks positive prices on the resources that will minimize the dual function. She seeks the lowest upper bound on the optimal solution that can be found using prices.

A potential outside buyer of the firm wishes to evaluate what the firm is worth. He is not knowledgeable enough to evaluate the price directly. He plans to simply displace the owner and retain the managers. Each time he sets a price vector, he can determine the resulting return, by getting the optimal response from each of the managers, which he interprets as a possible amount he would have to pay for the firm. Since he wants to pay as little as possible, he seeks to minimize that amount.

Optimality Conditions

A pair (x, λ) satisfies the *optimality conditions* (OC), for (P), if

$$\lambda \geq 0, \hspace{1.5cm} \text{(Positive Prices)} \hspace{1.5cm} (OC.1)$$
$$x \text{ maximizes } L(\cdot, \lambda) \text{ over } X, \hspace{0.5cm} \text{(Lagrangian Maximizer)} \hspace{0.5cm} (OC.2)$$
$$g(x) \leq b, \hspace{1.5cm} \text{(Explicit Feasibility)} \hspace{1.5cm} (OC.3)$$

and $\hspace{1cm} \lambda^{\mathsf{T}}[g(x) - b] = 0. \hspace{1cm}$ (Complementary Slackness) $(OC.4)$

Implicit feasibility is guaranteed by $(OC.2)$.

Theorem B.3   *If (x, λ) satisfies the optimality conditions, then x is optimal for the primal, λ is optimal for the dual, and the optimal values of the primal and the dual are equal.*

Proof   The Everett result guarantees that x is optimal for the primal, because b qualifies as a β in Theorem B.1. Since x is feasible for the primal, $f(x)$ is a lower bound on the dual objective function. By complementary slackness, the dual objective function equals $f(x)$. That is, the price vector λ is optimal for the dual. The optimal value of the primal is $f(x)$. The optimal value of the dual is also $f(x)$.   □

Example B.1 (continued)   We have seen that the point $(x_1, x_2, \lambda) = (3, 2, 4)$ satisfies the optimality conditions. We already know that $x = (3, 2)$ is optimal for the primal. We now know that $\lambda = 4$ is optimal for the dual and that these results are not coincidental. The optimal value of the primal and the dual is 21.

Karush-Kuhn-Tucker Conditions

Let (KKT) denote (OC) with the exception that $(OC.2)$ is replaced by

$$\nabla f(x) - \lambda^{\mathrm{T}} \nabla g(x) = 0. \tag{$KKT.2$}$$

A pair (x, λ) satisfies the *Karush-Kuhn-Tucker* conditions if it satisfies (KKT).

Theorem B.4   *(Karush-Kuhn-Tucker Sufficient Conditions)   If f is concave, g is convex (g_i is convex for each i), $X = \mathbf{R}^n$, and (x, λ) satisfies the Karush-Kuhn-Tucker conditions, then x is optimal for the primal.*

Proof   By Theorem A.1(b), $(KKT.2)$ implies that $(OC.2)$ holds, so all the results of Theorem B.3 hold.   □

Theorem B.5   *(Karush-Kuhn-Tucker Necessary Conditions)   (Zangwill, 1969:40,56)   Suppose that f and g are continuously differentiable, g is convex, $X = \mathbf{R}^n$, and there exists a feasible $a \in X$ such that $g_i(a) < b_i$ for all i. If x is optimal for the primal, then there exists λ such that (x, λ) satisfies the Karush-Kuhn-Tucker conditions.*

The usual version of the Karush-Kuhn-Tucker necessary conditions (for example, Zangwill, 1969:40) requires less of g: g must satisfy only what is called a *constraint qualification*.

Duality Gap

The *duality gap* is the difference between the optimal value of the dual and the optimal value of the primal. By Theorem B.3, if there exists a pair (x, λ) that satisfies the optimality conditions, such as in Example B.1, then the duality gap equals zero. However, in Example B.2, there is a strictly positive duality gap. Referring back to Figure B.1, the dual can be interpreted as follows: First, draw a vertical line through the given level, 13, of resources. Second, each dual variable corresponds to an array of parallel lines with that slope. The smallest of the lines that dominate the plotted points is automatically found when the Lagrangian is maximized given that dual variable. The value of the dual objective function equals the height of the vertical line where it is intersected by the minimal dominating line. The object is to find the smallest such value. In this case, the optimal value is 65, which exceeds the optimal value, 58, of the primal. A strictly positive duality gap indicates that there does not exist a (x, λ) that satisfies the optimality conditions. In short, an optimal solution cannot always be found by the Lagrangian approach.

In general, a strictly positive duality gap can arise not only from having a discrete set of feasible solutions but also from nonconvexities, either in the objective function or in the constraints. If there is a continuum of feasible solutions, then the set of feasible solutions, when plotted as in Figure B.1, will appear as a solid shaded area. If the upper portion of this set is not convex, then a duality gap can arise.

Suppose that the primal in this example is reformulated to allow randomizing among various possible (implicitly feasible) solutions, the objective is changed to maximization of the expected return according to this randomization, and the constraint requires only that the expected amount of resources used under this randomization be less than the amount available. Then the Lagrangian approach yields the optimal solution: Appropriately randomize among the Lagrangian maximizers. In this case, pick the solution corresponding to $(10, 53)$ with probability 0.4 and the solution corresponding to $(15, 73)$ with probability 0.6. The expected return is 65 and the expected resource usage is 13.

Gradient of the Dual Function

Theorem B.6　　*(Luenberger, 1973:313)*　*If f is concave, g is convex,*
$X = \mathbf{R}^n$, and $x(\lambda)$ maximizes the Lagrangian as a function of λ, and is
differentiable, then
$$\nabla L^*(\lambda) = b - g\big(x(\lambda)\big).$$

Proof　Taking the partial derivatives of
$$L^*(\lambda) = f\big(x(\lambda)\big) - \lambda^{\mathsf{T}}[g\big(x(\lambda)\big) - b],$$

we get

$$\nabla L^*(\lambda) = [\nabla f\big(x(\lambda)\big) - \lambda^{\mathsf{T}}\nabla g\big(x(\lambda)\big)]^{\mathsf{T}}\nabla x(\lambda) + b - g\big(x(\lambda)\big).$$

Because f is concave, g is convex, and $X = \mathbf{R}^n$, $x(\lambda)$ satisfies *(KKT.2)*,
so the expression reduces to the desired result.　　　　　　　　　　　　　□

Theorem B.7　　*(Geoffrion, 1971)*　*The dual function is convex.*

Proof　(Exercise B.11)　　　　　　　　　　　　　　　　　　　　　　□

Luenberger (1973:314) gets at this result by finding that the Hessian of the dual
function is positive semidefinite, which, by Theorem A.6(a) means that the dual
function is convex.

Example B.1 (continued)　　The dual function $L^*(\lambda) = 27 - 3\lambda + 3\lambda^2/8$
is clearly convex. Setting its derivative equal to zero leads to $\lambda = 4$, which
confirms that this point is optimal for the dual.

Interpretation

Regardless of the form of the primal problem, Theorem B.7 says that the dual
problem is a simple convex optimization problem: It has a convex objective
function and only nonnegativity constraints. Furthermore, by Theorem B.6, its
gradient is extremely easy to compute: At component i, it equals the amount
by which the constraint i is infeasible, evaluated at the current solution. If the
current solution requests less than what is available of a given resource, that
is, $g_i(x(\lambda)) < b_i$, then the partial derivative of the dual objective function is
strictly positive at that point. Increasing the corresponding price would increase

the objective function. As the dual seeks to minimize the dual function, the price on that resource should be reduced. That is, reduce the price on resources that are not being fully utilized—but not below zero. Similarly, increase the price on resources that are being overused (not enough is available to meet projected usage).

Consider the following transient behavior of a price system in a static economy in which multiple players each act to maximize their expected returns under limited resources. If, when requests (demand) for resources exceed what is available, the price is increased. Similarly, when requests for resources are less than what is available, and the current price is strictly positive, then that price is decreased. We can interpret this behavior as minimizing the dual to a problem in which the primal objective function is the sum of the expected returns over all players. Any solution to the optimality conditions is stable in the sense that no price changes would be made, and all the players would be happy with their plans at those prices. If there is no duality gap, then such a solution exists.

Exercises

B.1 *(Tom Newberry's Dilemma, 1971)* Consider the following single constraint optimization problem:

$$\min_{Q_1>0,\dots,Q_n>0} \sum_{j=1}^{n} \left(\frac{ca_j D_j}{Q_j} + \frac{h_j Q_j}{2} \right) \tag{B.2}$$

subject to

$$\sum_{j=1}^{n} \frac{a_j D_j}{Q_j} \le b, \tag{B.3}$$

where c, b, and all a_j, D_j, and h_j are strictly positive scalars. This problem arises in operations, with the following interpretation:

$D_j =$ demand rate, in units per week, for product j

$a_j =$ hours of setup labor required for a production run of product j

$h_j =$ cost per week to hold a unit of product j in inventory

$c =$ cost per hour of setup labor

$b =$ number of hours of setup labor available per week

$Q_j =$ lot size (length of production run) for product j

The objective is to minimize the sum of setup costs per week plus inventory holding costs per week, without using more of the setup labor than the amount that is available. If constraint (B.3) is ignored, then (B.2) decomposes into a separate problem for each product, and elementary calculus leads to the classical *EOQ* formula as the answer:

$$Q_j^* = \sqrt{2ca_j D_j/h_j}.$$

Let

$$\beta := \sum_{j=1}^{n} \frac{a_j D_j}{Q_j^*},$$

which is the number of hours of setup labor used per week by the unconstrained solution. If $\beta \leq b$, then clearly the unconstrained solution is optimal for the constrained problem as well. Suppose that $\beta > b$.

(a) Use the Everett result to derive an explicit optimal solution to the constrained problem.

(b) Show that the optimal solution to the constrained problem can be computed by simply multiplying the unconstrained optimal lot sizes by β/b. That is, show that

$$Q_j^0 = \frac{\beta}{b} Q_j^*,$$

where Q_j^0 is the optimal lot size (for product j) for the constrained problem, and Q_j^* is the optimal lot size for the unconstrained problem.

B.2   Find an explicit optimal solution to the following problem:

$$\max -2x_1^2 + 12x_1 + 10x_2 - 6x_2^2 + 3x_1 x_2 \text{ over } x_i \geq 0 \text{ for every } i$$

subject to

$$2x_1 + x_2 \leq 4.$$

B.3   Represent the level of resources in Exercise B.2 by the abstract quantity β. (Replace 4 in the right-hand side by β.)

(a) Determine the set of values of β for which the optimal values of the decision variables are both strictly positive.

(b) Specify the optimal values of the decision variables as functions of β for the set found in part (a).

B.4   Determine the set of values of β in Exercise B.3 for which exactly one of the decision variables is strictly positive in the optimal solution. Specify that variable and its optimal value as a function of β for that set.

B.5   Consider the following problem:

$$\max -x_1^2 + 36x_1 + 30x_2 - 3x_2^2 \text{ over } x_i \geq 0 \text{ for every } i$$

subject to

$$2x_1 + x_2 \leq \beta_1$$
$$x_1 + 2x_1 \leq \beta_2.$$

Specify the set of dual variables such that both Lagrangian maximizing primal variables are strictly positive.

B.6   Derive the form of the dual when the objective function of the primal is to be minimized, rather than maximized.

B.7   Show that if the explicit constraints of the primal are given by $g(x) = b$ rather than $g(x) \leq b$, then the Lagrange multipliers of the dual are unconstrained in sign.

Hint: Represent $g(x) = b$ by $g(x) \leq b$ and $g(x) \geq b$.

B.8   (*Linear Programming Duality*)   Suppose the primal is a linear program. That is, $f(x) = c^\mathsf{T} x$, $g(x) = Ax$, and $X = \{x \in \mathbf{R}^n | x \geq 0\}$. Show that the definition of the dual given by (D) yields the traditional linear programming dual:

$$\min b^\mathsf{T}\lambda \text{ over } \lambda \geq 0$$

subject to

$$A^{\mathsf{T}}\lambda \geq c.$$

B.9 *(Farkas's Lemma)*   Show that

(a) $c^{\mathsf{T}}x \leq 0$ for all x such that $Ax \geq 0$

iff

(b) there exists $\lambda \geq 0$ such that $c + A^{\mathsf{T}}\lambda = 0$.

Hint: Use Exercise B.8.

B.10 *(Shadow Prices)*   Let (D_β) denote the dual to (P_β). (The Lagrangian gets written as $L(x, \lambda, \beta)$ to clarify its dependence on β.) Suppose that f is concave, g is convex, $X = \mathbf{R}^n$, $x(\beta)$ is optimal for (P_β), $\lambda(\beta)$ is optimal for (D_β), and $x(\beta)$ and $\lambda(\beta)$ are partially differentiable. Show that $\nabla_i F(\beta) = \lambda_i(\beta)$. (The marginal value of resource i, when the vector β is available and used optimally, is the optimal value of the dual variable for that resource. This *price* for the resource hides in the shadows until the dual problem is solved.)

Hint: Assume first that $m = 1$ and show that $F'(\beta) = \lambda$.

B.11   Prove Theorem B.7 using Theorem A.3.

B.12 *(Ha and Porteus, 1995)*   Consider the following quadratic programming problem, consisting of a quadratic objective function and linear constraints: Find $x \geq 0$ and $y_i \geq 0$ for $1 \leq i \leq n$, to

$$\min \quad -x + \frac{a}{2}\sum_{j=1}^{n} y_j^2,$$

$$\text{subject to} \quad \sum_{j=1}^{n} y_j = T,$$

$$x \leq \alpha \sum_{j=1}^{i-1} y_j + \sum_{j=i+1}^{n} y_j, \quad 1 \leq i \leq n, \tag{B.4}$$

where $a, T > 0$, and $\alpha > 1$.

This problem arises in a model of concurrent engineering in which the objective is to minimize the expected time to complete a project that consists of a product design and a process design. Constants that are not affected by the decision variables are deleted from the objective function. The number n of progress reviews conducted during the time that the product design is carried out is a parameter in this formulation. The decision variable x represents the amount of process design work that has been completed by the time the product design is complete, and y_j represents the number of days of uninterrupted product design work that are carried out before the jth progress review is conducted.

(a) Show that the objective function is convex.

(b) Show that the Karush-Kuhn-Tucker conditions are as follows:

$$\lambda_i \geq 0, \quad 1 \leq i \leq n,$$

$$\sum_{j=1}^{n} \lambda_j = 1,$$

$$\lambda_0 - \sum_{j=1}^{i-1} \lambda_j - \alpha \sum_{j=i+1}^{n} \lambda_j + ay_i = 0, \quad 1 \leq i \leq n,$$

$$y_i \geq 0, \quad 1 \leq i \leq n,$$

$$x \geq 0,$$

$$\sum_{j=1}^{n} y_j = T,$$

$$x \leq \alpha \sum_{j=1}^{i-1} y_j + \sum_{j=i+1}^{n} y_j, \quad 1 \leq i \leq n,$$

$$\lambda_i \left(x - \alpha \sum_{j=1}^{i-1} y_j - \sum_{j=i+1}^{n} y_j \right) = 0, \quad 1 \leq i \leq n,$$

where a sum is assumed to vanish if the upper index (of the sum) is strictly less than the lower index.

B.13 (Continuation of Exercise B.12) Given n and $\alpha > 1$, let

$$r_n^k := \begin{cases} +\infty & \text{if } k = 0, \\ \frac{(\alpha+1)}{(\alpha^k-1)(\alpha^{k+1}-1)} \left[(\alpha^k - 1) + (n - k)(\alpha - 1)\alpha^k \right] & \text{if } 1 \leq k \leq n - 1, \\ 0 & \text{if } k = n. \end{cases}$$

(a) Show that r_n^k decreases in k.

(b) Show that if $r_n^k \leq Ta < r_n^{k-1}$ and $1 \leq k < n$, then the following solution is optimal:

$$x = \sum_{j=2}^{n} y_j,$$

$$y_1 = \left[T - \frac{(n-k)(\alpha-1)}{(\alpha^k - 1)a} \right] \Big/ \left[\frac{\alpha^k - 1}{\alpha - 1} + \frac{(n-k)(\alpha^k + 1)}{\alpha + 1} \right],$$

$$y_i = \begin{cases} \alpha^{i-1} y_1 & \text{for } 1 \leq i \leq k; \\ \frac{(\alpha^k + 1)y_1}{\alpha + 1} + \frac{\alpha - 1}{(\alpha^k - 1)a} & \text{for } k+1 \leq i \leq n. \end{cases}$$

Hint: Show that the first k constraints of $(B.4)$ are binding and the remaining are nonbinding. Thus, the first k Lagrange multipliers for $(B.4)$ should be positive, and the rest should equal zero.

References

Everett, H., III. 1963. Generalized Lagrange multiplier method for solving problems of optimum allocation of resources. *Operations Research.* **11** 399–417.

Geoffrion, A. 1971. Duality in nonlinear programming: a simplified applications-oriented development. *SIAM Review.* **13** 1–37.

Ha, A., E. Porteus. 1995. Optimal timing of reviews in concurrent design for manufacturability. *Management Science.* **41** 1431–47.

Luenberger, D. 1973. *Introduction to Linear and Nonlinear Programming.* Addison-Wesley, Reading, Mass.

Tom Newberry's Dilemma. 1971. Harvard Business School Case 9-672-058.

Zangwill, W. 1969. *Nonlinear Programming: A Unified Approach.* Prentice-Hall, Englewood Cliffs, N.J.

APPENDIX **C**

Discounted Average Value

Most of this appendix is based on Porteus (1985). It first reviews discounting and net present value (NPV) computations. It then introduces the discounted average value (DAV), which merely rescales the net present value into a uniform cost rate. After showing how the DAV can be useful in comparing cost streams that arise over different time horizons, this appendix shows how the DAV can be easily approximated. A useful such approximation corresponds to charging simple interest. This approximation is applied to the EOQ model of Chapter 1 to show that a conventional formulation of that model, which appears to be undiscounted, can be justified as the approximation to the DAV found here. In particular, the mathematical form of the DAV approximation is far simpler than the general expression for the NPV, which allows for explicit solutions and easily derived comparative statics. The EOQ model is an example of a regenerative economic model, namely, a model in which performance is measured using economic criteria and in which regenerations occur: Without getting formal, the process starts over again in some recognizable regenerative state, which in the EOQ model, is the point at which a new order is received. Thus, the approximating approach to the DAV in this appendix is offered as an option for analyzing regenerative economic models in general.

C.1   Net Present Value

Suppose that a cost is incurred (or revenue received) at the beginning of each of n consecutive periods of equal length. If n is small or the periods are very short, then simply totaling the costs over the n periods, or dividing that total by the number of periods, to get the average cost per period, is a reasonable approach for a single dimensional representation of these costs. However, in most economic settings, time is money, and costs incurred now are more costly than those incurred later. In particular, organizations often identify an *opportunity cost of capital*, expressed as an interest rate i per period, such that a dollar invested now (at the beginning of this period) will return $1 + i$ dollars at the beginning of the next period. (Note that i is a positive real number in this appendix and should not be confused with the imaginary number $\sqrt{-1}$.) Thus, we need put aside only $\alpha := 1/(1+i)$ now to pay one dollar at the beginning of the next period. Similarly, we need put aside only α^t dollars to pay one dollar exactly t periods from now. Thus, α is called the one-period *discount factor* and $\alpha^{t-1}c_t$ is the *present value* evaluated in terms of monetary units at the beginning of period 1 of having to incur cost c_t at the beginning of period t, which is $t - 1$ periods later.

Suppose that the cost c_t will be incurred at the beginning of period t for $t = 1, 2, \ldots, n$. Let v_{NPV} denote the net present value of that cost stream, namely,

$$v_{\text{NPV}} = \sum_{t=1}^{n} \alpha^{t-1} c_t.$$

Note that c_t need not be positive and that if $c_t < 0$, then we plan to receive net revenue in period t. The word "net" is used to clarify this fact. While there are more sophisticated approaches for combining cost streams into simple orderings, the (easily computed) net present value provides useful guidance in many operational settings.

Continuous Compounding

When costs are incurred (and revenues received) only at the beginning or end of discrete periods of equal length, then, given a discrete interest rate i per period and the corresponding (one-period) discount factor α, it is clear how to compute the NPV of any stream of costs and revenues. However, if financial transactions can occur in the middle of a period, there are periods of different lengths, or some costs are incurred continuously over time, specification of the NPV is ambiguous. We shall resolve this ambiguity by assuming that interest is compounded continously.

Suppose we have an interest rate i, which is expressed as the rate at which interest is paid per unit of time. For example, if the time unit is a year and $i = 0.2$, then the interest rate is 20% per year. If interest is compounded once a year, then one dollar will yield $1 + i = 1.2$ at the end of the year, so that $0.20 of interest is earned over that time. If interest is compounded twice a year (every six months) then, in the first six months, the interest rate of 20% per year will be applied for half the year to yield $0.10 in interest, for a total of $1 + i/2 = 1.1$. The earned interest is added to the principal, so the entire $1 + i/2$ earns interest for the second half of the year: The interest earned then is $(1+i/2)i/2 = 0.11$. The total available at the end of the year is $(1+i/2)^2 = 1.21$, so that $0.21 of interest is earned during the year. In general, if interest is compounded m times over $[0, t]$, at the end of equally spaced intervals, the total available at the end of the year is $(1+it/m)^m$. Equivalently, the present value (at time 0) of a dollar received at time t is

$$\left(\frac{1}{1 + it/m}\right)^m .$$

Continuous compounding amounts to letting m go to infinity. Unless stated otherwise, we assume continuous compounding henceforth. The next result shows that net present values are easy to compute under continuous compounding, regardless of when a financial transaction takes place. It is convenient to define the *equivalent discrete interest rate* i_{E} for a time period of a given length, as the interest rate that, if compounded only once per time period, yields the same net present values as under the continuous compounding when financial transactions take place only at the beginning of each time period.

Lemma C.1   *Suppose that interest is compounded continuously at the rate of i per unit time.*

(a) The present value (as of time 0) of x dollars received at time t is xe^{-it}:

$$\lim_{m\to\infty} \left(\frac{1}{1 + it/m}\right)^m = e^{-it}.$$

(b) The effective (one-period) discount factor, the present value (as of time 0) of one dollar received at time 1, is $\alpha = e^{-i}$.

(c) The equivalent discrete interest rate, is given by

$$i_E = e^i - 1 = i + \frac{i^2}{2!} + \frac{i^3}{3!} + \cdots.$$

(d) The present value (as of time 0) of incurring costs at a continuous rate of x dollars per unit time over the time interval $[0, t]$ is $x(1 - e^{-it})/i$.

Proof   (a) Exercise C.1.

(b) Set $x = t = 1$ in (a).

(c) By (b), the effective discount factor is $\alpha = e^{-i}$. Using the fact that i_E is defined through $\alpha = 1/(1 + i_E)$, solving for i_E and applying a standard expansion of e^x yield the desired result.

(d) Here, we have

$$v_{\mathbf{NPV}} = \int_{\tau=0}^{t} xe^{-i\tau} d\tau$$
$$= \frac{x(1 - e^{-it})}{i}.$$

$\square$

Thus, we can easily convert a continuous interest rate into an equivalent discrete rate and vice versa. For example, if one compounds using a simple interest rate of 20% per year $(i = 0.20)$, the resulting equivalent discrete rate (per year) is $i_E \cong 0.221$, namely, 22.1% per year.

Similarly, it is clear how to compute the NPV of a sequence of discrete costs incurred over time. Part (c) shows how to compute the NPV when a cost rate is incurred continuously over time.

C.2   Discounted Average Value

The *discounted average value (DAV)* (of a cost stream) over a specific time interval is the cost rate that, if incurred continuously over that interval, yields the same NPV as the actual stream. It simply reexpresses the NPV, which is a total, into a *rate* of expenditures per unit time (over the given time interval, assuming continuous compounding). Wagner (1969) calls it the *equivalent average return*. It is also called the *equivalent annuity value*.

We shall see that there are three main advantages of the DAV. First, it is directly comparable to *average cost*, the sum of all expenditures divided by the length of the time interval over which they are incurred. The DAV can be viewed as an adjustment of the average cost that accounts for the timing of the expenditures. If positive, the DAV goes up if the bulk of expenditures arise early in the stream, and it goes down if the bulk arise later in the stream. Second, the DAV allows for easy comparison across streams with different time horizons. Third, the DAV can be approximated easily (and accurately when i is small) by a form that is readily interpretable. Each of these advantages will be illustrated in this appendix.

Derivation of the DAV for a Deterministic Time Interval

Theorem C.1

(a) Given v_{NPV}, the NPV (as of time 0) of a given cost stream, the equivalent DAV over $[0, t]$ is given by

$$v_{\text{DAV}} = \frac{i v_{\text{NPV}}}{1 - e^{-it}}.$$

(b) The DAV is a decreasing function of the time at which any positive expenditure of the cost stream is incurred.

Proof

(a) Suppose that costs are incurred at the rate of v_{DAV} over $[0, t]$. Then, by Lemma C.1(d), the resulting NPV is

$$v_{\text{NPV}} = \frac{v_{\text{DAV}}[1 - e^{-it}]}{i}.$$

The result follows from expressing v_{DAV} in terms of v_{NPV}.

(b) If any particular positive expenditure of the cost stream is delayed, then the NPV of the stream decreases. Since the DAV is a fixed multiple of the NPV, the DAV decreases, too.   □

Numerical Example

Suppose that interest is compounded continuously at the rate of 2% per month, that we face the following three alternative cost streams, and costs are incurred at the beginning of each month.

Month	Alternative 1	Alternative 2	Alternative 3
1	1000	200	0
2	1000	1000	200
3	1000	1809	2812
Total	3000	3009	3012
Average	1000	1003	1004
DAV	1009.9	1002.1	995.1

Because we are discounting continuously, the effective single-period discount factor is $\alpha = e^{-0.02} \cong 0.98020$. The net present values, as of time 0, are therefore as follows:

$$v_{\mathbf{NPV}}(1) \cong 1000 + 980.2 + 960.8 = 2941.0.$$

$$v_{\mathbf{NPV}}(2) \cong 200 + 980.2 + 1738.1 = 2918.3.$$

$$v_{\mathbf{NPV}}(3) \cong 0 + 196.0 + 2701.7 = 2897.7.$$

To compute the DAVs for the time interval $[0, 3]$, we apply Theorem C.1 with $i = 0.02$ and $t = 3$, so that

$$\frac{i}{1 - e^{-it}} \cong 0.3434.$$

Hence

$$v_{\mathbf{DAV}}(1) \cong 0.3434(2941.0) \cong 1009.9,$$

$$v_{\mathbf{DAV}}(2) \cong 0.3434(2918.3) \cong 1002.1,$$

$$v_{\mathbf{DAV}}(3) \cong 0.3434(2897.7) \cong 995.1.$$

This example illustrates the first advantage of the DAV: Alternative 1 incurs 1000 in each month, but instead of doing so evenly throughout each month, the expense comes all at once at the beginning of each month. Thus, its DAV is higher than its average cost of 1000. (Exercise C.2 shows that the DAV is very close to 1000 if the 1000 is spent in the *middle* of each of the three months.) Although the average costs increase for the next two alternatives, their DAVs decrease, because the bulk of their expenditures occur later. In short, comparing the undiscounted average cost and the DAV reveals whether the bulk of the costs are incurred either (relatively) early or late.

C.2   Alternatives with Different Time Horizons

DAV is useful for comparing alternatives with differing time horizons. For example, suppose you need the capabilities of a certain machine for a long time (essentially an infinite horizon), you have two choices of machines, and your opportunity cost of capital is 2% per month (compounded continuously). One costs $1000 and lasts two months. The other costs $1488 and lasts three months. Both have exactly the same operating costs, quality levels, and so on. At the end of any machine's useful life, another machine must be purchased.

It is clearly inappropriate to base your decision on the basis of the NPVs of the machines over their different lifetimes: You will still need a machine in the third month, but the NPV for the two-month machine will only incorporate costs for two months.

In this example, it is fair to compute the NPV of the costs incurred over a six-month time horizon, because a new machine is required then regardless of the machine used. (There is a *common regeneration point* then, in the sense that both processes start afresh then.) Letting α denote the effective discount factor, the results are as follows:

$$v_{\text{NPV}}(1) = 1000 + \alpha^2 1000 + \alpha^4 1000$$
$$\cong 1000 + 960.8 + 923.1 \cong 2883.9,$$

and
$$v_{\text{NPV}}(2) = 1488 + \alpha^3 1488$$
$$\cong 1488 + 1401.3 \cong 2889.3.$$

Thus, the first machine is preferred. If, in general, there is a large number of machines (and corresponding lifetimes), so it is difficult to find a common regeneration point, then a simpler approach would be desirable. Computing the DAV is a simple and effective way to approach this problem, because, by Exercise C.3, the DAV for a given machine type will be the same regardless of how many lifetimes of the machine are used in the computation.

The results are as follows. For the first machine: $e^{-2i} = e^{-0.04} \cong 0.96079$, and $i/(1 - e^{-2i}) \cong .51007$. So the DAV is $0.51007(1000) \cong 510.1$. For the second: $e^{-3i} = e^{-0.06} \cong 0.94176$, and $i/(1 - e^{-3i}) \cong .34343$. So the DAV is $0.34343(1488) \cong 511.0$.

The first machine is, of course, still preferred. We didn't have to find a time horizon that would make the comparison fair. The numbers are higher than the undiscounted average values, because the expenditures occur at the beginning of each machine's useful life.

C.3   Approximating the DAV

We now explore how the DAV can be approximated by adjusting the average cost using simple interest based on the timing of the expenditures. This approximation, presented in Porteus (1985), is simple and, as we shall see, allows for useful analyses of certain regenerative problems arising in operations. Let $O(x)$ denote an arbitrary function $f(x)$ with the property that $\limsup_{x \to 0} |f(x)/x|$ is finite. In particular, $O(i^2)$ denotes a function that behaves like a constant times i^2 when i is small, and is therefore close to zero if i is close to zero.

Theorem C.2   *The DAV over the time interval $[0, T]$ for a single expenditure of x at time t can be expressed as*

$$v_{\text{DAV}} = \frac{x + ix(T/2 - t)}{T} + O(i^2).$$

Proof   The result can be obtained directly by finding the first two terms of the MacLauren series expansion of

$$f(i) = \frac{ie^{-it}}{1 - e^{-iT}}.$$

Doing so requires several applications of l'Hospital's rule. A simpler approach follows: We know that $f(i)$ has an expansion of the form $a_0 + a_1 i + O(i^2)$ (without knowing a_0 and a_1 yet), that $e^{-it} = 1 - it + (it)^2/2 + O(i^3)$, and that e^{-iT} has a similar expansion. Requiring that the expansions of $f(i)(1 - e^{-iT})$ and ie^{-it} be equal, term by term, allows us to determine the values of the coefficients: The expression $f(i)(1 - e^{-iT})$ has the form

$$\left(a_0 + a_1 i + O(i^2)\right)\left(iT - \frac{(iT)^2}{2} + O(i^3)\right) = i(a_0 T) + i^2\left(a_1 T - \frac{a_0 T^2}{2}\right) + O(i^3).$$

Similarly, the expression ie^{-it} has the form

$$i - i^2 t + O(i^3).$$

Thus, we must have $a_0 T = 1$ and $a_1 T - a_0 T^2/2 = -t$, from which it follows that $a_0 = 1/T$ and $a_1 = (T/2 - t)/T$.   □

Thus, the approximate DAV for a single expenditure of x at time t is

$$v_{\text{DAV}} \cong \frac{x + ix(T/2 - t)}{T}. \tag{C.1}$$

The first term in the numerator is the expenditure itself. The second term is called the *financial holding cost:* Identify the middle of the time interval, $T/2$, and charge simple interest for the time elapsing from making the expenditure until then, namely, for $T/2 - t$. If an expenditure is made early in the interval, we *charge* interest from that time until the middle of the interval. If it occurs later in the interval, we *credit* interest from the middle of the interval until the time the expenditure takes place. Once all that is done, we divide by the length T of the time interval to get the equivalent uniform stream.

Reexpressing (C.1) as

$$v_{\text{DAV}} \cong \frac{x}{T} + \frac{ix(T/2 - t)}{T}$$

shows that this approximation consists of taking the average cost, the total cost x incurred over the time horizon divided by the length T of the time interval, and adding the time averaged financial holding cost.

The approximation for a sum of expenditures can be found by fixing the time horizon and summing each of the approximate DAVs. This approach can be viewed as approximating the discounted present values with an undiscounted formulation. The timing effects of expenditures, and receipts, are accounted for by use of financial holding costs. Financial holding costs ignore compounding of interest, and other second-order effects.

Example

Consider the numerical example of Section C.2. For the first machine, the time interval is $[0, 2]$, which is the life of the machine. The middle of the interval is 1.0. The total cost is \$1000, and it is incurred all at the beginning of the period. Thus, simple interest for one month (up until the middle of the time interval) is charged, amounting to a financial holding cost of $1000(0.02) = 20$. Thus, the approximate DAV is

$$\frac{1000 + 20}{2} = 510.$$

For the second machine, the interval is $[0, 3]$. The middle of the interval is 1.5. The total cost is \$1488, and one and a half months of simple interest are charged, amounting to a financial holding cost of $1488(1.5)(0.02) = 44.64$. Thus, the approximate DAV is

$$\frac{1488 + 44.64}{3} \cong 510.9.$$

Based on this approximation, the first machine is preferable. Indeed, these results are very close to the exact ones, and the estimated gain from using the first machine is extremely close to the exact gain.

Accounting Interpretation

Suppose we are attempting to fairly represent the expenditures of a firm over a particular financial cycle, such as a fiscal year. This approach suggests that we charge financial holding costs on lump sum expenditures, from the time they are incurred until the middle of the financial cycle. If revenues are involved, treat them like negative costs: Give interest credit for revenues received early in the cycle and charge interest from the middle of the cycle on for revenues received late.

If costs are incurred at a constant continous rate over some subinterval, then determine the total cost expended over the subinterval, find the middle point of the subinterval, and treat the stream like a single expenditure made at that middle point.

This approach essentially sets up a bank that charges simple interest and requires that any payment be made at the middle time point of the cycle: If you want to incur a cost early, you borrow for the time you need it. If you want to incur a cost late, then you get credit for the time your bank can use the money. (No compounding of interest occurs.)

C.4   Application to the EOQ Model

Consider the classical EOQ model introduced in Chapter 1, in which production occurs instantaneously and the production cost consists of a setup cost K plus a proportional cost c. We assume, for clarity, that both such costs are incurred at the time of production, and, for convenience, that there are no physical holding costs, such as rental of space, heating, and so forth. As in Chapter 1, let λ denote the mean demand rate per week, and Q the lot size, which is our decision variable. In addition, let i denote the opportunity cost of capital per week.

We now apply Theorem C.2 to approximate the DAV for this model. As before, a cycle is the amount of time $T = Q/\lambda$ it takes to deplete the lot size. The middle of the cycle is $T/2 = Q/(2\lambda)$. The financial holding cost over the cycle is

$$i(K + cQ)\frac{Q}{2\lambda},$$

which consists of simple interest on the total expenditure of $K + cQ$, made at the beginning of the cycle, until the middle of the cycle. The sum of the expenditure and the financial holding cost is

$$K + cQ + i(K + cQ)\frac{Q}{2\lambda}.$$

Hence the approximate DAV is that quantity divided by the average cycle time:

$$\frac{K\lambda}{Q} + c\lambda + \frac{iK}{2} + \frac{ciQ}{2}.$$

Interpretation

The first term gives the setup cost per week. The second gives the direct (labor and materials) costs. The third gives the financial holding cost assessed on the setup cost. The fourth is the financial holding cost (rate) on the variable ordering cost. This is nearly the same expression that we got in our classical development of the EOQ model in Chapter 1. The only difference is that the classical development excludes the third term. However, that term does not affect the selection of the decision variable Q, so this approach can be viewed as support for the validity of the classical development. Hadley and

Whitin (1963:79–81) provide similar support by leading their readers through an exercise in which they show that the classical (undiscounted) EOQ is a first-order approximation to the optimal lot size in the discounted case.

Challenging the Conventional Approach

There is a conventional approach that is independent of the discounted average value approach and that leads to exactly the same four terms: The cost of ordering Q units is $K + cQ$, so the average unit cost is

$$\frac{K + cQ}{Q} = \frac{K}{Q} + c.$$

The average inventory level over time is $Q/2$. Thus, the average dollar value of that inventory is the product of the average unit cost and the average inventory level:

$$\left(\frac{K}{Q} + c\right)\left(\frac{Q}{2}\right) = \frac{K}{2} + \frac{cQ}{2}.$$

The financial holding cost is the opportunity cost of capital times this average investment value:

$$i\left(\frac{K}{2} + \frac{cQ}{2}\right) = \frac{iK}{2} + \frac{ciQ}{2},$$

which gives the third and fourth terms above. Adding the setup and direct costs per week leads to the same four terms.

However, this conventional approach, based on average physical inventory levels does not always work. For example, suppose you have a single customer who wants you to produce units at a fixed average rate over time. He will pay you a fixed fee over time provided you produce fast enough to meet his specified demand rate. However, he is willing to take your output as fast as you produce them. That is, if you produce faster than required, you can simply deliver the goods to him, and you need carry no physical inventory.

Because your physical inventory level is always zero, the conventional approach assesses no financial holding costs, so the objective function would consist solely of the first two terms, and the indicated optimal solution would be to produce an infinite amount immediately, which is ludicrous. The DAV approach leads to the same terms as before and suggests that the classical EOQ solution is still optimal. The moral of this story is that what matters is not the physical inventory level during the cycle, but the *timing* of the expenditures and receipts during the cycle.

C.5   Random Cycle Lengths

In this section we examine the general case in which the cycle time, the time between regenerations, is itself a random variable. We apply these results to the EOQ problem in the next section.

Notation

$T =$ cycle time (random variable).
$F =$ cdf of the cycle time.
$\tilde{F} =$ Laplace-Stieltjes transform of F:

$$\tilde{F}(i) := \int_{t=0}^{\infty} e^{-it} dF(t).$$

$\mu =$ mean cycle time.
$\sigma =$ standard deviation of cycle time.

Note that $\tilde{F}(i) = E(e^{-iT})$ can be interpreted as the expected present value of a dollar received at time T. In this setting, the DAV (of a cost stream) is the deterministic cost rate that yields the same NPV as the expected NPV of the actual stream.

Formulas

Theorem C.3   *Suppose one dollar is spent immediately and the cycle time is a random variable.*

(a) The DAV (over the cycle time) is given by

$$v_{\textbf{DAV}} = \frac{i}{1 - \tilde{F}(i)}.$$

(b) The DAV can also be expressed as

$$DAV = \left(1 + \frac{i\mu}{2} + \frac{i\sigma^2}{2\mu}\right) / \mu + O(i^2).$$

Proof (a) Given T, the NPV of paying a rate of x per unit time over $[0, T]$ is, by Lemma C.1(d), $x(1 - e^{-iT})/i$. Therefore, the expected NPV is $x(1 - \tilde{F}(i))/i$. Setting that equal to 1, the NPV of one dollar spent immediately, and solving for x leads to the result.

(b) Applying the method of proof of Theorem C.2, and using the fact that $\tilde{F}(i) = 1 - i\mu + i^2(\sigma^2 + \mu^2)/2 + O(i^3)$, leads to the result.

$\square$

The first term in the numerator of (b) is the dollar itself. The second is the (by now standard) financial holding cost on the time from the beginning until the middle of the cycle. The third term is the *financial variability cost*, which is one-half the product of the interest rate and the ratio of the variance to the mean cycle time. Dividing by μ converts the result into an equivalent rate over time.

C.6   Random-Yield EOQ Problem

In this section, we apply Theorem C.3 to an EOQ model in which some of the items produced in a batch may be defective. Whenever the stock level drops to zero, a new batch must be produced. Let β (< 1) denote the expected fraction of a lot that is defective, so that $\bar{\beta} = 1 - \beta$ is the (expected) fraction that is good. The problem is to determine the optimal batch size. We shall show that the distribution matters: the solution depends on the distribution of defectives.

Deterministic Case

Suppose that the same fraction β applies exactly to all lots, so $\bar{\beta}Q$ is the effective output size of the lot, rather than Q, the size of the input. The cycle length is now $T = \bar{\beta}Q/\lambda$. Using Theorem C.2, the approximate cost per cycle is

$$K + cQ + i(K + cQ)\frac{\bar{\beta}Q}{2\lambda}.$$

Thus, the approximate DAV is:

$$\frac{K\lambda}{\bar{\beta}Q} + \frac{c\lambda}{\bar{\beta}} + \frac{iK}{2} + \frac{ciQ}{2},$$

which is equivalent to the classical EOQ model corresponding to dividing the demand rate λ by $\bar{\beta}$, to get a higher effective demand rate. The optimal lot size is

$$Q^* = \sqrt{\frac{2K\lambda}{\bar{\beta}ci}},$$

which is strictly larger than the standard result (which corresponds to $\bar{\beta} = 1$).

Stochastic Case

Suppose, to consider the extreme stochastic case, you get 0 good units with probability β and Q good units with probability $\bar{\beta}$. If you get none good, you must start another lot immediately and incur the setup cost again. So the cycle time is 0 with probability β and Q/λ with probability $\bar{\beta}$. The mean cycle time is still $\bar{\beta}Q/\lambda$. Using the fact that $\text{Var}(T) = E(T^2) - E^2(T)$, the variance of the cycle time is

$$\bar{\beta}\left(\frac{Q}{\lambda}\right)^2 - \left(\frac{\bar{\beta}Q}{\lambda}\right)^2 = \bar{\beta}\left(\frac{Q}{\lambda}\right)^2(1 - \bar{\beta}) = \beta\bar{\beta}\left(\frac{Q}{\lambda}\right)^2.$$

Applying Theorem C.3, the resulting approximate DAV is

$$\frac{K\lambda}{\bar{\beta}Q} + \frac{c\lambda}{\bar{\beta}} + \frac{iK}{2\bar{\beta}} + \frac{ciQ}{2\bar{\beta}}.$$

The first and second terms are as in the deterministic case above. However, the third and fourth terms now also have $\bar{\beta}$ in the denominator. The optimal lot size for this problem is the same as the unadjusted EOQ (with no defects). Thus, because this result differs from the case of a deterministic yield, the yield distribution affects the results!

Exercises

C.1 Given that $e := \lim_{m\to\infty}(1 + 1/m)^m$, prove Lemma C.1(a).

C.2 Suppose, in the numerical example in Section C.2, that the costs are incurred in the *middle* of each of month, rather than at the beginning. Compute the resulting DAV for alternative 1.

C.3   Verify the following statement made in Section C.3: "The DAV for a given machine type will be the same regardless of how many lifetimes of the machine are used in the computation."

C.4   The approximation in Theorem C.2 is of the form $a_0 + a_1 i + O(i^2)$ and is called a first-order approximation. Derive the second-order approximation, of the form $a_0 + a_1 i + a_2 i^2 + O(i^3)$. (That is, determine a_2 explicitly.)

C.5   Consider a single expenditure of x made at time t in a problem with cycle length T. For convenience, assume that an asset is obtained by virtue of the expenditure.

Suppose, first, that $t = 0$. A conventional approach might apply straight-line depreciation to the expenditure, valuing the asset at x at time zero and at 0 at time T. Thus, the average value of the asset during the cycle is $x/2$. Therefore, one can argue that the opportunity cost of capital should be applied to that amount to obtain $ix/2$, which consists of the financial holding costs. Thus, the cost rate per unit time for this problem is $x/T + ix/2$, which is exactly what we get in Theorem C.2.

Now consider arbitrary t, not necessarily equal to zero. Suppose the value of the asset is depreciated on a straight-line basis over the period $[t, a(t)]$. Charge the opportunity cost of capital on the average value of the asset, averaging over the entire cycle, assuming the value is zero outside the interval $[t, a(t)]$. Determine the analogous cost rate per unit time. Determine what $a(t)$ must be for this cost rate to equal the approximate DAV of Theorem C.2. Under what conditions does $a(t) < t$? Interpret this system of costing in this case.

C.6   The streams of costs and revenues in the table below are incurred at the middle of each month. Time 0 is the beginning of month 1, and the opportunity cost of capital is 2% per month. Determine the NPV as of the beginning of month 1 and the DAV over $[0, 12]$ for each stream. (The DAV for the revenue stream should be very close to 43.6.) Approximate the DAV for each stream using financial holding costs as specified in Section C.4. (The approximate DAV for the revenue stream will equal the average cost per month, 43.6.)

Month	Revenue	Cost
1	43.6	17.5
2	43.6	20.5
3	43.6	23.5
4	43.6	26.5
5	43.6	32.5
6	43.6	41.5
7	43.6	50.5
8	43.6	59.5
9	43.6	58.0
10	43.6	46.0
11	43.6	34.0
12	43.6	22.0

C.7 Provide the details of the proof of Theorem C.3(b).

C.8 Consider the EOQ model of Section C.5. Suppose that payment of the labor and materials cost can be delayed for two time units (weeks) after the beginning of each cycle. What is the optimal lot size now? How much has been saved? How much has been saved, expressed in percentage terms? Work out a numerical example to illustrate each answer.

C.9 Suppose that cost is incurred at a rate of xt at time t for $0 \le t \le T$ and that the cost of capital is i.

(a) Show that the NPV of that cost stream is

$$\int_{t=0}^{T} e^{-it} xt \, dt = \frac{x}{i^2} \left(1 - (iT + 1)e^{-iT} \right).$$

(b) Show that the DAV over $(0, T)$ of that stream is

$$\frac{x \left(e^{iT} - iT - 1 \right)}{i(e^{iT} - 1)}.$$

(c) Show that the DAV in (b) can be expressed as

$$\frac{xT}{2} - \frac{ixT^2}{12} + O(i^2).$$

C.10   Consider the EOQ model of Section C.5. Suppose that an additional physical holding cost of h per unit of on-hand inventory is charged per unit of time (week). Compute an approximate DAV for this model.

Hint: The present value of the physical holding costs incurred in a cycle of length T is $\int_{t=0}^{T} e^{-it} h(Q - \lambda t)\, dt$. Use the first term in Exercise C.9(c) to compute the approximate DAV for the physical holding costs and add that to the objective function.

C.11   Consider the following modification of the random-yield model of Section C.7. The expected fraction defective continues to be β. However, there are three possible outcomes involving the number of defects in the lot size: (1) Exactly half the lot size Q is defective with probability α, (2) all units in the lot size are defective with probability p, and (3) none of the units is defective, with probability $1 - \alpha - p$. Using Theorem C.3 to approximate the DAV, what is the optimal lot size now?

Hint: Solve for p in terms of α and β.

References

Hadley, G., T. Whitin. 1963. *Analysis of Inventory Systems.* Prentice-Hall, Englewood Cliffs, N.J.

Porteus, E. 1985. Undiscounted approximations of discounted regenerative models. *Operations Research Letters.* **3** 293–300.

Wagner, H. 1969. *Principles of Operations Research.* Prentice-Hall, Englewood Cliffs, N.J.

Preference Theory
and Stochastic Dominance

Many useful insights into operational problems can be obtained by assuming the objective is to minimize expected costs or to maximize expected returns. In the language of preference (utility) theory, this approach assumes that the decision maker is risk neutral and therefore ignores risk preferences. However, it is well understood that incorporating attitudes toward risk is essential in building adequate theories in many other fields. For instance, modern portfolio theory in finance would be nearly vacuous without doing so. The role of such attitudes in operational problems is still quite undeveloped. This chapter presents some of the basic concepts of preference theory. The connection between the important concepts of first- and second-order stochastic dominance and preference orders is given. It also presents the concept of variability developed by Rothschild and Stiglitz (1970) that is closely connected to second-order stochastic dominance. Finally, it applies these concepts to the newsvendor model, revealing that newsvendors who are risk neutral with respect to monetary outcomes are risk averse with respect to the probability distributions of demand that they face.

D.1   Basic Concepts

Assuming that you have preferences over lotteries and obey reasonable axioms of behavior, von Neumann and Morgenstern (1944) proved that there exists a utility function u, defined on the outcomes of those lotteries, that can be used to represent those preferences: If X and Y are two lotteries, then you prefer X to Y if and only if $Eu(X) \geq Eu(Y)$. Such utility functions are invariant under strictly positive linear transformations: Identical preferences are represented before and after. Heyman and Sobel (1984) discuss the axioms, give results and proofs, and discuss some of the paradoxes. You should interpret a lottery as a general random variable that can represent virtually any kind of uncertainty that may be faced in a decision-making setting. For example, it can represent (uncertain) demand for a product, delay in accomplishing an activity, defects arising in a production process, and so on.

Raiffa (1968) gives an excellent, readable introduction to the area. If the best and worst possible outcomes are finite, the values of the utility function can be assumed to be between zero and one and can be interpreted as probabilities. In particular, imagine a lottery ticket with a probability stamp p on it, meaning that, like it or not, you face a simple lottery in which the probability that the best outcome occurs is p and the probability that the worst outcome occurs is $1 - p$. Your utility $u(x)$ of receiving return x can be interpreted as the probability stamp on such a ticket that makes you indifferent between receiving that fixed return (x) and undergoing the lottery. You would strictly prefer the lottery if the probability is increased and you would strictly prefer the fixed return if the probability is decreased. Raiffa (1968) goes on to discuss reasonable ways to assess someone's utility function.

Your *certainty equivalent* for the uncertain return X is the certain amount, $C_{\mathbf{E}}(X)$, that yields the same expected utility as the uncertain return:

$$u(C_{\mathbf{E}}(X)) = E[u(X)].$$

With Raiffa's interpretation, the expected utility of an uncertain return simply amounts to the simple lottery ticket that is equivalent to the compound lottery: Suppose the uncertain return consists of n possible values, $x_1, x_2, \ldots, x_n$, with probability q_i for outcome i. Then

$$E[u(X)] = \sum_{i=1}^{n} q_i u(x_i),$$

which, when interpreting $u(x_i)$ as the probability of receiving the best outcome (and otherwise receiving the worst outcome), can be seen as the equivalent probability of receiving the best outcome.

Your *risk premium* for X is $E(X) - C_{\mathbf{E}}(X)$, the amount of the expected return that you are willing to forgo to obtain your certainty equivalent. You are *risk neutral* if your risk premium is zero: $C_{\mathbf{E}}(X) = E(X)$. You are *risk averse (seeking)* if your risk premium is positive (negative). You are risk averse [seeking, neutral] for all lotteries X if and only if your utility function is concave [convex, affine]. See Arrow (1971) and Pratt (1964) for more depth in this regard.

The *Pratt/Arrow measure of absolute risk aversion*, evaluated at point x, is

$$\rho(x) = \frac{-u''(x)}{u'(x)}.$$

The measure is zero if you are risk neutral. The larger the measure is, the more risk averse you are: The larger the risk premium is on a given lottery.

If $\rho(x)$ is a decreasing function of x, then the risk premium decreases on a given lottery as your wealth increases. (Adding a fixed amount to each outcome lowers the risk premium.) Constant absolute risk aversion means linear or exponential utility, which have the powerful characteristic of facilitating consistent decisions regarding risk in an organization with decentralized decision making, a compelling setting for many operational problems.

The measure of *relative risk aversion* is $x\rho(x)$. It measures risk aversion for lotteries whose payoffs are fractions of your wealth.

A quadratic utility function reduces to tradeoffs between the mean and variance of the returns from the lottery. This utility function forms the underpinnings of the Capital Asset Pricing Model (CAPM) in finance.

D.2   Stochastic Dominance

Suppose you are advising a friend who faces two lotteries, X and Y, and you haven't yet assessed your friend's utility function. You wonder if there are ways to determine which lottery is preferred without assessing the actual utility function. For instance, you might speculate that if the two lotteries have the same mean payoff and your friend is risk averse, then your friend would always prefer the one with the lower (statistical) variance. However, Exercise D.1 shows that you would be wrong: It is possible to have a concave increasing utility function u, and random variables X and Y such that $E(X) = E(Y)$, $\text{Var}(X) < \text{Var}(Y)$, and $Eu(X) < Eu(Y)$.

However, stochastic dominance, of which there are several useful kinds, can be useful in this regard. We first introduce the concepts and follow with their relationship to preferences. (We restrict discussion to only first- and second-order stochastic dominance, FSD and SSD, in this chapter.)

Let F and G denote the distribution functions, and f and g the densities, for X and Y, respectively. We say that X *dominates* Y *under FSD* (and that F *dominates* G *under FSD*) if

$$F(x) \le G(x) \quad \text{for every } x.$$

When it is clear from the context (only FSD is being considered) we also say that X is *stochastically larger* than Y.

Under FSD, for any arbitrary payoff you select, the dominating lottery has a smaller [larger] probability of yielding at most [least] that payoff. The cumulative of the dominating lottery is below the other, as seen in Figure D.1. Similarly, the dominating cumulative distribution is to the right of the other: The pth fractile of the dominating distribution is larger for every probability p. For example, if X is uniformly distributed over (the interval) $(3, 4)$ and Y is uniform over $(2, 4)$, then X dominates Y under FSD.

We say that X *dominates* Y *under SSD* if

$$\int_{z=-\infty}^{x} F(z)\, dz \le \int_{z=-\infty}^{x} G(z)\, dz \quad \text{for every } x.$$

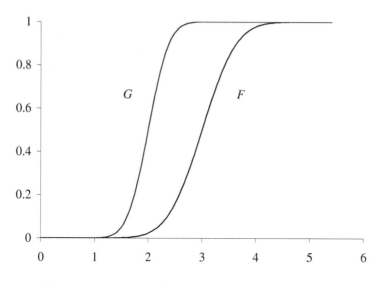

Figure D.1   First-Order Stochastic Dominance

Under SSD, the cumulative of the cumulative of the dominating lottery is below
the other. Clearly, if X dominates Y under FSD, then X dominates Y
under SSD as well. However, the contrary is false. For example, if X is
uniformly distributed over (the interval) $(2, 4)$ and Y is uniform over $(1, 5)$,
then X dominates Y under SSD but not under FSD: Figure D.2 illustrates
that the cumulatives cross. However, the cumulatives of those do not.

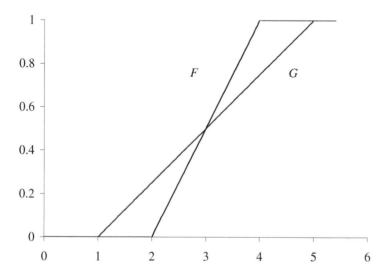

Figure D.2   Second-Order Stochastic Dominance

The concepts of third- and higher-order stochastic dominance are defined analogously. See Milne and Neave (1994) for a nice presentation of the basic results for discrete random variables, including a proof of the following result.

Theorem D.1

(a) X dominates Y under FSD iff $Eu(X) \geq Eu(Y)$ for every increasing function u.

(b) X dominates Y under SSD iff $Eu(X) \geq Eu(Y)$ for every increasing concave function u.

(c) Suppose $E(X) = E(Y)$. Then X dominates Y under SSD iff $Eu(X) \geq Eu(Y)$ for every concave function u.

Part (a) says that if you prefer more to less, then you will always prefer a lottery that dominates another under FSD. It also says that if one lottery is preferred to another by every person who prefers more to less, then the first lottery dominates the second under FSD.

Part (b) says that if, in addition to preferring more to less, you are risk averse (or risk neutral), then you will always prefer a lottery that dominates another under SSD. In particular, because the function $u(x) = x$ is increasing and concave, it also says that if one random variable dominates another under SSD, then it has a higher mean. There is also an analogous statement for the "if" part of the result.

Part (c) says, in part, that if the means of the two lotteries are the same and you are risk averse, but don't necessarily prefer more to less, then you will always prefer a lottery that dominates another under SSD.

Interpretations

We first examine a result that will prove useful in characterizing second-order stochastic dominance.

Lemma D.1   If X is a positive random variable with distribution function F and density function f, then, for each $y \geq 0$,

$$E\big(\min(X, y)\big) = \int_{x=0}^{y} [1 - F(x)] \, dx. \tag{D.1}$$

Proof   Recall from the Preface that $z \wedge y := \min(z, y)$. Then

$$\int_{x=0}^{y} [1 - F(x)] \, dx = \int_{x=0}^{y} \left(\int_{z=x}^{\infty} f(z) \, dz \right) dx$$

$$= \int_{z=0}^{\infty} \int_{x=0}^{z \wedge y} f(z) \, dz \, dx$$

$$= \int_{z=0}^{\infty} (z \wedge y) f(z) \, dz. \qquad \square$$

By setting $y = \infty$, Lemma D.1 includes the following commonly used alternative representation of the mean of a positive random variable:

$$\int_{x=0}^{\infty} [1 - F(x)] \, dx = \int_{x=0}^{\infty} x f(x) \, dx = E(X). \qquad (D.2)$$

Parzen (1960:211–2) has a nice geometric interpretation of the general version of this representation.

Lemma D.1 also yields a newsvendor interpretation, which is used to derive (1.1), of the partial integral of the anticumulative: Interpret X as demand for a product during a period and y as the stock level available before observing demand. Thus, $\min(X, y)$ is the number of units sold, so (D.1) gives the expected number of units sold in that period.

Theorem D.2   *Suppose that X and Y are positive random variables with distribution and density functions. Then X dominates Y under SSD iff*

$$E \min(X, y) \geq E \min(Y, y) \quad \text{for every } y \geq 0.$$

Proof   Let F and G denote the distribution functions of X and Y, respectively, and let

$$T(y) := \int_{x=0}^{y} [G(x) - F(x)] \, dx.$$

Then, by definition, X dominates Y under SSD can be written as $T(y) \geq 0$ for every $y \geq 0$. Thus, we have

$$T(y) = \int_{x=0}^{y} [G(x) - F(x)] \, dx$$

$$= \int_{x=0}^{y} [1 - F(x) - 1 + G(x)] \, dx$$

$$= \int_{x=0}^{y} [1 - F(x)] \, dx - \int_{x=0}^{y} [1 - G(x)] \, dx.$$

The result then follows from Lemma D.1.   □

Thus, among positive lotteries, there is an interesting equivalence between second-order stochastic dominance and the newsvendor problem: Interpreting the lotteries as demand distributions, one lottery dominates the other (under SSD) if and only if it yields a higher expected number of unit sales, for every possible initial stock level y.

D.3   How to Define Variability

As was indicated earlier, defining variability as the statistical variance of a random variable is not satisfactory in a decision-making context. In particular, we want a coherent concept of "variability," so that if we keep the mean the same and increase the variability, then a risk-averse person will prefer the one with less variability. Theorem D.1(c) provides the key to this issue: If we have two lotteries, say X and Y, with equal means and all risk-averse persons prefer X to Y, then X dominates Y under SSD. We would therefore like to say that Y has more variability than X. This section explains why this labeling makes sense and sheds insight into the difference between this concept of variability and statistical variance.

Following Rothschild and Stiglitz (1970), we say that Y has *more variability (in the sense of RS)* than X if $E(X) = E(Y)$ and there exists a random variable Z such that Y and $X + Z$ have the same distribution and $E(Z \mid X = x) = 0$ for all x. That is, Y has the same distribution as X plus a (zero mean) noise term.

Continuing to follow Rothschild and Stiglitz (1970), we also define a *mean preserving spread* as a transformation to a given random variable that takes weight out of the center of its density (or probability mass function) and distributes it in the tails, keeping the mean unchanged. The result is a new random variable with the same mean and a larger variance. Milne and Neave (1994) call this a perturbation with zero mean disturbance terms. The following result justifies introducing these notions.

Theorem D.3   *(Rothschild and Stiglitz, 1970)   Suppose X and Y are positive random variables with equal means. Then X dominates Y under*

SSD iff Y has more variability in the sense of RS than X iff Y can be obtained from X by a sequence of mean preserving spreads.

Milne and Neave (1994) generalize this result to the case in which the means need not be equal. The important consequence of Theorem D.3 is that we should think of variability in terms of sequences of mean preserving spreads rather than (statistical) variance. In short, if one random variable has more variability in the sense of RS than another, then it has a larger variance, but the converse is false: If two random variables have the same mean but different variances, it isn't necessarily the case that the random variable with the larger variance can be obtained from the other through a sequence of mean preserving spreads. Indeed, every solution to Exercise D.1 illustrates pairs of such random variables.

D.4   Application to the Newsvendor Problem

Suppose, in the context of the newsvendor problem of Section 1.2, you are offered the choice of two different probability distributions of demand, Φ_1 and Φ_2, with densities ϕ_1 and ϕ_2, respectively. You seek to maximize the expected contribution, so you are risk neutral among lotteries whose outcomes are monetary returns. The expected contribution you get from a particular distribution defines an *induced preference* on probability distributions: You prefer the distribution that yields the higher expected contribution. We explore the consequences of this induced preference in this section.

Recall from (1.1) that the expected contribution, as a function of the stock level y and the demand distribution Φ, can be written as

$$v(y, \Phi) = pE \min(D, y) - cy. \tag{D.3}$$

Thus, the expected contribution can be written as $v(y, \Phi) = Eu(y, D)$, where $u(y, \xi) := p \min(\xi, y) - cy$. Examining the partial derivative of u with respect to the quantity demanded, we have

$$u_2(y, \xi) = \begin{cases} p & \text{if } \xi \leq y \\ 0 & \text{otherwise.} \end{cases}$$

That is, for a given stock level y, the utility function is concave increasing in the quantity demanded. Thus, you are risk averse among lotteries whose outcomes are quantities demanded. In short, you are risk averse among demand distributions. Indeed, because the utility function is *not* affine, you are not risk neutral. That is, even though you are risk neutral among monetary lotteries, you are not risk neutral among demand lotteries. (You would evaluate demand distributions solely by their means if you were risk neutral among demand distributions.) Exercise D.7 provides a different context in which your induced preferences are risk seeking: you prefer more variability.

Suppose Φ_1 dominates Φ_2 under FSD. Because the utility function is increasing in the quantity demanded, Theorem D.1(a) ensures that you prefer Φ_1, regardless of what y you select. Thus, you will always prefer the first-order stochastically larger demand distribution.

Theorem D.2 reveals another interesting connection between second-order stochastic dominance and the newsvendor problem. Suppose we fix the initial stock level y. If Φ_1 dominates Φ_2 under SSD, then, by Theorem D.2, you prefer Φ_1. Furthermore, if, as a risk-neutral newsvendor, you prefer Φ_1 to Φ_2 for every y, then Φ_1 must dominate Φ_2 under SSD.

Additional Unit Stockout Penalty

Suppose, as in Exercise 1.19, that there is an additional stockout penalty $\pi > 0$ for every unmet demand. In this case, the expected contribution, as a function of the stock level y and the demand distribution Φ, is $v_A(y, \Phi) = Eu_A(y, D)$, where $u_A(y, \xi) := u(y, \xi) - \pi(\xi - y)^+$. Here, the utility function u_A is concave but *not* increasing in the quantity demanded. It is clear that if demand is deterministic (and strictly positive), and the stock level $y = 0$ is fixed, then you strictly prefer the (first-order) stochastically smaller demand distribution. Thus, we cannot conclude, as we did when the utility function was increasing, that you will always prefer the stochastically larger demand distribution. Exercise D.8 demonstrates even more: Even after selecting the optimal stock level for each demand distribution, you can strictly prefer the stochastically smaller demand distribution. However, if the two demand distributions have equal means and Φ_1 dominates Φ_2 under SSD, then, by Theorem D.1(c), you prefer Φ_1.

Exercises

D.1   Identify a concave increasing utility function $u(\cdot)$ and two random variables X and Y such that $E(X) = E(Y)$, $\mathrm{Var}(X) < \mathrm{Var}(Y)$, and $Eu(X) < Eu(Y)$.

Hint: Use discrete lotteries with only two possible payoffs each.

D.2   Verify that if X is uniformly distributed on $[a, b]$, then

$$F(x) = \begin{cases} 0 & \text{if } x \leq a \\ (x-a)/(b-a) & \text{if } a \leq x \leq b \\ 1 & \text{otherwise,} \end{cases}$$

and

$$F^{(2)}(x) = \begin{cases} 0 & \text{if } x \leq a \\ (x-a)^2/[2(b-a)] & \text{if } a \leq x \leq b \\ x-(a+b)/2 & \text{otherwise,} \end{cases}$$

where F is the distribution function for X and $F^{(2)}(x) := \int_{z=-\infty}^{x} F(z)\, dz$.

D.3   Suppose that X_1 and X_2 are statistically independent, and that X_i is uniformly distributed on $[a_i, b_i]$ for each $i = 1, 2$. Provide the necessary and sufficient conditions (on the parameters) for X_1 to dominate X_2 under SSD.

Hint: Use Exercise D.2.

D.4   (Derman, 1970)   Suppose that P is an n by n stochastic matrix. Use Theorem D.1 to prove that if $\sum_{j=k}^{n} P_{ij}$ is an increasing function of i, for each $k \leq n$, and $g(j)$ is an increasing function of j, then $f(i) := \sum_{j=1}^{n} P_{ij} g(j)$ is an increasing function of i.

D.5   (St. Petersburg Paradox)   Consider a lottery in which a fair coin is flipped until heads appears for the first time. If heads appears on the first flip, then you receive \$2. If heads appears for the first time on the nth flip, then you receive 2^n dollars.

(a) What is the expected amount you receive from this lottery?

(b) What is the least you (personally) would be willing to sell your rights to such a lottery for? (This is your certainty equivalent for this lottery.)

(c) Why do you think this problem is called a paradox?

(d) The classical way in which this paradox is resolved is to insist that people are not risk neutral. Furthermore, it can be shown that if one has an unbounded utility function, a lottery can be constructed that yields infinite expected utility. So the classical resolution is to insist that people's utility functions must also be bounded. What follows is another possible resolution.

One might plausibly argue that you can never be paid more than the value of the world. Suppose we estimate the value of the world to be $\$2^m$, for some integer m such as $m = 60$, so that the maximum payoff of the lottery can be assumed to be 2^m. Thus, if heads appears for the first time on the nth flip and $n \geq m$, then you receive only 2^m, rather than 2^n. Compute the expected payoff of this lottery as a function of m. How can this be interpreted as another resolution of the paradox?

D.6   A risk-averse investor faces a single period opportunity to invest in any of n different projects. Let x_i denote the amount she invests in project i and r_i the (uncertain) amount she receives from each dollar invested in project i. One of the projects can be interpreted as retaining her current fixed assets. Thus, her wealth at the end of the period can be expressed as

$$w = \sum_{i=1}^{n} r_i x_i = r^\mathsf{T} x.$$

Let $u(w)$ denote her concave utility function of wealth. Let X denote the admissible investment vectors: She must select $x \in X$. Assume that X is a convex subset of $\mathbf{R}^n$. Let $\bar{r} := Er$ denote the expected unit payoff for each project and let $\bar{x}$ denote the optimal investment vector for the deterministic problem obtained by replacing the random returns by their expectations. That is, $\bar{x}$ is assumed to exist and maximizes $u(\bar{r}^\mathsf{T} x)$ over $x \in X$.

Prove that

$$Eu(r^\mathsf{T}\bar{x}) \leq \max_{x \in X} Eu(r^\mathsf{T} x) \leq \max_{x \in X} u(\bar{r}^\mathsf{T} x).$$

D.7   Consider the owner of a linear firm. That is, her problem is to solve the following linear program: Find an n-vector x to

$$\max c^\mathsf{T} x \quad \text{subject to} \quad Ax \leq b, x \geq 0.$$

Let $v(b, c)$ denote the optimal value of the objective function as a function of the m-vector b of resource levels and n-vector c of unit contributions.

(a) Suppose that b is an m-vector of random variables and that the owner observes b before x must be selected. Prove that the owner is averse to variability in b. (She is risk averse in quantities.) That is, prove that the induced utility $v(b, c)$ is concave with respect to b for each fixed c.

(b) Suppose that c is an n-vector of random variables and that the owner observes c before x must be selected. Prove that the owner prefers variability in c. (She is risk seeking in prices.) That is, prove that the induced utility $v(b, c)$ is convex with respect to c for each fixed b.

D.8   Consider the newsvendor problem of Section D.4, in which, as in Exercise 1.19, you also incur a unit penalty cost of $\pi > 0$ for every unit short (unmet demand). In this case, your objective function is $v_A(y, \Phi) := v(y, \Phi) - \pi E(D - y)^+$. Suppose Φ_1 dominates Φ_2 under FSD. Let y_1 and y_2 denote optimal stock levels for Φ_1 and Φ_2, respectively. Construct a numerical example in which $0 < v_A(y_1, \Phi_1) < v_A(y_2, \Phi_2)$. That is, even after you implement the corresponding optimal policy for the distribution you select, you do not necessarily prefer the first-order stochastically larger demand distribution.

Hint: Consider demand distributions with only two outcomes, let Φ_1 differ from Φ_2 only in the size of the larger outcome, and select parameters so that the optimal stock level is the same for both (equal to the smaller outcome).

References

Arrow, K. 1971. *Essays in the Theory of Risk-Bearing*. Markham, Chicago.

Derman, C. 1970. *Finite State Markovian Decision Processes*. Academic Press, New York.

Heyman, D. M. Sobel. 1984. *Stochastic Models in Operations Research, Volume II*. McGraw-Hill, New York.

Milne, F., E. Neave. 1994. Dominance relations among standardized variables. *Management Science*. **40** 1343–52.

Parzen, E. 1960. *Modern Probability Theory and Applications*. Wiley, New York.

Pratt, J. 1964. Risk aversion in the small and in the large. *Econometrica.* **32** 122–35.

Raiffa, H. 1968. *Decision Analysis. Introductory Lectures on Choices under Uncertainty.* Addison-Wesley, Reading, Mass.

Rothschild, M., J. Stiglitz. 1970. Increasing risk: I. A definition. *Journal of Economic Theory.* **2** 225–43.

von Neumann, J., O. Morgenstern. 1944. *The Theory of Games and Economic Behavior.* Princeton University Press, Princeton, N.J.

Index

CPSIA information can be obtained
at www.ICGtesting.com
Printed in the USA
BVHW031506101019

560632BV00028B/50/P

9 780804 743990